A Year of Wine

A Year of Wine

PERFECT PAIRINGS, GREAT BUYS,

and

WHAT TO SIP FOR EACH SEASON

Tyler Colman

ILLUSTRATIONS BY **ALEX EBEN MEYER**

SIMON SPOTLIGHT ENTERTAINMENT
New York • London • Toronto • Sydney

Simon Spotlight Entertainment
A Division of Simon & Schuster, Inc.
1230 Avenue of the Americas
New York, NY 10020

First Simon Spotlight Entertainment hardcover edition November 2008

SIMON SPOTLIGHT ENTERTAINMENT and colophon are trademarks of Simon & Schuster, Inc.

For information about special discounts for bulk purchases, please contact Simon & Schuster Special Sales at 1-800-456-6798 or business@simonandschuster.com.

Designed by Jaime Putorti

Manufactured in the United States of America

10   9   8   7   6   5   4   3   2   1

Library of Congress Cataloging-in-Publication Data

Colman, Tyler.
  A year of wine : perfect pairings, great buys, and what to sip for each season / by Tyler Colman.
      p. cm.
  Includes bibliographical references and index.
  1. Wine tasting. 2. Seasons. I. Title.
  TP548.5.A5C65 2008
  641.2'2—dc22   2008038980
  ISBN-13: 978-1-4169-4815-5
  ISBN-10:   1-4169-4815-5

For Michelle and the boys

CONTENTS

PART ONE: WINTER

PART THREE: SUMMER

PART FOUR: FALL

INTRODUCTION

A Call for Context and a Way to "Drink Different"

One January evening, my wife, Michelle, and I were watching the sun setting over the Caribbean. We were on vacation and were having dinner at a purportedly good restaurant with swanky black-and-white decor, techno music pulsing quietly, and flowing linens in place of walls. We could hear the waves breaking on the beach, smell the sea salt on the breeze, and I even felt a little tinge of sunburn from where the sun had penetrated my impenetrable sunscreen that afternoon on the beach. I had been looking forward to dinner all afternoon while pondering lofty subjects such as which wine goes with conch, be it grilled or fried.

But reviewing the wine list, something seemed out of place. Cult Cabernet from California followed listings of Merlot and Shiraz. Big reds dominated the list. This isn't always a big disappointment, but in a hot climate? It just didn't add up. The wine list clashed with the context. It would have been fine back home in New York, perhaps, with a fire in the background and hearty fare on the table but here I wanted a lighter wine. The few whites on the wine list were all pretty uninspiring, so we ordered one glass of big red and a Pellegrino. At the end of the meal, the red was still sitting there and the Pellegrino had been refilled several times.

Fast-forward a few years to a vacation Michelle and I spent in southern France in the height of the summer. After hiking in the rolling hills all afternoon, we returned to the house where we were staying and poured a couple of glasses of the local rosé. The pink color popped, the condensation quickly appeared on the outside of the glass, and we munched on tapenade and bread. The wine itself may not have scored highly in a blind tasting, but it was refreshing and exactly what the occasion called for—the wine and the moment fit together perfectly.

Context is wildly underrated when it comes to enjoying wine. Where we are, whom we're with, what time of year it is, what we are eating, when in the wine's life—and ours—we are drinking it, and even how we are drinking it all influence our perceptions of wine. But for some reason, such a fundamental and obvious point has been overlooked in how we think, discuss, and most importantly, drink wines. Too often, it's tempting to go with the known and reach for the same wine even if the context varies. And too often, a wine itself is taken as fixed and unchanging because of a numerical rating that a critic gave it and that it carries with it from meal to meal, year to year. But we must remember that there's a lot of diversity out there in the wine world today, and we need to explore it to find great pairings of wine, mood, and food.

So the thesis of this book is: drink different. If you always ask for the same wine—be it a Chardonnay or a Cabernet—resolve to change your wine choices (at least occasionally) to reflect something other than your comfort zone, such as the occasion, geographical location, food, or season. I guarantee it will change the way you enjoy and appreciate wine.

At root, plotting a seasonal arc to your wine consumption is simple. In the wintry months embrace warming, big wines. And serious wines too. I'm in a more contemplative mood during the winter, perhaps because of fewer distractions from the great outdoors. And the winter menu often calls for big wines since the foods featured tend to be stews, roasts, and risottos, all hearty and warming. If I'm in an igloo, I don't want a rosé, I want a Cabernet or a Barolo (and, presumably, a blanket).

The summer, by contrast, is all about lightness, being carefree at the beach or the park. It's hot out so these wines are often throw-it-back sort of wines, usually chilled for maximum refreshment. But they are almost always enjoyed when with friends, or when dining outside eating farm-fresh fruits and vegetables. So the setting has an impact on the moment and on your selected bottle. Simply put, if it's 90 degrees outside and I'm on the deck under an umbrella eating a salad, I don't want a Cabernet. But I do want that rosé.

Yes, winter and summer are the two extreme seasons, so the choice of wine might seem a bit obvious. But spring and fall, transitional seasons, have corresponding wines as well. In the spring, I like serious whites that have good aromas and concentration to them. In the late summer and fall, I tend to start to crave reds again and transition back through some lighter-bodied wines. It's all about preparing myself for the months ahead, staying in tune with the current, often rapidly changing weather, and acknowledging the changes that tend to accompany these transitional times of year.

In addition to seasonality, the particular moment you're experiencing while taking a sip can drastically alter the way you regard a bottle for the rest of your life. For example, the Champagne you had after winning a championship or closing a big deal never tasted so good. But really, it could have been some humble bubbly rather than a $75 bottle, because the situation dictated the euphoric mood. However, if you're on a first date and not sure how things are going, opening the dinner with a glass of beautiful Champagne might just push things to the next level.

Why doesn't the wine someone had on vacation in Provence or Tuscany taste as good back at home in Chicago or Seattle? A lot has to do with context: The vacation is over, you have to do your own shopping and cleaning up, and the warm breezes off the lavender fields may have been replaced by biting winds.

Wine importer Kermit Lynch sums it up when talking about a wine from Cassis (not the liqueur): "Of course Cassis tastes better at Cassis! Debussy sounds better after a walk through the foggy, puddle-riddled streets of Paris. You are in the midst of the atmosphere that created it. The wine is not different; the music is not different. You are."

And the reverse is true: Great wine has never tasted as bad as the time you drank it as your partner dumped you. At the end of the movie *Sideways*, do you think Miles enjoyed his 1961 Cheval Blanc that he drank from a Styrofoam cup while sitting under the fluorescent lights of a burger joint? No, he guzzled it, and it could have been Carlo Rossi for all he cared. It was a deliberate insult to the injured wine lover since he thought his romantic dreams were shattered.

All of this context—the mood and the food, the place and the people—creates a culture of consumption, an ambience. *Terroir* is the term grape growers use for the distinctive combination of where the grapes are grown, including the soil, the sun, and the wind. What often gets overlooked is that how and where wine gets consumed affects how well we enjoy it, perhaps even more than the *terroir*. Sometimes a Beaujolais is better than a cult Cabernet.

Drinking seasonally and, by extension, mindfully of the time, place, and mood of the moment, brings us closer to the world around us. It makes us take account of our surroundings, instead of ignoring them as we sometimes do with our food and our wine choices. In fact, what's often most appealing about drinking seasonally to me is that the foods on my plate change and the wine in my glass needs to change to keep up. Consider seasonality the wine drinker's addendum to eating locally grown foods, arguably the current biggest trend in fine restaurants and for home cooks.

Drinking locally is not always a viable option or not enough to capture the interest of curious wine lovers. Instead we can celebrate the diversity of the global marketplace. In fact, even if some wine enthusiasts do not have many local wine offerings, the market tends to be fabulously diverse. Such is the case in many parts of America today as wines from Hungary, Slovenia, and South Africa compete for shelf space with the more traditional regions of France, Italy, and California. So let's resolve as wine drinkers to follow one of the most pervasive trends in dining and eating today, and add a dose of vitality and seasonality to our glasses.

Is this possible if you only like reds? Or if reds give you headaches and you can't stand even the sight of them? Yes! At root, this annual rhythm is about weight (how appropriate for a New Year's resolution!), with fuller, richer wines in the winter and lighter wines in the summer. If you want to sketch your seasonal arc composed of only white wines or only reds, it's very possible to do that. In fact, many regions such as Burgundy or categories such as German Riesling have richer, fuller wines, as well as lighter wines. So you can conceivably drink seasonally within a narrow category of your favorite style.

I enjoy wines of all colors and degrees of bubbles. So throughout the year in wine sketched in these pages, I'll draw on the diversity that exists in the wine world and celebrate the seasons and different regions. But no matter your tastes, you'll find something perfect for your palate in every month. Unlike chef Gordon Ramsay, who has pushed to outlaw out-of-season produce because it is not a locally sustainable choice, I'm not a militant who will pry your Cabernet out of your sweaty fingers by the pool—I'll just offer you a glass of Moscato and see if you make the switch yourself.

And because I am a blogger at DrVino.com and cyberspace is a place of discussions rather than monologues, I am thrilled to weave in the voices and opinions of thirteen leading sommeliers who offer their thoughts on selecting good wines for the seasons throughout the book.

A final note on points: Where are the scores? In this book, I don't score wines since all the wines that I recommend are just that—wines that I would recommend. Points are about removing wine from context and are generally awarded during rapid tastings, usually conducted in the morning, by experts under cold office lights with one hundred other wines. In the same way that a rock concert would drown out a piano sonata, these tastings tend to favor bigger, bolder wines that overwhelm more subtle or delicate wines. And tacking a score on a wine won't tell you whether it is the best wine for your lunch on the deck. While I think comparative blind tastings have some value and even suggest you try them at home to sharpen your own sensory perceptions, what I seek to do here is to recommend great wines and perhaps the perfect context for enjoying them.

Before we get started on our twelve-month journey, I lay out a few basics for getting the most out of wine in the following pages. These are tips for all seasons. A first step is thinking about wines by style, or by flavor profile, which leads to better pairings with food and the mood. Next, I give some suggestions on how to find a good wine shop near you and how best to use it as a resource. You may have trouble finding some of the wines I recommend. Don't fret if you can't find a specific bottle—even though I fret trying to find wines all the time, since American wine retailing laws make it so difficult to find the exact wine I'm looking for. Just go to your local specialty shop, and oftentimes you'll be able to find something in the category that turned you on if the exact pick is not available. I'll also talk about good stemware and whether it is worth breaking the bank for some very breakable crystal glasses. And finally, I suggest some general tips on how to make the most of a winery visit. For every month of the year, I've selected a fun destination for wine tourism, so this is just a preface to those individual adventures.

A Note on Prices

Wine prices vary by retailer and by state. So I include a general pricing guide that corresponds to these brackets:

$:	Under $12 a bottle
$$:	$12–$25
$$$:	$25–$50
$$$$:	over $50

A Year of Wine

THE BASICS

Don't Judge a Wine by the Grape— Judge a Wine by Its Style

When you walk into a Best Cellars wine store, you won't find a section for California Cabernet. Or Bordeaux. Or New Zealand Sauvignon Blanc. What you will see signs for are sections such as Big, Fresh, and Fizzy. Wine, you see, has got style.

Best Cellars was a pioneering shop in a burgeoning movement toward organizing wine by style, or flavor profile, instead of by grape variety or the region in which it was grown. On the whole, this is a consumer-friendly way to organize a store since, after all, shoppers probably want a wine that fits a certain flavor profile, and the grape variety or the region is a subset of that. (However, if the descriptive terms get too goofy or you know what you want already but are not sure where the bottle is displayed, then the system can be a little annoying.)

It is helpful to think about wine as we enjoy it—in the glass—as opposed to getting too caught up in the language of producers, especially for those just starting out on the voyage of wine discovery. So think about wine styles along a simple axis of light, medium, and full. Let's go through it once for whites. Then lather. Rinse. Repeat with reds. Understanding style is especially useful for our seasonal approach, since, just like in fashion, certain qualities make a wine better for one time of year than another. Thinking about wine by style complements our seasonal approach: light in the summer, heavy in the winter, with the middleweights for the transitional months. So, with that in mind, read on and enjoy your year of wine.

Flavor Profiles: Whites

Light whites are very popular now. They're unoaked, so the generally fresh aromas of the grape and where it was grown shine through. Pinot Grigio has notes of flowers. New Zealand Sauvignon Blanc has a piercing intensity of citrus that I think can make it taste freshly squeezed. Torrontés from Argentina has wildly intense aromatics yet is dry on the palate. I tend to enjoy these wines most in the spring and summer.

Midweight wines are more serious. Instead of the fresh fruits and grass of the quaffers, they introduce more—perhaps light oak and some minerality. What's minerality? Zinc and iron? Close, but probably more like chalk and calcium. The soil where the grapes are grown can give the resulting wine a different character and for minerally wines, that can taste like wet rocks. It's a safe bet that you have never put wet rocks in your mouth, but try a Chablis or a Sancerre—especially compared to their new world analogues, a hot climate Chardonnay or Sauvignon Blanc—and you can taste the stony, flinty character. These are perhaps the best all-season whites.

Richer, fuller whites have more heft. They can be sweet, which makes a wine feel richer, or dry, when the richness is often achieved with aging in oak barrels. Riesling and Pinot Blanc can typify the first category, and the classic American Chardonnay is emblematic of the second. I tend to prefer these wines in the winter, with heavier foods and when there's more time for reflecting on the wine.

Flavor Profiles: Reds

Turning to the reds, drop some acid and fruit with these light wines: They're great with food since they have higher acidity and bright, fresh fruit in their composition. A lot of hugely enjoyable wines fall into this category, such as reds from the Loire, cru Beaujolais, Barbera, some Pinot Noir, and unoaked Malbec. (In case it isn't obvious, I really like this style of wine.) These are often reds for all seasons, but in my experience they are perhaps best enjoyed with certain meals or occasions, which I'll discuss throughout the book.

In the middleweight ring are reds that have seen more oak and still have some fruit, but might have had a little work done. A nip and tuck, so to speak—maybe some oxygen was added in the fermentation tank to soften the tannins and make the wine plush (in the case of a California Merlot or an oaked Malbec, for example). But there can be natural beauties in this category as well, such as some wines from the grape Nebbiolo or even a spicy Zinfandel.

Finally, the heavyweights. Big, dark fruit aromas and flavors dominate, with perhaps some leather or black truffle. Tannins, those elements in wine that make it feel chewy and make you want to go *chomp, chomp,* are very apparent, and as the wines age, the tannins become silkier and these big reds can offer ample rewards. Examples from this style often come from Cabernet Sauvignon or Syrah, thus the regions of Napa, Bordeaux, or the Rhône. These wines often need the fat and proteins of meat, and I tend to prefer them to help enliven long winter evenings.

LIGHT WHITES	MIDWEIGHT WHITES	HEAVY WHITES	LIGHT REDS	MIDWEIGHT REDS	HEAVY REDS
Pinot Grigio	Chablis	Riesling	Beaujolais	Californa Merlot	Cabernet Sauvignon
New Zealand Sauvignon Blanc	Sancerre	Pinot Blanc	Barbera	Oaked Malbec	Syrah
Torrontés		American Chardonnay	Pinot Noir	Grape Nebbiolo	
			Unoaked Malbec	Zinfandel	

Pairing Wine with Food

Pairing wine with food is the ultimate conundrum. For a long time the rules were simple: red with meat, white with poultry and fish. Then people started experimenting, and suddenly "red wine with fish" became A-OK!

But even that once revolutionary proclamation now seems somewhat outdated. Although we still eat meat and fish, the world of flavors is now so rich and readily available (when chicken tikka masala became the unofficial dish of Britain, you knew a page had been turned in the world's cookbook). All of a sudden the question, Which wine goes with the food we're having? has become much more complicated. Have we entered into an era of "impossible" food-wine pairings? When pondering which wine goes with pad thai or chips and salsa or a breakfast burrito, the answer to the question seems to be yes.

On the one hand, there are vague generalities: Drink the wines you like and eat the foods you like. It's hard to argue with that. But that rule of thumb is not exactly pushing you to explore new terrain—and in the worst cases, some of your favorite wines might be disastrous on the palate when consumed with your favorite foods. Consider eggplant: One time I was sipping a full-throttle Zinfandel at a casual dinner. Then along came some grilled eggplant, which I tried and deemed tasty. Going back to the wine— yikes! What happened?!? The tannins in the eggplant reacted horribly with the wine, and the wine was effectively ruined. I had a similar experience with chips and salsa: Michelle and I had hosted some friends for a Sunday lunch, and as I was cleaning up, I noticed some grand cru Chablis still left in the bottle. I had a sip and it was great, with pleasant acidity and a lingering mineral character. Then I wandered into the next room where the chips and salsa were sitting on a side table and, for some reason, I couldn't resist. Then I took another sip of grand cru Chablis—bad idea. The elegant wine was ruined by the salty, corny, tomatoey, spiciness that is chips and salsa, which had been fun earlier with a zingy, lighter wine.

Another approach to tough food-wine pairings is to get specific, VERY specific! Some people are rigid, and they only follow very specific recommendations for food and wine matchups. I've even seen a food-wine pairing generator that can make 360,000 suggestions!

I prefer a middle ground. Here are my four suggestions for pairing wine with food:

1. Try matching big with big and light with light. Then switch.

2. Try having a wine with higher acidity than the food.

3. Sweet helps tame spice.

4. If it grows together, it goes together.

Let's put some meat on these bare bones. If you're eating a steak, you'll want a big red to go with that fat and protein. (In fact, there are so many big red wines available today that their producers probably wish everyone ate steak for breakfast, lunch, and dinner.) A rich lobster with butter calls out for a big, oaked white, such as a white Burgundy or California Chardonnay done right. Foie gras is ideally served with the rich sweet wine most associated with Sauternes. Similarly, light white fish would go great with a Pinot Grigio, for example.

The obverse of complementing styles is the also successful strategy of contrasting styles of food and wine. Consider burritos. You could confront them head-on with a big Zinfandel. Or you could bow to their supremacy and go with a leaner and lighter wine. I have a fruit-forward, unoaked Bonarda from Argentina that I keep as my house burrito wine. As a good rule of thumb, the heavier of the two, the food or the wine, will win out.

Having higher acidity in the wine than the food keeps the food fresh the same way a squeeze of lemon makes a piece of fish taste better. Generally, wines from cooler climates have higher acidity, but it can vary by grape variety. This rule of thumb helps explain why it is so difficult to pair wine with salad and vinaigrette since it's hard to top vinegar for acidity.

Now, for the spicy-sweet combo. Sweet wines, such as Riesling, are often overlooked in a stampede to Chardonnay. Slightly sweet wines, also known as "off-dry," actually pair well with spicy foods as they provide a soothing blanket of relief to the tongue, especially when the wines have some core of acidity. Riesling is the ultimate wine to pair with spicy takeout.

Finally, "if it grows together, it goes together" is an aphorism in the world of local food. The same is true with wine. If a wine comes from the Old World, try pairing regional wines with regional foods—Europeans have been doing this for generations and chances are they're onto something: jamón serrano with Rioja; Alsatian sausages with Gewürztraminer; fresh chèvre with Loire wines red and white; Muscadet and oysters; mortadella and Lambrusco. These are all fantastic pairings that have withstood the test of time.

Pairing food and wine does pose (probably undue) anxiety for many people. If I had to pick one "go to" wine for pairing with food, Champagne would probably just edge out Riesling. Sadly, the budget cannot always provide for such a luxury, and some serviceable substitutes can be found in Cava from Spain, American sparkling wines, and Prosecco from Italy. But Champagne pairs so well with such a wide range of foods, from sushi to popcorn, that it's really a host's ace in the hole. Further, the bubbles provide an uplift to even mundane occasions.

Working the other way, if I had a bottle of wine that I had to serve and didn't know what to serve with it, roasted chicken is always a safe bet. It's got fat, it's got protein, and it could go in a number of different wine directions, red or white.

So getting back to the aforementioned chicken tikka masala. What would you pair with that? Stay tuned, or if you're anxious, check the September chapter.

Dr. Vino's Favorite Food-Friendly Grape Varieties

WHITE	RED
Sauvignon Blanc	Pinot Noir
Chenin Blanc	Gamay
Riesling	Cabernet Franc
	Barbera
	Mencia

Broken Glass: The (Un)Importance of Great Stemware

It's not often I find a box from UPS on the doorstep, open it, and smash the contents in the sink. But that's what I did recently when some crystal glasses I'd ordered arrived.

Had I lost all sense with too much Sancerre? No, I was testing out the "impact resistant" claim of some glasses I had purchased, the Tritan Forte by Schott Zwiesel, which have titanium infused in the crystal for strength.

Since I didn't want to have shards of crystal flying around the kitchen, I wimped out and only dropped one stem about three inches, a distance that would have shattered many an ordinary crystal stem. In fact, many crystal stems are so delicate that if you even *look* at them the wrong way they will shatter. But this Forte lived up to its name and withstood the blow.

The shelves of many wine enthusiasts' cabinets sparkle with complete sets of crystal stems. Georg Riedel (rhymes with "needle"), a tenth-generation Austrian glassblower, had the ingenious idea of designing a different glass for each specific grape variety on the theory that each glass would not only augment the aromas but also send the wine to the appropriate spot mapped on the tongue. In fact, his company has come out with an *Oregon* Pinot Noir glass, overlaying place on top of grape. If that keeps up, dedicated enthusiasts will have to add some more cabinets.

Is all this stemware necessary? Well, *Gourmet* magazine ran a story called "Shattering Myths" in which the author asserted that Georg was pulling the wool over discerning drinkers' eyes. The reason wine in Riedel stems tastes better is not because of a tongue map—it simply tastes better because we believe it should. That's an important point.

But since I'm making the argument in this book that context matters, little adds to the immediate sensation of wine to lips as much as proper stemware. Crystal stemware, tall and thin with a generous balloon, sloping in at the top, is the way to go. They can be had for less than $10 a stem, and they will upgrade your Tuesday night wine to feel like a Saturday night wine.

Riedel's glasses are well made and beautiful but, like much fine crystal stemware, they sometimes seem to break if you even sneeze in their general vicinity. That's what led me to the nine dollar per stem Tritan Forte line. And unlike Riedel's, which require perilous hand-washing (during which many of the breakages occur), the Tritan Forte can be tossed in the dishwasher, almost literally. Ravenscroft also makes a handsome Classics line that is lead-free crystal for about eight dollars a stem.

Whether or not you need a set of specific glasses for each grape is up to your tastes and storage space. A nice set of big glasses (Bordeaux) is good to have, as well as a set of smaller ones (Chardonnay). I gave my parents a set of each recently, and now they can enjoy nice glasses throughout the year. (And I can enjoy the good stemware when I visit.)

Waiter, Someone Stole My Stem!

Maximilian Riedel, eleventh generation in his family's crystal company, decided to make his mark: He lopped the stem and the base off a perfectly good glass.

These squat crystal tumblers, known as the Riedel O, now rest sturdily on the counter at many wine bars and restaurants. While they're sleek and slightly irreverent, their biggest drawbacks are fingerprint goobers and body heat.

For a normal glass, holding the stem eliminates those goobery fingerprints on the crystal bowl itself, allowing you to see the wine in all its colorful glory. But the stemless Riedel O gives you no choice but to goober up the bowl, and at the end of a cocktail party, these glasses look a little worse for wear. Plus, holding the bowl heats up the wine. That's fine for cognac, but not for Chablis.

Finding a Wine Shop to Savor

I have a cranky friend who doesn't trust wine magazines—he says they're too conflicted due to the fact that they sell ad space and recommend wines. So whom does he trust? His local wine shop.

Sure, the wine shop has inventory to move. But the staff also wants repeat business, so my cranky friend feels that they're less likely to make a bad recommendation.

And I think he's onto something: Finding a good wine shop can be worth its weight in, well, wine. Unfortunately, most wine in America is sold through supermarkets where all too often wine gets about as much thought from the section's buyers as laundry detergents. However, the number of wine shops in the U.S. is increasing. Here are some indicators that you've found a good shop:

❉ Knowledgeable staff: It's extremely important to befriend someone that you trust at a good shop. Describe to them what you like, what you're looking for, and what you'll be eating. Listen to their suggestions and heed their recommendations. Taste the wines with dinner. Report back to them. Repeat. It's a system destined to bring you many fine evenings.

❉ Free tastings: If a wine store is serious about their recommendations, they'll open up a few bottles, sometimes once a week, sometimes every day (sadly, free in-store tastings are not legal in all states—but they should be!). Taste through all the wines available, even if you think you don't like the wine offered—come on, this is free wine we're talking about, people! The more you taste, the more refined your palate will become.

❉ Great selection: The selection doesn't have to be big, it just has to be good. There's a small shop in Brooklyn that I would love to live around the corner from. It has about three hundred wines—not many, but almost all that I'd like to try. As a rough, superfast indicator, I usually judge the strength of a shop by their Loire selection, since many reds and whites from the Loire are so food-friendly.

❋ Staff-written shelf-talkers: Have you ever wandered down the aisle of a wine store, only to be accosted by little flaps of paper bearing a barrage of numerical scores clipped from magazines? Well, these can be a good or bad feature, depending on your personal view. Generally, I find these flaps, known in the industry as "shelf-talkers," to be poor substitutes for good, knowledgeable staff members—paper is cheaper than well-trained humans, after all. But some shoppers don't like interacting with the staff, even at a small shop, particularly for low-priced wine. So it's not that shelf-talkers are necessarily bad, it's just that if they are staff-written and attributed to a member of the staff, there's more of a chance for interaction with a fellow human to get better wine suggestions the next time.

❋ Good in-house writing: If the staff loves wine, then they should be able to articulate why and how the wine works for them. This doesn't have to be limited to the above-mentioned shelf-talkers—print catalogs, e-mail blasts, and Web sites are great mediums for wine-related writing too.

❋ Reasonable pricing: If they want you to come back, this makes sense, no?

❋ Bonus points: A store with an original design or layout. Crush Wine in Manhattan has a serpentine wall of wine bottles, resting horizontally and backlit. Valhalla in Chicago (which actually closed prematurely) had one bottle of each wine with a funny description available out on a dining room table under a chandelier, and its staff would retrieve the wine of your choice out of the back when asked. It's not that a shop with fluorescent lights and a linoleum floor can't be good—1960s decor just doesn't provide the context for wine experience that we are looking for.

When You Should Be Loyal and When You Should Shop Around

Carla Bruni said that she was "bored to death by monogamy." And that was just weeks before Nicolas Sarkozy, president of France, married the former model and aspiring singer.

Sometimes it pays to channel your inner Carla Bruni while wine shopping. So I encourage you to choose a specific wine that you like, plug it into a specialized wine search engine such as Wine-Searcher.com, WineZap.com, or Vinquire.com. Each site will generate a list of retailers in your area that stock the wine, and then you can sort by price and go to the stores with the lowest prices. Shopping around and doing your homework can pay off.

But there are benefits to a more monogamous approach to wine shopping. Besides the rapport and trust you can develop with a clerk that you know and knows you, there's the fact that being known and, frankly, spending a good chunk of change at a store, should get you some perks. Just as airlines reward their frequent fliers, many wine shops want you to be loyal and offer incentives to frequent customers. Some stores have deals that give you discounts for spending a certain amount or buying a certain number of bottles. Other shops may be able to get different size bottles for their best customers, find them the most hard-to-find futures, or let their best customers know about the best wines for them before they even hit the store shelves.

Frankly, in my opinion, most wine shops need to work harder on customer loyalty. If they are too big to know a loyal customer, which is not itself a problem, there's simply no excuse to not have software that can remember which wines a customer bought (or even better, liked) the last time they paid the store a visit. E-mail campaigns can be tailored to customer desires and less "check out what just landed in the warehouse" in tone and theme. And sure, the standard case discounts are nice, but if a "gold" customer goes to the shop, even for a couple of bottles, shouldn't she get a discount? Stores should provide service, selection, or incentives to keep us loyal and prevent us from channeling our inner Carla Bruni.

Making the Most of Wine Travel:
Find Rare Wines, Call Ahead, and Avoid the *Schlepfaktor*

Visiting a winery is lots of fun for many reasons: seeing the site where the grapes are grown, talking with the people who make the wines, and participating in a wine tasting that would be hard, if not impossible, to recreate at home. As great as it is to go to wine country, wherever that is, there are also some ways to enhance the experience.

Don't forget to call ahead no matter where you are in the world. Some wine producers will welcome drop-ins, and I've had plenty of fun, spontaneous "ooh, this place we're driving by right now looks interesting" kind of visits. But you significantly raise your chances of getting better treatment (or getting in at all) if you have a reservation. Try to schedule two visits for your day in wine country that will serve as anchors to your schedule. Then you won't feel rushed, you'll be sure to hit some places you've had your eye on in between, and you'll still have time for a few drop-ins. Also, try to do your serious tasting early in the morning, since thirsty crowds tend to build later in the day. When you're visiting a winery, try some of the rare wines. Warm up on the introductory wines to make sure you like the house style, but remember you are at the winery, and it's perhaps the only place to try older wines or even special blends they might sell through the tasting room. They're not going to all be worth buying, but they're often worth tasting.

Keep in mind that ultimately you're probably going to want to take home something tangible from your trip, and this is most likely going to be wine itself. Fortunately, the FAA

TIP: PHONE FIRST

If you buy wine from an Internet retailer, it can help to call the store before clicking the purchase button. Because it is often expensive and time consuming to keep the Web site current, I've had situations where I have seen a wine listed on the site and gotten excited, only to call and find it's no longer available. But I've also had good experiences where there was less than a case of a certain wine left in the store—too little to put on the Web site—and the staff member tipped me about it on the phone and let me purchase a few bottles. Don't underestimate the power of human interaction!

now prevents wine tourists from making the same mistake I made when I first went to Napa and Sonoma, since carry-on rules have changed since then. After a weeklong tour of wine country, Michelle and I schlepped cases of wine through the San Francisco airport and onto the plane. They were heavy, and Michelle was not pleased. But what made matters worse was that when we went back to our local wine store at home, many of the wines were right there on the shelves. And for lower prices. Ouch.

So always consider the *schlepfaktor* when buying wine at a winery. Ask yourself, Is it worth it to carry this wine back?

Fortunately, now many domestic wineries, eager not to see tasting-room sales plummet thanks to the liquids ban on planes, offer visitors deals on shipping. Take advantage of this by buying and shipping wines not available in your home market. A quick Internet search or a call to a store at home will verify whether the wines you are contemplating fit the bill (the winery may also be able to tell you). But if you can't verify whether popular bottles are or are not available at your local shop, there's almost always a surefire way to get something special at the winery: Choose some older, "library" wines or go for a nonstandard size bottle, such as a half-bottle or a magnum.

If your travels take you to wineries in the summertime, you'll want to think about just how much wine you want to buy and then keep in the hot car all day (a hot trunk can kill a Cabernet in a couple of hours). Some die-hard wine enthusiasts bring an ice-filled cooler to keep the wines from getting cooked.

Finally, if you go to a small, family-run winery, consider buying a bottle of something, especially if you didn't pay a tasting fee. Obviously it's not essential—there was no quid pro quo when they poured you the wines—but direct-to-consumer sales can yield three times the profit for a winery as selling to distributors.

Before you embark on your year of wine, here's a typical overview of a year on the vine in the Northern Hemisphere.

NOVEMBER, DECEMBER, JANUARY, AND FEBRUARY: A period of low activity in the vineyard. The vines are dormant, but they do need to be pruned so that new canes can grow with new fruit in the following season. Workers toil in vineyards around the world in these winter months, collecting great piles of pruned vine wood. These piles are often burned, creating plumes of smoke from the vineyards. Apparently vine wood can make for good barbecuing too!

In the winery, the maturing wines may be shifted from one barrel or tank to another from time to time, a process of clarification and hygiene. So if you visit a winery at this time you may see people cleaning tanks. Yay, exciting!

MARCH AND APRIL: Break out the buds! I'm not talking beer. The delicate buds start popping out on the vines in a time known as "bud break." This new growth heralds the coming of a new vintage, but it is also risky since there is still the chance of frost through April (or later in some regions), which could kill the new shoots. To prevent this, growers may use wind machines—or even helicopters!—to circulate warm air onto the vines.

MAY: The new growth on the vines has shot out leaves, and the rows of vines look beautiful from a distance. But up close there's something missing: grapes! By mid-May, the vine starts to flower, developing clusters of tiny proto-grapes in a period known as "fruit set." Unlike many plants, grapes don't rely on insects such as bees for pollination; instead, they rely on the wind. Thus, a risk for this time of year is too much wind, particularly storms that also bring unwanted humidity.

JUNE: Green harvest is perhaps the most striking difference between grape growers and corn growers. In the vineyard, workers pass down each row and cut off bunches of the very young, green grapes. The ground between the vines is littered with fruit that might have been turned into wine. But it would have been bad wine. By reducing the amount of crop—something a corn grower would never want to do—the quality increases as the vine concentrates more on the remaining grapes, ultimately resulting in better wines. It must have been tough for the first person to drop all of that fruit on the ground in the name of quality!

Back in the winery, the wines from previous vintages that are maturing in the barrel or tank may be bottled at this time to make room for the new wines arriving at the end of summer.

JULY: Grapes—even those that make red wine—are green up until July. Then in about a week in mid-July, they change from hard and green to soft and blue-purple. In France they call this time *véraison*, and English-speaking vineyard hands thought this was the perfect term so that's what we call it in English too. The grapes get a sugar rush during this time, as sugars in the fruit naturally increase, acidity falls, and the berry size starts to grow. The vineyard manager may drop more of the fruit at this time if some bunches are lagging behind others.

AUGUST, SEPTEMBER, AND OCTOBER: Now is the time when things start humming in the vineyard and the winery. Different grape types are ready for harvest at different times; for example, Sauvignon Blanc is an early ripening grape while Cabernet Sauvignon is late. When to pick will ultimately depend on winemaker style. The overall trend has been to pick fruit later, when it is high in sugars and polyphenols for the reds. In order to determine the harvest date, both the vineyard manager and the winemaker take many samples a day from throughout the vineyard: He will pick a berry and put it in a device called the refractometer, which tells the sugar levels. Or not—some winemakers prefer to rely on taste, and when the fruit and seed taste right in the mouth, the fruit is ready to be picked.

Harvesting is backbreaking work and often relies on migrant labor. All wine-growing regions resolve the labor needs of harvest differently. Some rely solely on migrant laborers, but since they are in high demand from other vineyards, they may not always be available on the day the winemaker wants to pick. Other wineries from Sonoma to Portugal provide housing for a core crew who labor in the vineyard much of the year. One creative solution is Château Palmer in Bordeaux. Starting in 1997, a Danish high school teacher arranged for a bus load of his students to come and live on the property for several weeks and work the harvest, including the grapes for the top wine, which has sold for $300 on release in recent vintages. Bernard de Laage of Château Palmer told me that their lack of wine knowledge is actually an asset since they "have no bad habits" and can be easily trained. Sounds like my kind of work-study.

The harvested grapes go to the winery where their treatment varies with the winemaker's style. Some are taken to the crushpad in the back of the winery, sprinkled with sulfur (an antioxidant) and then put through a crusher-destemmer, a giant metal bin with what looks like an enormous screw at the bottom. Passing through here removes the stems and material other than grapes, known as "MOG." Other wineries use a more expensive treatment called "triage," where workers manually pick out the bad berries off a conveyor belt.

Crushing the fruit puts the sugars from inside the grape in contact with the yeasts that naturally occur on the outside of the grape. The yeasts eat the sugars during fermentation to create alcohol (and carbon dioxide). *Et voilà*, wine!

Well, that's a condensed version of winemaking. It clearly varies by wine type, since the skins and seeds are usually removed from white wine prior to fermentation, while reds ferment with the lovely tannins found in the seeds and skins. And most winemakers actually render the natural yeast inert and introduce commercial yeast strains. Left to their own devices, the natural yeasts might be too few in number to consume all of the sugar, thus leaving the wine with an undesirable amount of sweetness, or residual sugar. So almost all wineries use commercial yeast to have greater control over fermentation. Some even use yeasts developed to confront a local problem, such as yeasts that thrive on the high sugars found in warm areas. A small fraction of winemakers dare to roll the dice that Mother Nature gave them, using only the yeasts found on the skin of the grapes. I admire their bravery and dedication to "natural" winemaking and often find these wines to have great vitality.

Winemakers in different wine regions confront different problems. In cooler climates, such as Germany, the trouble has historically been trying to achieve high enough natural sugars in the grapes (although this appears to be changing as climate change warms these northerly vineyards). So they are allowed to add sugar. By contrast, winemakers in warm climates such as California or Australia confront the issue of having too much sugar and may resort to steps to reduce that sugar, either by adding water (somewhat of a legal gray area) or deploying technology to bring down the alcohol level of the wine. Warm-climate winemakers may also add tartaric acid.

After fermentation the wine is racked, a process that does not involve a torture device, but instead merely siphoning off the freshly fermented wine from the top of the fermentation tank, leaving behind the debris (lees, or spent yeast cells). Many white wines continue their maturation in stainless steel tanks. Fine reds and whites are often put in oak barrels for further barrel aging, usually between six and twenty-four months depending on the wine type and winemaker.

The wine can be racked and clarified (filtered with natural fining agents, such as egg whites) several times before bottling, but generally the winemaker keeps exposure to oxygen at this stage to a minimum.

Now that you've covered some of the basics, prepare to embark on your year of wine. . . .

PART ONE

Winter

The dark days of winter provide many opportunities for celebrating with friends and family. My per bottle cost definitely increases in the winter, but it's not just because of the celebratory nature of the holidays—with the rich foods and many hours spent at the table instead of playing outside as in summer. I prefer serious wines worthy of contemplation. The following are my staples for staying warm and drinking well in the winter months.

❋ Serious and Celebratory Wines for Dark Winter Days and Festive Evenings

CHAMPAGNE: A staple in my cellar during winter. Somehow the bubblies from other parts of the world that I enjoy in the other three seasons recede and let Champagne take prominence for the winter months. The great acidity, the chalky minerality, the excellent pairings with shellfish, and the tremendous crowd appeal all make me pop the cork throughout the winter. See February for more specifics but, in short, look for Diebolt-Vallois, Larmandier-Bernier, Louis Roederer, Charles Heidsieck for nonvintage and, of course, the vintage Champagne.

RIESLING: This wine isn't just for summer. I like fuller-bodied Riesling with some sweetness and perhaps some age. Try producers from southern parts of wine-growing Germany, such as the Pfalz (try Müller-Catoir or Fitz-Ritter). Riesling with age on it makes for a great wine experience since the sweet wines can lose their sweetness but retain their richness. And they still remain relative bargains in the world of mature wine.

BARREL-AGED WHITES: The richness of barrel aging makes for lovely whites of great weight and depth for the winter weather and food. Try the richer whites from Burgundy such as Meursault or even some grand cru Chablis. Joseph Drouhin makes some very good whites and reds from the region. Domaine Leflaive makes prized and pricey white Burgundies.

FINE RED BURGUNDY: The wonderful poise, delicacy, and acidity of red Burgundy go so well with the cooler months. Unfortunately, that Burgundy is excellent isn't exactly a secret, and the demand for fine Burgundy outstrips the tiny supply. If you're looking for a reliable producer try Joseph Drouhin, Domaine Faiveley, Louis Jadot, or Bouchard Père et Fils, which all have wines that run the gamut from affordable to not very affordable, very good to extraordinary. Verget also offers some very solid whites. If you are going to splurge, somehow, someway, try a wine from Domaine Leroy or Domaine Dujac.

BAROLO: Barolo is a marvelous choice for the fall and winter. The wines are subtle, profound, and tremendously age-worthy. Try the Mascarello Monprivato, a personal favorite and an old-school producer. Giacomo Conterno and Cappellano are also wonderfully traditional. Vietti makes some compelling wines that are more modern in style.

NORTHERN RHÔNE: Syrah gets serious in the northern Rhône appellations of Hermitage, Côte Rôtie, and Cornas. Unfortunately, word has gotten out and the prices have run up for Jaboulet, E. Guigal, and Jean-Louis Chave among other top producers. J.L. Chave makes towering reds (and whites) from the Hermitage, but since the mid-1990s the prices have escalated to hedge-fund manager levels. Fortunately, he makes some lower priced wines such as the excellent St. Joseph, another Northern Rhône appellation that makes serious yet more affordable reds.

CABERNET SAUVIGNON: For the best in Cabernet Sauvignon (try the Médoc region of Bordeaux (see December for details). But there are other regions in the world making exciting Cabernet without the price tag. Here are three under $20: BenMarco Cabernet from Argentina comes from a leading grower and has good varietal character, notes of tea leaf, and red fruits. The Ex Libris from Washington State packs a punch with heavier oak treatment. The Cousiño Macul from old vines in the Maipo region of Chile has tremendous power, dark fruits, and lingering intensity. Enjoy all with a big steak.

ZINFANDEL: Winter is the best time in my view for enjoying this burly American wine. A. Rafanelli makes a rich, textured yet balanced version; Ridge has several single-vineyard bottlings (Lytton Springs, Geyserville) that are also tasty and have the benefit of being easier to find.

SWEET WINES: They're rich, thick and supersweet! But the best sweet wines are redeemed by some balancing acidity to offset the sweetness. They're best enjoyed in small quantities, which is why they are often sold in half bottles (375 ml). Here are a few you should consider trying this winter:

Sauternes: The granddaddy of sweet wines, the Sémillon and Sauvignon Blanc grapes hang on the vine until they shrivel and experience botrytis, or "noble rot," when a benevolent gray fungus forms. The resulting wine is golden in color, unctuous, rich, and sweet. Château d'Yquem is the top producer and incredibly expensive. Other creditable choices are available from Château Suduiraut and the nearby region of Monbazillac, where Château Tirecul la Graviere is a leading producer.

Sherry: Turning more to the amber-colored sweet wines, from the sherry region, it's common to blend multiple vintages in a "solera," a system of interconnected barrels. Although only trace elements can remain from the original year, they often get bottled as such. One that I poured at an extended family reunion to much success was the Alvear PX 1927 because that was the year my grandfather graduated from college. (PX stands for Pedro Ximénez, the main grape.) The relatives loved the sentimental connection as well as the thick, almost treacly, taste. But I had the last laugh since the wine only cost me $18.

Muscat from South Australia: It's also made in a solera system like sherry and is also amber in color. Chambers Rosewood Muscat and Campbell's Rutherglen Muscat are the leading producers and both under $20 for a half-bottle.

PORT AND COGNAC: These are such good wintry choices that I wrote whole sections on them! (See January.)

JANUARY

With the New Year comes new resolutions. Why not channel your energy to make changes by resolving to take better wine notes and learn about more grape varieties? Those are two of the things I propose for January. The cold weather also makes it a good time to try some warming drinks, port and cognac (both made from grapes), settle in and be studious by the fire, and reflect on the effects of oak in red wines. And, of course, the best way to beat the January cold is to simply get away, which is why this month's travel suggestion is to go down under for Australia Day.

A Resolution: Taking Better Wine Notes

In addition to resolving to "drink different" this year, you've resolved to keep better wine-tasting notes. Come on, you've got to keep better track of the expanding line item labeled "wine" in Quicken!

Even if wine doesn't appear in your household accounting program (yet), taking notes is foundational to learning about wine. It helps you re-

JANUARY TIP

This month, stock up at sales! Many wine stores clear out inventory at this time of year. Back up the truck! One wine writer once told me that he buys most of his year's supply of wine at sales, particularly in spring and fall, buying eight to ten cases at a time. Whoa! If you've got the space, it's a great way to stretch your wine dollar.

member which wines you enjoyed and which ones you hated, and it also sharpens your ability to describe wines.

You can jot your notes anywhere, on paper, in the computer, or in your handheld. At our house, Michelle and I have some spiral sketchbooks that we fill up with our notes. It's fun to have guests contribute their thoughts too (but there's no obligation!), since that way our tasting book also serves as a guest book. Flipping through it brings back memories of good times as well as good wines.

In addition to taking notes, sometimes I float labels off particularly memorable bottles in a bowl of warm water with a drop of dishwashing soap and then tape them in our tasting guest book. Unfortunately, glue technology has improved so many labels don't float off anymore. In those cases, I snap a digital picture instead. It's less romantic, but it is faster, cleaner, and easier to tag in a digital library for future searching. Or you can take pictures of labels with your cell phone and store the shots in a "wine" file on the phone, so you can refer back to past faves while in the wine store.

But the thorny issue remains: Just what should you write about the wines?

One of my pet peeves in restaurants is when you ask a server about a dish and she responds, "It's great!" While long on enthusiasm, such a description comes up short in terms of actual, objective detail—who's to say the server's definition of great is the same as mine? Applying that notion to wine notes, you could simply write "great stuff!" and be done with your entry. And if that works for you, since you know your own definition of "great," then so much the better. But when you get the next vintage of that same wine and want to see how it compared to the previous, such a short description may not be enough to help you make a good comparison. So I suggest being a bit more objective and descriptive in your notes. It may seem like a chore at first, but trust me, you'll soon get the hang of it and be glad you put in the extra bit of effort.

To improve your note-taking, you need to really tune in to your impressions of the wine in your glass from start to finish. In Paris I stumbled upon an antique print shop that had a multipanel print about wine appreciation. The print depicted a jolly old man in each moment of wine appreciation: first with the eyes, then the nose, then the mouth. The final panel read "appreciation" and pictured the man relaxing in a comfy chair.

Simple as the illustration was, it conveyed a good order for approaching wine tasting: First consider the appearance, then the aromas, then the taste. Fortunately, the anatomy of the face is such that it's easy to remember since your eyes, nose, and mouth appear in that same descending order. It also serves as a good basis for what you should try to write about the wine that will help you remember it in the future. Here's a further breakdown of what to include in your tasting notes:

COLOR is often an overrated characteristic to use to judge wine because it's not always accurate in terms of its predictions. Color can, however, be a quick indicator of age. For Cabernet Sauvignon, for instance, an older wine is more brick red and often more transparent, while a younger wine is inky purple and opaque. On the other hand, I've had plenty of wines ranging from Pinot Noir to Nebbiolo to Pinot d'Aunis that are light in color, transparent, and have aggressive, youthful tannins. And I've had rich, golden wines that I thought would be sweet but were actually dry. So color can fake you out. But it's still worth noting what a wine looks like.

AROMAS are often underrated in tasting notes, but they merit close attention before you go stampeding for the palate. We can perceive many more aromas than we can taste, by a factor of about one thousand to one. In fact, there's one California winemaker who doesn't drink wine anymore—he makes his wine, which sells for $300 a bottle, entirely by selecting and blending aromas. Don't take your nose for granted! In fact, for the sake of experimenting, clothespin your nose and then see how hard it is to differentiate between wines. If that sounds painful, take heart: Some researchers already enlisted subjects to do that, and they had tremendous difficulty even distinguishing red from white without the use of their olfactory sense. The nose knows!

TASTE is often overrated. Granted, this is where it has to all come together: The mouthfeel, balance, and weight the wine has in the mouth, are the important parts of tasting. But we can really perceive only about four discrete tastes: sweet, sour, salty, and bitter. So your notes on taste can't be superficial—you need to pay attention and try to capture the entire arc of the wine in your notes. The best wines have a beautiful arc. The arc is broken down into three stages: the "attack," the midpalate, and the finish. Think about plotting this on an X-Y axis and sketching at what point the wine is most intense. Many young wines today are all attack and then fall flat. However, some of the best Pinot Noirs and Rieslings, for example, are all finish, and linger for over sixty seconds in the mouth. Great stuff. Anyway, if words escape you, maybe plotting the arc visually will help.

So as you embark on a new year, try to start jotting down notes of the color, the aromas, and the tastes of the wines you discover. At first it might all taste like "wine," but as you taste more, you'll gain more points of reference and write more precise notes. As you taste more wines, your tasting notes can include references to other wines that remind you in one way or another of the one you are tasting. This is the kind of writing assignment you shouldn't really mind.

VOLATIZING THE ESTERS

This impressive-sounding phrase explains why wine geeks are always swirling and sniffing. The fact is we all have much better noses than we do tongues. We can perceive a huge amount of aromas—upward of five thousand—while we can only taste four discrete tastes. So as much as we might want to get down to the actual tasting part of trying wines and foods, our noses can often tell us more than our tongues.

People swirl wine in the glass to volatize the esters, which are small aromatic compounds that like to lie on the surface of the wine. Swirling shoots them out of the glass and toward your nose. (Practice swirling on a tabletop before attempting at a cocktail party.)

One time at a wine-tasting lunch, I sat down at my place at the table and put my small, black, leather-bound notebook, a Moleskine, down on the table in front of me. Then another writer sat down next to me, and he put down a Moleskine, although his had a binding on the top, making it more of a notepad. We were joined by a third writer who pulled out yet another, slightly larger version of the Moleskine black notebook.

Clearly, this Italian notebook is the unofficial pad of wine writers. Get a small one and keep it in your bag. Take it out whenever you're tasting wine. It will make you look like a pro, and nine out of ten servers in restaurants will take you more seriously. It's clinically proven.

Of course, you can also use a fifty-nine-cent pad from the drugstore. I did that for a long time, but then I left one full of notes on a plane and it was never returned. So I started to spring for the $11 fancy notebooks. I figure if I ever lose one, it looks substantial and official, so someone might bother to return it to me.

High-tech tasters can use an iPhone, BlackBerry, or Treo for digital convenience (and don't forget about the camera phone for capturing label images). The only drawback to the high-tech note-taking is that the sommelier may think you're banging out e-mail or text messages and assume you're distracted from the meal and the wine. Bottom line: Get convenience and respect with the little black book.

Variety Is the Spice of Life:
Do a Wine Century

Variety, varietal. If there's one guy who knows the difference, it's Steve De Long.

Steve and Deborah De Long are on a worthy mission to educate wine consumers about grape varieties beyond Chardonnay and Cab. To achieve this goal, they compiled the handsome De Long Wine Grape Varietal Table, a poster that graphically arranges, from heaviest to lightest, the descriptions of

184 grape varieties. If I owned a wine shop, I'd hang it somewhere the customers could linger and take it all in.

But since I don't have a shop, I have instead taken an interest in their Wine Century Club. Drink wine from one hundred different grape varieties and you're in (blends count)! Membership in a club has never been so easy. The application, which asks you to list the one hundred varieties you've sampled, relies on the honor system. As the application form states, "Should you lie, may the wrath of Bacchus curse your palate!"

I hand out the application to my students at the beginning of my six-week classes. We usually fill up about a third of the form, and participants often bring enough experience to get to the halfway mark. Then the going gets tough. But there are always some participants who really get into it. They start searching out free tastings at shops around town to try indigenous varieties such as Ribolla Gialla, Greco di Tufo, and Aglianico from Italy (and with over two thousand to choose from, many could qualify several times over from Italy alone); some hit the Greek section of the store to try Moschofilero, Assyrtiko, and Xinomavro; and some dive down the Spanish aisle to try Godello, Albariño, and Verdejo.

So get out of your groove and start trying some new grape varieties. Without belaboring the point, a wine can be made from a single grape variety, say Cabernet Sauvignon, and then become a varietal wine (e.g., labeled by the grape variety instead of a blend). So just remember that variety, as in grapes, is the spice of Steve's life—don't call them varietals since that's an adjective. You don't want him to revoke your membership before you're even in the club.

If you'll excuse me, I'm off to find some Scuppernong from North Carolina. . . .

Note: There is no physical address for this virtual club, so don't expect to be able to relax over a glass of recherché Romorantin with other members in a clubhouse. Once you're in, though, you do get a handsome plaque mailed to you and a sense of satisfaction.

Lush or Rustic: A Malbec Taste Test

After tasting my tenth red wine of the morning at a panel tasting in New York City, I overheard a fellow taster declare it "rustic." Was that a compliment or a slam? I wondered.

The more I thought about it, the more I thought, It depends. If the Cabernet were a $100 bottle from Napa Valley, no doubt "elegant" or "sleek" would be more along the lines of what the winemaker was hoping for. But if it were a French country red, the comment would be most apt. A lot of times rustic wines have a great deal of character and charm and are more food-friendly, values that the French appreciate. But the fact of the matter is, Malbecs often fit both descriptions.

This January, as you resolve to taste more thoughtfully and take better notes, grab two bottles of Malbec—a perfect winter wine—and taste the two ends of the rustic–sleek spectrum yourself. The Malbec grape makes inky black wines and exemplifies the different styles between the Old World and the New. And its history and heritage are as full of contradictions and complexities as the wine it bears.

The ancestral home of Malbec is Cahors, a region deep in the heart of southern France. Although the winemakers had geographic access to other countries through the rivers to the sea, the powers in Bordeaux historically resisted allowing the winemakers to use these easy routes to the world and imposed high taxes on the wines of the interior. Thus, the wines remained mostly regional and their character to this day remains, oftentimes, rustic. The acidity of the grape grown in Cahors might be higher than the Malbec grapes in other regions, the tannins a tad raspy, and overall less approachable without decanting or food.

In Argentina, by contrast, new producers came into this wine country and crafted wines explicitly for the export markets. They are often sleek and stylish with sometimes excessive oak treatments, a vaguely sweet taste, and higher levels of alcohol. The grape, grown in the high desert, tends to make a wine that has sweet fruit on the attack, a meaty midpalate, and soft, supple tannins on the finish. Add a malolactic fermentation, a way of increasing the smoothness of the wine by converting tough malic acid into creamy lactic acid (think milk), and you end up with just what the export markets wanted, a big, luscious red that can be consumed on its own or with hearty food, such as grilled meat.

So invite some friends over on a cold night and pour a bottle from each region to taste the differences. From Cahors, Clos La Coutale is from a family-run estate and makes a good value wine for under $15. Clos de Gamot is also a good, traditional producer but slightly higher in price. From Argentina, try the Terrazas de los Andes Malbec Reserva or the Catena Zapata Malbec for good examples of the oaked, Argentina style at around $15. (The Clos de los Siete, made by the controversial winemaker Michel Rolland, is also around $15, but has a Syrah and Cabernet blended in to make it all throttle and no finesse—the Ford Mustang of Malbecs.) For bonus points, you can remove the foil at the top of each bottle, put the bottles in bags to conceal their identities, and pour the wines "blind." Then try them with dinner and see how they taste with food.

Try the experiment again a few weeks later with other red grapes from two different producers in two different regions. Soon, you'll know when and whether you're into rustic charm, and you'll be well on your way to drinking different in the new year.

Port: A Stealth Weapon for Providing Winter Warmth

Port has fallen on hard times today as global demand for dessert wines has softened. People are pushing back from the dinner table without drinking a sweet wine. It's a pity because port today is better than ever. It is also a drink that craves the right ambience for consumption, and that ambience is best achieved on a cold winter night. So add port to your January wine list. On its own, port can be very good. Add a sharp cheese, such as Stilton or blue, some walnuts, and a roaring fire, and enjoy port's warming kick. The rest is up to you.

So what is port? Like sherry and Champagne, port is a blend of grapes from different vineyards. The grapes must come from a zone up the Douro River in Portugal, a trip that took three days by mule in the old days, but is now about a two-hour drive. The British set up warehouses known as "lodges" in Villa Nova de Gaia, across from the river Porto, and bottled and blended port from there, which is how it got its name. (Port was all the rage in the eighteenth century. The British shipped barrels of it home from Porto, making it the most popular wine in Britain for two centuries.)

Harvested from the steep slopes of the Douro, the red grapes are put in open-top fermentation vats made from granite called *lagars*. Then a bunch of men in short-shorts start stomping them under their bare feet, singing while they work.

Nothing beats the human foot for crushing grapes for port wine. The foot crushes the grape delicately without bursting the seed and releasing its bitter tannins. The honor of being trodden underfoot is reserved for only 2 percent of all port—the best, vintage ports—since the process is twice as expensive as using mechanized crushers. In tribute to feet everywhere, the mechanized crushers are actually built to emulate the human foot, with a soft underside on each of the firm pistons. (They don't have toes, though.) These mechanized crushers are, however, beginning to give feet a run for their money as the technology improves. David Guimarerns of the Taylor-Fladgate Partnership, a leading producer, told me that in five years the technology will have improved so that tasters won't be able to distinguish the mechanized-trodden from foot-trodden.

The fermentation is "stopped" while the wine is still sweet and fruity by adding some clear brandy. This also raises the alcohol level to 20 percent. While that's higher than dry table wines, it's at a more drinkable level than, say, cognac, which has a 40 percent alcohol level.

Port is phenomenally age-worthy, which for me makes it fun to collect and explore. When tasting and purchasing port, keep in mind that not every year is declared a vintage since "vintage port" is a designation saved for the best. Vintage ports spend the least amount of time in the big maturation barrel, since they must be bottled within thirty-three months. So most of their aging occurs slowly in the bottle. And once you pull the cork—sometimes with special tongs that, when heated, cut through the neck of the bottle, cork and all—try to drink it that day or in the next two to three days.

Our first son was born in 2003 when heat waves baked Europe vineyards, leading to wines that are likely to only be good in their youth, if at all. This posed a problem for me since I wanted to get some wine for us when we celebrate our son's twenty-first birthday. Fortunately, the heat did not harm the 2003 vintage for port, which was widely regarded as a very strong year, so I got some bottles of 2003 vintage port. Sweet now, I know that in the year 2024 they will have mellowed beautifully. Good thing, since they set me back a pretty penny, ranging from $50 to $90 a bottle.

But there are two cheaper ways to explore the charms of port from a vintage. The first is to get an "LBV" or "late bottled vintage" port. These spend about double the time in the big barrels as vintage port, which speeds up their evolution. They are released after about five years. Then there is Colheita, a style of port that spends even more time in barrel but still receives the stamp of the vintage. These are easier to drink upon release but are still age-worthy in the bottle—I've tried a Colheita that was forty years old and drinking beautifully. Both a good LBV and a good Colheita start at about $18 a bottle.

Tawny ports are also worth exploring. These are blends from multiple vintages, aged in barrels. Where vintage ports tend to have more of a ruby hue with fresher more intense fruits, tawnies are more, well, tawny in color and have more mature fruits and greater delicacy earlier. They're not meant for you to age in the cellar (the producer did that for you already); rather they are for drinking within a few weeks of opening. They often come in ten- and twenty-year-old bottlings. Going for thirty- or forty-year tawnies, which can easily start at $80, is overkill, in my view. If you're going to pay that much, you might as well buy mature vintage port.

Finally, there's ruby port. Mostly ruby port doesn't have a lot going for it since it is often too young and too sweet. While it's sometimes found in desserts or as an apéritif, ruby is especially great for one thing: Christmas smoking bishop, mulling port with the juice of roasting oranges. A ladle of this was what turned the mood of Ebenezer Scrooge in *A Christmas Carol*.

✳ *Five Great Ways to Use Port to Your Advantage this Winter*

QUINTA DO NOVAL NACIONAL: Perhaps the best vintage port, the Nacional is certainly one of the most expensive. Noval is now a unit of AXA Millésimes run by Christian Seeley, who also oversees Suduiraut in Sauternes and Pichon-Longueville (Baron) in Bordeaux. $$$$

NIEPOORT: Dirk Niepoort has taken over this family-run house and the results are outstanding across the board. His 2003 is excellent in its sweet intensity; the 2005 I like even better, although at this stage, it's very young. Check back in twenty years. $$$$

TAYLOR FLADGATE: This premier house makes elegant vintage port ($$$$); the twenty-year-old tawny is also very good, at a lower price point ($$$).

DOW'S: The LBV here is often a great value, rolling in under $20. It's especially good for friends who work in equities since it has the word "DOW" on the label. $$

QUINTA DO INFANTADO: João Roseira makes his port only with grapes from his own vineyards, using foot-treading. The ruby is a great value. $$

XOXO: From Cognac, with Love

What do Kim Jong-il, Winston Churchill, and Jay-Z have in common? The answer is not much, except for their love of cognac. And cognac is another perfect antidote for winter.

With a list of fans as diverse as this, how could you not be curious to learn what attracts powerful people to the drink? If you need more incentive, consider this: Samuel Johnson threw down a challenge to us wine geeks more than two hundred years ago when he was offered a glass of claret. According to his chronicler, Boswell, he replied, "No, sir, claret is the liquor for boys; port, for men; but he who aspires to be a hero must drink brandy." Well, I don't know if I aspire to hero status, but I'm not going to settle for being a mere "boy"!

Perhaps no grape-based drink is so defined by those who consume it rather than those who make it. Cognac, like Champagne, is in fact a place. And like Champagne, big brands dominate. The biggest distiller, Hennessy, is a part of LVMH, which is also the parent company of the biggest Champagne house, Moët. Care to guess the best-known wine and spirits brands according to *Business Week*? Hennessy is the top with Moët in second place. Both brands involve master blending and master marketing.

Even more than Champagne, cognac is the ultimate bling bottle. For instance, as if the Louis XIII from Rémy Martin were not expensive enough at $1,400 a bottle, the house released Black Pearl, a $10,000 bottle. Hennessy retaliated with Beauté du Siècle, which it sells complete with a display case designed by ten artists, for $220,000. Delivery is included—a member of the Hennessy board will bring it over in a stretch Hummer. Seriously.

But beyond the bling, cognac is a delicious and aromatically intense distilled spirit that has a finish that just won't quit. Growers in the region grow grapes (Colombard and Ugni Blanc mostly) at abundant yields that would make a thin, white wine if they chose to stop there. Instead, distillers send the thin wine through a traditional copper still, and it comes out at 35 percent alcohol. Then they distill it again to get 70 percent alcohol. (I once visited a distillery and tasted the fiery spirit right out of the still. At that point, it is clear and 70 percent alcohol. Much to my surprise, it was possible to perceive aromas distinct to the vineyard, potent as it was.)

The spirit is then moved to oak barrels where it ages for up to an astonishing fifty-five years. Since wine only ages for at most two or three years in a barrel, this seems like an eternity. As the cognac ages in the barrel, it gains color and intensity up to the fifty-five year apex before going downhill. Then the cognac gets transferred to "demi-johns," large glass jugs wrapped in wicker to keep any light out, which preserve the cognacs as they were when they came out of the barrel, frozen in time. The very best of those get placed in the inner sanctum of the cellar, known as *paradis*, or "heaven." These make up the bling bottlings.

Here's the quick and dirty about the various levels of cognac:

❖ VS: The youngest cognac and usually quite rough. I haven't quite worked out what to do with this grade. Add soda?

❖ VSOP: Cognac starts to get serious here and is great for cocktails and some are even ready for sipping.

❖ XO: The oldest cognacs that are widely available. These are for sipping. Just try not to use a ridiculously large snifter—leave those for Kim Jong-il to look silly with.

Some of the smaller producers don't even use this system. But the general rule still applies: The older a cognac is, the more suitable it is for sipping instead of mixing.

✤ *Four Cognacs that You Don't Have to Be a Hip-hop Artist or a Dictator to Enjoy*

HINE VSOP: At less than $50 a bottle, this is a good bottling from an excellent smaller house. Great in Sidecars or for sipping. $$$

DELAMAIN: This producer buys mostly maturing barrels from the best growers and continues to age them in the cellar where time stands still. They make beautiful, delicate cognacs without the bling renown but still a little bling in price (about $250). They are one of the few producers to pursue a vintage program, which makes their cognacs a great birth-year gift. $$$$

FRAPIN: The biggest grower-blender who exclusively uses their own fruit from their five hundred acres of vineyards. The beautiful aromas of their Château Fontpinot XO (about $100) are worthy of contemplating on a wintry evening in front of a fire. Beautiful stuff—I've converted quite a few cognac skeptics with this. $$$$

PAUL GIRAUD: Giraud, a former racecar driver, grows his own grapes in a prime part of the region, hand harvests, and does his own distillation. His VSOP (about $40) has great character—and handles corners well. $$$

*M*aking cocktails from wine is almost always a losing proposition—with the notable exception of the French 75, a classic cocktail made from a Champagne base and a dash of gin. So if we are to join the cocktail fad, my best advice is to hop on and ride a sidecar to victory. This olde tyme cocktail is mercifully not made from still wine, but it is made from grape-based cognac.

To make a sidecar, pour two ounces of a good cognac (the Hine VSOP is great) over ice in a cocktail shaker, add a half-ounce of fresh (essential!) lemon juice and a half-ounce of Cointreau. Add simple syrup (1 cup sugar dissolved in one cup water) to taste if at all, and shake for longer than you would think necessary. Or pour into a small martini glass with a sugared rim. You'll never order a cosmo again.

Travel to: *Australia—Shake Off the Winter Blues with a Trip Filled with Sun and Fun Down Under*

Whether you visit over the holidays or for Australia Day on January twenty-sixth, the hot days, diverse wines, and cheery people make for a great getaway in January. So ditch the cold and get down in Australia for some post-holiday R and R and Riesling.

Speaking of, Jeffrey Grosset is the rock star of Riesling. Hailed as one of the top ten white winemakers in the world by Britain's *Decanter* magazine, this winemaker with a shaved head is also a *terroirist*—that is to say, an ardent believer in *terroir,* a French term that has no ready English translation but roughly means a "sense of place." Grosset even points out that the indigenous people of Australia have used the word *pangkarra* for thousands of years, a word that similarly refers to the characteristics of a certain place.

In the eyes of the American wine consumer, Australia is known for lighthearted critter labels and consistent wines that jostle with each other on the shelves of supermarkets. A large country that has a land mass equivalent to the United States but a population of only around 20 million, the wine producers have looked to the export markets to soak up the tankers full of Shiraz and Chardonnay.

But to discover the *pangkarra* and people like Grosset, it's necessary to travel out of the supermarket aisle, all the way Down Under, and about three hours by car up the Main North Road from Adelaide in South Australia. Even though Grosset's two main vineyards, Springvale Watervale and Polish Hill, are only four miles apart, he describes the first as a "soft rock site" with red loam over limestone and the second as a "classic hard rock site" with shale, slate, sandy loam, clay, and gravel. (See what I mean about him being a rock star?) The Springvale produces Rieslings more accessible in their youth, and the more expensive Polish Hill is more age-worthy.

Age is not something that one might associate with Australian wine. But the top wines can easily rack up decades. Jacob's Creek Steingarten Riesling, widely considered one of the country's top wines, generally starts to come into its own after seven years. Penfolds' Grange, the country's iconic red wine, is not even released for six years after the vintage and can mature for decades.

Competing with the Great Barrier Reef and the sights and vibe of Sydney, South Australia might not be at the top of your itinerary for Australia, but the state makes almost half the country's wines—including all those mentioned thus far. Adelaide, the country's fifth largest city and capital of the state, is a pocket-size home to one million people and has a cosmopolitan feel with its leafy, Victorian neighborhoods bisected by tram lines. The site provides a convenient springboard to the surrounding wine country.

Practically no winery is closer—a mere fifteen minutes from downtown into the Adelaide Hills—than the fabled Penfolds Magill Estate, which still has the original Dr. Penfold's cottage and is the site where winemaker Max Schubert first blended Grange in 1951. Tastings of the top wines are available by appointment; those who just show up at the tasting room can enjoy the other wines and the views from the site, a sweeping five-acre Shiraz vineyard in the foreground as well as views down to the city and the Gulf Saint Vincent. Have dinner at the restaurant, considered among the country's finest, and soak up the view through the wall of windows. With the exception of Champagnes and dessert wines, the entire wine list comprises Penfold's wines, including a vertical tasting of Grange dating back to 1970. However, at $2,000 and for my birth-year wine, I wouldn't have much of a vacation left if I were to order it.

Only about thirty-five miles from Adelaide up the Sturt Highway lies Barossa, arguably Australia's best known growing region, which makes singular, intense, high-octane Shiraz. The sun beats down, the grapes ripen quickly, and the resulting wines often pack a punch with high alcohol levels and a sweetness and smoothness that often comes from finishing fermentation in American oak barrels. The small stone Lutheran churches that dot the valley reflect the German roots of the original settlers who fled religious persecution in the 1840s (as do the various bakeries, butcher shops, and pubs).

Barossa wineries range from multinationals to family-owned. Visiting Jacob's Creek with their elaborate welcome center (and petting zoo to keep kids occupied) provides a chance to taste some of the high-end wines in the VIP tasting. Dropping by the Grant Burge estate offers a chance to see one of the remaining holdouts still using cork closures—with cork trees planted on the property to boot. To check out a small, family-owned producer, dropping by the cellar door at Glaetzer will bring you to the big Shiraz of another shaven-headed winemaker, Ben Glaetzer.

Back in the cooler Clare Valley to the north, the tan, rolling hills with the green leaves of vineyards are punctuated by tall eucalyptus trees. Known for Riesling, such as the Grosset, as well as Pikes and Mount Horrocks (made by Stephanie Toole, a Kiwi and the life partner of Jeffrey Grosset), it's also home to good B and Bs and old country pubs, and a slower pace than Barossa. When you start to shake off the jetlag, you just might think about staying awhile and cracking open a cold one—a dry Riesling, that is.

✳ **TASTING TERM:** Winery visits happen at the "cellar door," or public tasting room.

✳ **TASTING FEES:** There are mostly none. I guess they figure if we head all the way down there, the least they can do is give us a taste of the wines for free? The wineries often expect you to taste in their suggested order, but feel free to just do whites or reds if you like. And chat with the staff since they often have tips about the best local dining spots as well as their wines.

✳ **CULTURAL NOTE:** Although it is fading somewhat, Australia has a vibrant and widespread culture of BYO ("bring your own"). With roots dating back to a period when it was hard to obtain a liquor license, they now remain largely because of tradition—and it is a great tradition since it means that it's possible to enjoy fine food without extravagant markups. Even Tetsuya's, a French-Asian fusion restaurant that has long been a culinary standard-bearer for Australia, still allows BYO, though for a $50 corkage fee. It's best to call ahead and confirm the policy to avoid disappointment. But BYO remains much more widely acceptable here than in the U.S.

✳ *Some Other Australian Regions, in a Nutshell*

HUNTER VALLEY: The closest region to Sydney, thus the weekends can be busy. Boatloads of Chardonnay, but some nice Sémillon too. Tyrrell's is a beautiful and very Aussie winery (watch the kangaroos bound by). Go in through the screen door that's been there for sixty years, and they'll pour the whole line of wines for you. McWilliam's is a good family-owned spot.

RUTHERGLEN: A small region between Melbourne and Sydney that came to be with a gold rush in the 1850s and today appears somewhat as a dustbowl that time forgot. The unctuous sweet wines known as "stickies," fortified wines from Muscat and Muscadelle grapes, hail from here. Be sure to check out Chambers Rosewood Vineyards, which has received several scores of 99 and 100 from Robert Parker, and consider how this humble property compares to other 100-point properties from France or Napa.

MELBOURNE: Here you'll find many great restaurants for wine lovers, and many wine regions are perfect for day trips. The Mornington Peninsula should be on the itinerary of all wine-loving golfers.

TASMANIA: A cool growing climate, this island state is making some good sparklers and some interesting Riesling.

MARGARET RIVER: All the way in Western Australia, wine-loving surfers should be sure to check out Margaret River. Leeuwin Estate produces some notable whites and reds; Evans & Tate has some good values; Moss Wood and Cullen make serious Cabs.

✤ *Be Sure to Taste:*

SPARKLING SHIRAZ: This distinctive purple fizzy wine is an Australian tradition at Christmas. Try the examples from Seppelt, a leading producer that isn't exported much.

COONAWARRA CABERNET: This is a leaner red for those who find the ultra-ripe Borossa Shiraz overbearing. Not much of it is exported to the U.S. so look for it at local shops, restaurants, and wine bars.

When to go: Mid-December to the end of January are the summer holidays Down Under so expect to book early for hotels and restaurants. Harvest roughly occurs between March and May, which can be a fun period with the fall colors. The biggest harvest festival is the Barossa Vintage Festival, which usually coincides with Easter. The mild climate makes it a great year-round destination.

Getting there: No matter how you try it, the trip down under is long. If you've got the time, particularly if you're flying from the East Coast of America, try an "around the world" ticket to mix up the return with another stop. And if you're redeeming miles for the trip, try to book as far in advance as possible.

SOMMELIER SURVEY

Rajat Parr,

Wine Director, The Michael Mina Group, San Francisco, California

How does context matter for enjoying wine?

I think it is the most important thing. Where you are, who you are, and what mood you are in—these things matter as much as anything. How much you know about the wine is not important, as long as you love it. It's all about enjoyment.

What is one of your favorite food-wine pairings?

Dungeness crab with drawn butter and Lafon Meursault.

How important is pairing wine with the seasons?

I like to think of the seasons as two entities, cold weather and warm weather. I think it has a lot to do where I live: In San Francisco we don't really have a summer. It is always cool.

If you had to have one wine per season, what would it be?

Winter: Côte Rôtie
Spring: Red Burgundy
Summer: German Riesling
Fall: Barolo

If you had to pick one season for drinking wine, what would it be? And why?

I love the fall. It's harvest time, there are warm days and cold nights, and you can enjoy great German Riesling for lunch and then a hearty red.

What's one of your most memorable food-wine occasions where the location or company really mattered?

It was last summer in a restaurant in Axpe (Spanish Basque country) called Extebarri. Everything was cooked on a grill. I was with a good friend, and we drank a great Txacoli and a 1995 Vega Sicilia Unico. The simple cooking in the countryside was among the best I have had.

FEBRUARY

To paraphrase Thomas Hobbes, February may be nasty and brutish but it is, thankfully, short. And fortunately there are all sorts of wine-inclusive events throughout the month to help us overcome the winter days, including the traditional Valentine's Day for popping Champagne corks and the entirely made up Open That Bottle Night, an excuse for midwinter indulgence. Of course, the Super Bowl is a big drinking holiday, during which you should attempt to replace that beer mug with a Champagne flute and try not to get ejected while doing so. And, it's a great time of year to indulge in some travel to the wine country of Sonoma before the crowds of summer descend upon the region.

Super Bowl: When the Chips Are Down, Don't Raise a Beer!

With the Super Bowl looming after weeks of playoffs and hype, some wine geeks may be wondering what to drink during the event. Never fear, there are solutions, so don't go reaching for that six-pack!

Impossible Super Bowl Food-Wine Pairing: Chips and Salsa

Beer, beer, beer: It's everywhere you look during the Super Bowl. We must fight back beer's dominance and make inroads into this important social event! It is the most viewed television event of the year, we must best beer drinkers on their own culinary turf with the ultimate TV snack food: chips and salsa!

Here's what I suggest: Take a page from the beer playbook and add bubbles or go sweet. Or both.

On the bubbly side, go with Prosecco or Cava instead of Champagne. Not only are they a better match for the finger food, it's also cheaper to spray your living room with them when your team wins. (Okay, I'm kidding, but my patented Dr. Vino spycam has revealed that most club owners go for cheap bubbles to spray in locker rooms, not the good stuff.)

Cava and Prosecco generally have a faint sweetness that will help cut the spiciness of the salsa. Try Mionetto Prosecco ($) or 1+1=3 Cava ($) with your Super Bowl snack. The good thing about cheap bubblies is that if you don't like them on their own, you can always make a mimosa.

The only problem with having a flute of bubbly among the traditional beer-drinking sports fans is the possibility of ridicule. But, come on, it's brut! And there's always bubbly in a can (yes, Francis Ford Coppola has one called "Sofia," named after his daughter), but that could be seen as pandering.

Another way to go is just sweet, without the bubbles. Try a nice Riesling like the Geil, Leitz Dragonstone, or "Dr. L." Rieslings tend to be good newbie wines too, and there may be some newbies at your Super Bowl gathering that you can convert to Team Grape. The final option is to add zing. Like a slice of lime in a Corona, you can add zing to the chips and salsa with a crisp, zingy white such as Sauvignon Blanc from New Zealand, or Albariño or Verdelho from Spain.

Champagne: The Big and the Small of It

When dreaming up big Valentine's Day plans, besides flowers, Hallmark, and chocolate, one other element usually springs to mind: Champagne. While bubbles are always impressive, so is being able to pick out a great bottle, which doesn't always have to have "Moët" or "Veuve" on the label. Here's a quick rundown on how to score big with the bubbles:

When you're shopping for Champagne, there are the big names, and then there's everything else. And by "everything else," I mean grower Champagnes. Grower Champagnes may lack the flash of their better-known counterparts, but you wouldn't know it by looking at their price tags, which are just as high-profile. So, why spend the same on an unheard of producer when you could buy one of the better-known brands? In a word: taste. In two words: wine geekdom.

Before diving into the topic of grower Champagne, let's go with the known. And few others are as well known as LVMH, the global luxury goods company that has a 60 percent market share of Champagne sales in the U.S. Their brands include such well-known names as Veuve Clicquot, Moët, Dom Pérignon, and Krug. Yeah. They're big. As with all the other best known houses, known as *grandes marques*, Moët & Chandon (as it is known) has been fabulously successful thanks to buying mostly other people's grapes and then blending wine. In fact, the brand management has been so well executed that the big Champagne houses are among the most successful brands in the wine business: They enjoy wide name recognition and a relatively high volume, and sell at a high price point. They've hit the economic sweet spot. Moët & Chandon sold 600,000 cases in 2005 in the U.S., and the average retail price of each bottle was $43.50. That's definitely the other end of the spectrum from Two Buck Chuck.

As indicated above, the big houses do two things extremely well: They are master blenders and master marketers. A master blender (or a team of blenders) blends the fermented juice from Chardonnay, Pinot Noir, and Pinot Meunier grapes to aim for consistency, an established house style. That way, a bottle of Veuve Clicquot tastes just like the next bottle of Veuve Clicquot (although they can tweak blends for different markets, for example, by adding more residual sugar to the American bottling). This consistency applies to their top Champagnes as well as their entry-level Champagnes, which also blend wine from different vintages, resulting in a final blend bottled as "nonvintage" or "NV." Champagne bottled from a single vintage, even from a big house, is meant to reflect that vintage character within the house style. As to the marketing, just open the December issue of any glossy magazine for a taste of that aspect.

On the other end of the Champagne continuum is a merry band of small growers. No, they're not elves—they just don't make a lot of bubbly. But that's also a point of difference. Like a traditional château, and unlike the big houses, they grow their own grapes and make their own wine.

A champion in America of this sort of "farmer fizz" is the erudite importer Terry Theise. He has a portfolio of very good grower Champagne so check the back label for his name; you'll likely end up with a good example of the style.

Theise argues (check out his extensive and articulate catalog) that the appeal of grower Champagne has three components: value, ethics, and taste. The value, he claims, comes because these farmers are not spending money placing their products in the latest James Bond film. The ethics of buying Champagne from the grower mean that you are supporting a family business, rather than some rapacious, leather bag–toting, silk scarf–wearing global corporation. (Okay, those weren't exactly his words, but you get the idea.) As to taste, many of the best grower Champagnes are dry, meaning that they have little residual sugar. Theise claims to have done analyses of bottles from store shelves and found some of the big houses have the sweetest brut (dry) Champagnes available. He suggests they are often out of balance and too sweet. While that may be the case with some (Moët White Star is best to be avoided unless it comes with a chaser), it's a tad too easy and self-serving of him to paint with a broad brush.

For all of these reasons, grower Champagnes are the darlings of cutting-edge wine writers. However, when I have served them at tastings to consumers, they have often received a middling "meh" because of the sometimes piercing acidity. The lack of sweetness can be jarring; other times, it's a refreshing difference that some consumers can enjoy in part as a counter-trend.

Grower Champagnes often improve with food and certainly can elevate the mundane dish or occasion into something more celebratory—but that's true of the big houses as well. In that way, they are the opposite of still rosé wines, which often depend on the context—warm weather, food, friends—to make them taste great. Champagne is a powerful transformer of mood and the moment. Sharpen up your Champagne knowledge and taste through a few.

HOW TO OPEN A CHAMPAGNE BOTTLE

IF YOU WANT TO LOOK LIKE AN AGGRESSIVE MORON: Remove foil and wire basket around cork. Clasp bottle with both hands by the neck and work cork out with both thumbs. Shaking optional. For safest results, this method is only recommended when aiming the bottle off the side of a boat.

IF YOU WANT TO LOOK LIKE A SOMMELIER: Remove foil and wire basket. Place palm of left hand over cork. Clasp and gently twist cork. Pour chilled Champagne into nearby flute. Switch hands if you're left-handed or want a "10" for degree of difficulty.

IF YOU WANT TO LOOK LIKE A NINJA SOMMELIER (CHAMPAGNE SABER-ING): Remove foil completely from the neck of the bottle as well as the wire cork basket. Find the seam of the bottle with your thumb. Find a saber, machete, or other swordlike instrument lying around. Holding the bottle firmly in your left hand, position the sword at the base of the neck of the bottle on the seam. Swiftly move the sword up the seam and strike the glass lip right where it meets the seam. Ideally the entire top portion of the bottle will fly off with the cork inside it. Note: best done outside. Also note, this will require much practice before attempting in front of a crowd. Can be done with a mere knife too, but, come on, how cool is a saber?

✤ Seven Grower Champagnes That Merit Attention

VILMART NV: This small producer has the first fermentation in oak barrels, which adds richness. The nonvintage is fantastically sophisticated, golden-hued with aromas of warm brioche, and a lingering complexity on the palate. The vintage Champagnes are even richer in color and flavor and are age-worthy; they start at about $60. $$$$

LARMANDIER-BERNIER BLANC DE BLANCS NV ($$$), AND THE NONDOSAGE TERREDE VERTUS ($$$$): The Blanc de Blancs Brut Premier Cru NV is very lively with a straw color, a fine bead, pleasant acidity reminiscent of green apples, and lovely balance. The Terre de Vertus bottling is slightly more expensive and has the rare distinction among Champagnes to be bottled without a dosage (most Champagne receives a top-up of a small amount of still wine and sugar syrup before the final cork is added in order to balance the wine's naturally high acidity). It has excellent purity and is crisp, dry, and food-friendly. It is the shazam, just great stuff.

PIERRE PETERS: Great value. This Champagne's excellent acidity makes it very food-friendly. It's got great verve as an apéritif too—I've poured it to people who, when I told them the price, wanted to buy a case. When I poured it out of a magnum for a man whose daughter was getting married in a few months, he wanted to know where he could get more magnums of it for the occasion. $$$

DIEBOLT-VALLOIS: A beautiful nonvintage wine, gentle and smooth, with great depth. This would be a great wine to pour blind against a Champagne from a larger house at the same price point to show how in Champagne, like rental cars, the little guys try harder. $$$

GIMONNET BRUT BLANC DE BLANCS PREMIER CRU NV: With great notes of yellow apple, this is a great apéritif. It's a popular choice among New York City sommeliers. $$$

JEAN MILAN BRUT BLANC DE BLANCS NV: This Champagne demonstrates the acidity commonly found in grower Champagnes. It is mouthwatering. Try it with sushi. $$$

❋ *Four Nonvintage Champers from Big Houses*

LOUIS ROEDERER: The nonvintage brut is a superlative wine, with huge crowd appeal. Consider it a slam-dunk Champagne as the creamy richness wins every time. If you really want to crank things up, opt for the vintage Cristal from the same house. Yes, it is the ultimate bling wine, and, yes, it is terrific, made in small quantities and deserving of the price. $$$

BOLLINGER SPECIAL CUVÉE: As with Roederer, cautionary flags went up in my mind because this is the current "James Bond's choice." The Special Cuvée has delicate green apple notes with a great zest of chalk. The vintage Grande Année is an exceptional value for vintage Champagne, but it also often needs time in the cellar (about $90). $$$

CHARLES HEIDSIECK BRUT RESERVE NV: A great name to go to for brut non-vintage since the house generously ages the wine significantly before release. This provides a richer, fuller bodied style that is great for toasting promotions and loved ones. $$$

RECOMMENDED ACCESSORY: CHAMPAGNE STOPPER

When the genie is out of the lamp and the toothpaste is out of the tube, we know there's no going back in. Is that the same for Champagne corks? Yes. To withstand the pressure in the bottle, corks for Champagne bottles flare at the bottom. And because they're rounded at the top, there's no sticking them back in the bottle upside down. So what to do if you can't finish a bottle of bubbly? Invest in Champagne stoppers. They are special devices with a rubber stopper and two metal clasps that reach down and secure under the lip of the bottle. They are surprisingly effective and can keep you raising a glass of bubbly—with bubbles!—for three consecutive nights.

DELAMOTTE NV, $35: This is the baby brother of revered producer Salon. For some reason, this Champagne house flies under the radar. The nonvintage has wonderful depth and texture, while some vintages (about $70) even rival Salon for one-quarter of the price.

Rosé Champagne: It's Not Just for Heart-shaped Jacuzzis Anymore

Oysters, rose petals, chocolate, chili peppers, licorice, star anise, strawberries: I'm sorry, but if you're in need of these supposed aphrodisiacs, you might as well check your spam folder for some discount pharmaceuticals. One thing will do the trick, however: Champagne.

The white bubbly is plenty sufficient. But February often calls out for added oomph. So why not make it pink?

A few decades ago, pink Champagne was relegated to schlocky hotel Jacuzzis in Niagara Falls. But recently, rosé Champagne sales have been on a tear, doubling in just three years. Nobody is quite sure why, but Slate wine columnist Mike Steinberger has suggested that it could have to do with club-going fashionistas, or it could be a general acceptance of having pink wine in the glass—a pretty good guess, given the rehabilitation of rosé in recent years (see July).

Sadly, with all things trendy and euro-denominated, the prices have shot up for this former ugly duckling turned belle of the ball. But are they worth the high prices?

Generally not. The pink premium is often double the price of the regular non-rosé for the same house and to me, that's just too

> **INSIDER TIP**
>
> To tell the difference between a grower Champagne and a larger house at a glance—well, a glance and a squint—take a look at the front label. In a tiny font, usually along the bottom, there's a marking that says "RM" or "NM." The first means that they grow and make Champagne (*recoltant-manipulant* if you want to get technical); the second means they buy and blend Champagne (*négociant-manipulant*). Unfortunately, even if a small portion of the grapes is purchased from other growers it must state "NM," but it's generally a good quick and dirty method for telling the difference.

high a price to pay, pretty as it is. To its credit, rosé Champagne generally has a bit more stuffing, thanks to either extended contact with the seeds and skins of the red Pinot Noir and Pinot Meunier grapes or the addition of still red wine to the blend (both methods are allowed; the results are nearly impossible to distinguish though the former seems better intuitively). This means that it pairs better with richer foods than the white counterpart and makes a more full-bodied apéritif. Come to think of it, maybe *that's* why it is more popular.

✳ *Four Pink Bubblies to Try*

BILLECART-SALMON BRUT ROSÉ NV: A touchstone for rosé Champagne, this flamboyantly pink wine has a great red fruit (strawberries, what else?!?) and rose petals on the aromas while it has an excellent balance between richness and acidity on the palate. Put another log on the fire, baby, it's going to be a long night! Unfortunately, the price has risen now that word has gotten out about it. $$$$

NICOLAS FEUILLATTE, BRUT ROSÉ NV: A solid value (yes, a $40 "value"—we must be talking about Champagne) with fine bubbles and notes of strawberries and faint citrus zest, but a little disappointing on the finish. $$$

ROEDERER ESTATE, ANDERSON VALLEY, NV: It has bubbles, it's pink, but it's not Champagne since it hails from cool Mendocino County. It's got nice fruit thanks to 60 percent Pinot Noir and good acidity and focus with 40 percent Chardonnay. This bubbly has still Pinot Noir added for color, if you're keen to see if you can taste the difference between this and the other method. $$$

JUVÉ Y CAMPS BRUT ROSÉ CAVA, NV: This wine has surprised me more than once with clean fruit and a fine bead. It won't get you a home run like the Billecart-Salmon, but you're definitely on base. Try with food too, particularly salty appetizers. $$

Pairing Wine with Chocolate, If You Must

Wine. Chocolate. Two fine things, indeed. But why do so many smart people insist on pairing them when it's generally such a disastrous idea? Some people may try to convince you of the virtues of Cabernet Sauvignon. Others may suggest late-harvest this and sticky that. If you're stuck and you *must* pair them, as often happens around the Hallmark holiday of Valentine's Day, I have one word for you: Banyuls. This dark, viscous sweet wine can make good chocolate taste great in a pairing of intense flavors.

Perched high above the Mediterranean, where France blends into Spain and the Pyrenees sag into the sea, terraced vines scar the hillsides in horizontal lines. The vines are difficult to cultivate because it's hard to access them on the steep slopes under the hot sun, and agricultural workers are hard to come by as they get lured away by service sector jobs. This is Banyuls country.

Yet the grape vines have managed to survive in this environment, with some of the oldest vines now topping one hundred years. The predominant grape in this wine is Grenache, a versatile red grape that is a workhorse in its youth and a miser in old age, producing bunches of intense grapes that, harvested late, make the sweet nectar of Banyuls. The grapes are often harvested in October partly shriveled, which adds to the intensity.

The oak-aged grand cru Banyuls must spend thirty months in barrel. This makes them amber in color with notes of nuts and toffee. They can then age for thirty years in the bottle. The non–grand cru Banyuls can be aged in barrel or in bottle and are often red in color. These in particular can be rich, thick, and chocolatey with notes of super-ripe dark fruit. Bittersweet chocolate is a clunky pairing on the whole; try to pair with good semisweet chocolate instead.

❋ *Three Banyuls Producers Worth Seeking Out*

LA CAVE DE l'ABBÉ ROUS: I poured the Helyos bottling at an event one time and a participant excused himself, stepped out of the room, and returned a few minutes later with a chocolate bar from a vending machine. He and his wife broke the bar with this wine and deemed it a superlative pairing. The wine is 100 percent Grenache and has seen time in new and old oak barrels, which gives it a dark color and great intensity. Best for groups but it will keep for a week if not consumed at once. $$$

DOMAINE LA TOUR VIEILLE: Christine Campadieu and Vincent Cantié make their Banyuls from Grenache with a third Syrah. The grapes are hand-harvested and the wine is made traditionally. $$ for 500 ml.

EY: The youthful Jean-François Ey (rhymes with the letter "A"), whose favorite grape is Grenache, ping-pongs across the Atlantic. He lives in America but makes and buys some Grenache wines in Roussillon and then imports them to the U.S. under his label, Ey. His Vigne d'en Traginer comes from a single vineyard and is a delicious way to finish a meal with notes of mocha, toffee, and roasted coffee beans. Try pairing with a chocolate soufflé or one of those molten chocolate cakes. $$ for 375 ml.

President's Day: The Sorry History of Wine in the White House

Wine lovers never had a better friend in the White House than Thomas Jefferson. The third president acquired a taste for the fruits of the vine as an American envoy to France, where he toured the major wine-producing regions (he covered Italy too, for good measure), amassing quite a collection of fine wine, which he brought back with him and poured liberally at the White House.

Jefferson rejoiced in pouring wine because he considered it a drink of moderation, an alternative to the "ardent spirits" and the "bane of whiskey" of his day. Even after leaving the White House, Jefferson tended his grape vines back at Monticello. Even though his Virginia grapes produced only mixed results in the glass, he found grape growing compatible with his vision of a yeoman democracy.

White House Wines Fit for the Queen of England

On May 7, 2007, the Queen dropped by for a formal dinner at the White House. The teetotaler-in-chief broke out his tux and decided to go with a youthful, all-domestic—nay, Napatastic!—lineup. Here was their menu, with wine pairings.

Spring Pea Soup with Fernleaf Lavender
Chive Pizzelle with American Caviar
WINE: Newton Chardonnay Unfiltered 2004

Dover Sole Almondine
Roasted Artichokes, Pequillo Peppers, and Olives

Saddle of Spring Lamb
Chanterelle Sauce
Fricassee of Baby Vegetables
WINE: Peter Michael Les Pavots 2003

Arugula, Savannah Mustard and Mint Romaine
Champagne Dressing and Trio of Farmhouse Cheeses

"Rose Blossoms"
WINE: Schramsberg Brut Rosé 2004

But the list of wine-friendly residents of the White House starts and pretty much ends with Jefferson (although Jackie Kennedy threw a mean party). Consider some of the other occupants: George Washington left office to become one of the largest whiskey distillers on the East Coast; Ulysses S. Grant was a close friend of the bottle, but not the wine bottle; Benjamin Harrison at least served wine at an official dinner in San Francisco in 1891—

but slighted the domestic industry in its own backyard by pouring French wines; and George W. Bush is a teetotaler.

Given this long and largely desultory history of wine and presidents, what exactly is the state of the White House wine cellar? When I asked former executive chef Walter Scheib, hired by Hillary Clinton and fired by Laura Bush, he said it was the state of California!

Actually, the White House has quite a modest wine cellar. That's right: It might have a bowling alley and a movie screening room, but the wine collection could fit in a wine fridge since it is only about three hundred bottles. Instead of having a large collection, Scheib said that they outsourced the wine needs as necessary. Whenever they needed wines for a state dinner, they would work with a winery to obtain their best wines, often from the vintner's personal collection. The White House rotates wines often so no one wine could be considered the ultimate "house" wine, even if they are always American now. And they do source from states other than California.

Open That Bottle Night

You know that special bottle that you have been keeping around for ages, packing up and taking with you every time you move? Well, it's finally time to pull the cork! Why? Well, no apparent reason other than it is Open That Bottle Night—the perfect way to finish February.

John Brecher and Dorothy Gaiter of *The Wall Street Journal* urge their readers to open that special bottle they've been saving on one coordinated night of the year, the last Saturday in February, when our spirits need a lift. I'm endorsing that idea. So go ahead and open a fun bottle or two with friends or loved ones for no particular reason. In fact, try to do this more than once a year. I'd vote for it once a week if it were up to me.

Travel to: Sonoma—Off-Season Means More Time for Wines and Less Time for Lines

As I meander along the narrow and winding Dry Creek Road in Sonoma, yellow mustard flowers punctuate the rows of dormant, old vines just below me. Spring is coming and I only have a Gore-Tex jacket—no sweater—as a caution against the low cloud that hangs over the hilltops. Wineries, mostly small, regularly appear on either side of the road. I stop at one and then another to swirl, sniff, sip, and chat.

Poking around Sonoma is fun at any time of year since the area offers a wide range of practically everything: grape varieties, boutique and supermarket wines, delicious cheese and ice cream, and even hotels ranging from the serviceable Holiday Inn Express to luxurious lodges. While Napa is very fun in its own bling way, I find the diversity of Sonoma very appealing. Plus, it is more affordable and can serve as a base for forays into Napa, which is just a short drive over the beautiful ridge through the petrified forest. The town of Sonoma can serve as a good beachhead for exploring the area, particularly around Sonoma Mountain. But I particularly enjoy Healdsburg, slightly farther north, with its more intimate plaza, great restaurants, and small hotels.

But Sonoma is big, so it pays to specialize in one wine-growing area and explore it in depth. (Why spend hours in the car driving up and down 101 when you could spend that time tasting wine?) The Russian River Valley produces some excellent Pinot Noirs, the Dry Creek Valley some full-throttle Zinfandel, the cooler Alexander Valley has still and sparkling wines, and the Sonoma Coast is attracting top producers of Pinot Noir to take their chances on the difficult but potentially very rewarding terrain.

If you visit Sonoma in February, as I have done a couple of times, you will have it practically all to yourself. Because the vines have already been pruned and the tourists have yet to arrive in droves for the festivals and summer events and the wines are resting in tanks and barrels, chatting with a winemaker is easier in the off-season, which is what I did when I stopped by A. Rafanelli. This family-owned winery on Dry Creek Road has made their name in making serious Zinfandels. But unlike other producers who crank out high-octane editions, the Zins at Rafanelli are rich and intense without being overdone. Since the typical way to get Rafanelli wines requires you to wait about two years to even get on the mailing list, a visit to the small, handsome winery is particularly worthwhile since visitors can taste through the wines and purchase a limited amount (cash or checks only). However, visitors must book an appointment in advance, which leads to a wonderfully personalized visit, usually hosted by a family member.

Incidentally, February also makes a good time of year to drink Zinfandel. Many commentators are quick to suggest Zinfandel as a great barbecue wine, particularly on the patriotic occasion of the Fourth of July. But I've never bought that theory. The grape often produces a full-bodied wine that is high in alcohol—the type of big red that is fun in the winter. But combine it with the heat of July, and your guests are likely to end up sleeping in the chaise longues before the first firework is launched. Shelly Rafanelli agrees: She told me that she particularly likes drinking Zins in the winter and often opts for a refreshing beer in the summer.

And it turns out that patriotism has also been misplaced: Even though Zinfandel is often touted as *the* American grape variety (Governor Schwarzenegger tried to have it become the official grape of California), tests of the genetic structure of the grape have shown that it is actually related first to Primitivo of Puglia, Italy, and even further back to Crljenak Kaštelanski, a grape found on the Dalmatian Coast of Croatia. But then again, America is a nation of immigrants so maybe it should revise its claim to citizenship as a naturalized one.

Some of the Zinfandel in the Dry Creek Valley has been "dry farmed" (without irrigation) and grows untrellised, shooting canes from gnarly stumps. Jim Forchini, owner of the Forchini vineyards and winery, wistfully showed me just such a block of one-hundred-year-old Zinfandel on his property on top of the ridge that looks down onto the Dry Creek Valley below. His enthusiasm for having such vines was tempered by the fact that two decades earlier, he had uprooted some of those old vines to plant more fashionable Cabernet Sauvignon. Now the Zinfandel produces the most valuable fruit.

At the very end of the Dry Creek Valley, Lou Preston makes wine from ninety-year-old Carignan vines, among others, at his winery Prestons of Dry Creek. With a bushy gray beard and a floppy hat, he removed an organic loaf of bread from a wood-burning stove as he told me about his one hundred acres of certified organic vines. Although he's cut back production from 25,000 to 9,000 cases, he still has a wide array of wines, mostly from little-known grapes such as that Carignan, more often found in the Languedoc in the south of France. They're all certified organic, which is a way of life for him since he sells the wines mostly through stores and restaurants that share his green philosophy. He encourages people to come and picnic at the tables outside the winery.

In the spirit of diversity that prevails in Sonoma, Preston also has 1,500 olive trees on his property. Freshly baked bread, diverse wines, local olive oil (which Preston calls "chaste maiden")—what more could you want?

When to go: Any time of year is a good time to visit Sonoma, but I've suggested this off-peak time of year to beat the crowds.

Getting there: The San Francisco airport has many carriers providing service, while Oakland can also be a good choice if you can bypass some traffic. Sacramento is a little far from Sonoma if you are heading directly there, but some people like the discount airline service to that airport.

Juliette Pope,

Beverage Director, Gramercy Tavern, New York, New York

How does context matter for enjoying wine?

Incredibly—the company, the occasion, the physical setting. Context sets the tone and tells you what makes sense in selecting and enjoying your wine to the fullest.

What is one of your favorite food-wine pairings?

Manzanilla sherry with toasted almonds and green olives.

How important is pairing wine with the seasons?

Less important than tuning it in to the food, which in turn is far less important than tuning in to your guests/company to choose what will be most suitable and thus pleasurable. But insofar as you are eating seasonally, then in that sense my wine pairings for work or for play are reflective of the season.

If you had to have one wine per season, what would it be?

Winter: **Northern Rhône Syrah**
Spring: **Riesling**
Summer: **Tough call between dry rosé and Lambrusco**
Fall: **Red Burgundy**

If you had to pick one season for drinking wine, what would it be? And why?

As I am most passionate about white wines, I suppose convention would have it that I would answer spring or summer, but the fact is that I love it all year round. That is no answer, I realize.

What's one of your most memorable food-wine occasions where the location or company really mattered?

Dinner at an end-of-the-country-dirt-road trattoria in the dark Tuscan countryside, where carafes of the property's own Chianti, which was surely not a particularly distinguished wine, went down beautifully and far too easily with my and my husband's roasted guinea hen and potatoes on a hillside patio on a breezy summer's eve. . . .

PART TWO

Spring

Perhaps no changing of the seasons is so spectacular—and so welcome—as winter turning to spring. Snow melting, daffodils and tulips blooming, and daylight savings. In addition to the weather improving and the days lengthening, this seasonal transition also sparks a change in the wines in our glasses. As Eric Asimov of *The New York Times* wrote one April, "the tulips on Park Avenue are blooming in gorgeous yellows, pinks, and reds, confirmation that spring has finally arrived in New York City. My own seasonal signpost is an annual thirst for German Rieslings."

Because spring ping-pongs between gorgeous sunny days and cool, rainy days, I find it a great transitional season to try many wine styles. Particularly alluring are the aromatic whites, such as Riesling, but also Pinot Gris and the exotic Kerner. I also like minerally whites, such as Muscadet and Chablis, and Chenin Blanc from the Loire in all its guises. The higher acidity reds of Barbera, Cabernet franc, and Gamay have such food-friendliness that it's hard to find just one season for them. But if you haven't been enjoying them thus far, it's time to crack some open. Here's a list of wines to help you spring into gear:

BUBBLY: With its notes of warmer climate fruits, the warmer days of spring are a good time for sparkling wine from California. Roederer Estate is a great value for $20, and Schramsberg Blanc de Blanc is also a good way to go though at a higher price. For the cooler days, I stick with Champagne.

MUSCADET: A great category of white wine that remains one of the best bargains of the wine world. The region lies where the Loire River meets the Atlantic, and the wines seem to have a faint saline quality to them making them the affordable choice for oysters and seafood. Made from the Melon de

Bourgogne grape (another one for the Wine Century Club, natch!), the sub-zone of Muscadet de Sèvre-et-Maine is where the best action is. Look for the producer names Domaine Luneau-Papin, Domaine de la Pépière, Domaine de la Louvetrie, and Guy Bossard—they are the leaders in the qualitative revolution. It's really a fantastic white for all seasons especially since the wines range from about $10 to $20. But if it has to fit in just one season, spring is the best to enjoy its superb pairing with shellfish and refreshment value as the weather warms.

DRY RIESLING: Aromatic whites also herald the arrival of spring. They are, indeed, a great way to go when the weather warms up. Try a young Kabi-nett or *trocken* wine since those are also easiest on the wallet. Some excellent producers from Germany that make wines of a crystalline purity and preci-sion are: Dönnhoff, Schäfer-Fröhlich, Knebel, and Keller. Although in a different style, the Leeuwin Artist Series Riesling is a good value dry Riesling all the way from Margaret River in Western Australia.

PINOT GRIS: Better known as "Pinot Grigio," this wine welcomes spring with its voluptuous aromas of melon, pears, and apples. From Oregon, Adelsheim makes a particularly gorgeous version, beautifully soft, yet sprightly. Some other good producers for under $20 are WillaKenzie, Bethel Heights, and Cooper Mountain. These wines are generally best while young. An excep-tional, rich, but not overwhelming Pinot Gris from Alsace is the Réservé Personnelle from Trimbach. Fire up some seared scallops and taste the magic!

THREE MORE EXOTIC AROMATIC WHITES: Pinot Bianco (better known as Pinot Blanc) from Alois Lageder in Alto Adige in Italy is an affordable spring pleasure; Friulano, also from northern Italy, has alluring aromatics of tropical fruits (Channing Daughters on Long Island makes a rare American example of the grape); Kerner, also a grape that offers lush aromatic appeal—I particularly look for the Abbazia di Novacella. I also like Grüner Veltliner in the spring, particu-larly the younger, less expensive ones since they pair well with many spring vegetables (for more details, see the section on Grü Vee on page 93).

BURGUNDY: These wines have many spring charms. The stunning purity, minerality, and freshness of the wines from the northerly Chablis region connect with the spring vegetables since most wines from this French region have a very gentle oak treatment. I like the entry-level wine from the small producer Gilbert Picq; the wines from Verget and Drouhin, two larger producers, are also reliable and worthwhile. And the white Aligoté, an unheralded white grape, also has a racy purity; look for Mikulski for a superior example. On the red side, I like the juicy, accessible reds of Mercurey in the springtime, particularly from A. & P. de Villaine and Faiveley.

BARBERA: A marvelous red grape that makes wines with naturally low alcohol and higher acidity. Try a comparison of the excellent Paitin Serra Boella from Piedmont, the grape's ancestral home, and the Palmina from Santa Barbara County. They're both gulpable yet serious wines, and you'll be able to spot the effect of the different growing areas. And Pinot Noir is another red that greets spring with enthusiasm (see the section on value Pinots on page 178).

MARCH

In like a lion, out like a lamb, March is the ultimate transitional month, usually marked by warm and cold swings. The hints at the warm weather to come remind us that it's time to get motivated for spring cleaning, to dust off the winter blahs, and make way for a sunnier time of year, so in this chapter I'll give you some tips for proper wine storage and sprucing up your cellar for spring. Since this month also holds the holy occasions of Passover and Easter, I'll suggest some wines to pop open to mark those events. And finally, if you find March going in like a lion and going out like one as well, check out the travel section on Argentina—it's a great time to visit the southern hemisphere.

Spring for Chenin Blanc from the Loire

When the snows of winter melt into slush, and it's springlike one day and wintry the next, I'm ready for the chameleon of whites: one of the best white grapes in the world, Chenin Blanc from the Loire. Whether March comes in like a lion or a lamb,

Chenin Blanc has got you covered. Unlike Sancerre and Muscadet, the other dry whites of the Loire, Chenin Blanc comes from the heart of the Loire and can run the gamut from dry to sweet.

When it's cold and you're feeling contemplative, put your fist to your chin and your elbow on your knee and think about a glass of Savennières. This incarnation of Chenin Blanc is always dry, floral on the nose, and totally fills the mouth with a rich intensity, minerality, and acidity. The wines are always rewarding and are so tremendously long-lived many fans suggest not even touching them for seven years after the vintage; others always decant them.

Of the three famous Savennières vineyards, the Clos de la Coulée de Serrant is the most well-known—it even has its own appellation, or growing area. Once hailed as the "Yquem of Anjou" and one of the top five white wines of France, the semicircular schist vineyard site is spectacular, the corduroy lines of vines folding over themselves and running down toward the Loire. Nicolas Joly took over the estate two decades ago from his mother and converted the vineyard to biodynamic farming, a form of chemical-free farming that weaves in a dose of spirituality. Joly himself is the high priest of the movement and travels the world in the name of biodynamics. The controversial wines are not always for newbies, however, and Joly recommends decanting them at least twenty-four hours in advance of consuming.

The Domaine des Baumard is another celebrated Savennières vineyard. By contrast, Clos du Papillon is more immediately likeable, especially the elegant one from des Baumard. I poured one bottle at a lunch consisting of nonwine friends on a March day and the wine, poised between delicate and intense, with fascinating mineral verve, enraptured the group and the bottle was quickly emptied. Madame de Jessey also makes a very good wine from this vineyard for her Château des Vaults. Both are particularly long-lived.

But for a wine that requires less thought and has an easy-to-understand appeal, enjoy a touch of honey or honeysuckle in your Chenin Blanc with the wines of Vouvray. The wines from this postage stamp–size town on the north banks of the Loire, an hour's drive upriver from Savennières, show the true expression and versatility of Chenin Blanc—dry, sweet, and sparkling. The best of all forms have fantastic aromatic expression, a veritable field of flowers to greet you on a spring day. And they have good acidity that give the wines tremendous verve and the perfect balance to offset the sweetness in the richer versions.

Such is the case with the legendary Domaine Huet. Noel Pinguet makes a dry sparkling wine that has wonderful purity that I would love to drink at a garden party—or with some smoked salmon. The still wines from the biodynamically farmed single vineyards have excellent mouthfeel, and the sweeter ones add tremendous depth and richness. Think of green apple with a touch of honey. The sweet wines come from grapes harvested later, sometimes as late as November, so not every year has the sweetest and most spectacular wines, the *moelleux*. Sometimes too rich in their youth, the wines are fantastically age-worthy and can easily give Cabernet Sauvignon and Merlot a run for their money in the aging department, reputedly retaining freshness and vitality for well over a century. Jacqueline Friedrich, a leading authority on the wines of the region, has written that the Huet 1947 *moelleux*, tasted many decades later, was what made her fall in love with Vouvray, Chenin Blanc, and the Loire, where she then bought a house. Powerful stuff.

Also of particular note is François Chidaine, who is based in Montlouis on the south side of the Loire but who also has vineyards in Vouvray, on the north side of the river. Some of the wines are dry, such as the Clos Baudoin, which Chidaine took over in 2002, and the ones from Montlouis, which tend to be more off-dry yet with excellent aromatics, depth, and concentration. I particularly like the Les Tuffeaux, which is just a faintly sweet, wildly gulpable apéritif. And practically his whole line of wines is under $25.

Serious winemaking, which often comes without the hefty price tag. I'll drink to that, rain, snow, or shine.

Protect Your Stash This Spring: Storing Wine in Apartments and in Mansions

With the warm weather approaching, it's important to keep any wines, and especially age-worthy ones, in proper conditions so they don't get cooked.

Apartment Storage Tips

Say you're one of the millions of city-dwellers who live in a small apartment. Where should you store wine?

First off, you should bear in mind that the enemies of wine are heat, vibration, and ultraviolet light, in that order. So the worst place to keep wine is on top of the fridge, which vibrates and is hot. Near the stove or radiator are areas that are not good places for your bottles either. And keep your wine off the windowsill, where temperatures fluctuate and the sun pours in.

If you have the space, a wine fridge is clearly the best and most obvious solution for storing your special bottles. In fact, many new apartments are hardly considered complete without a wine fridge. Just be sure that the unit you purchase is sufficiently quiet so that it doesn't bother anyone in the same room and that it is vibration-free so that the wines don't get shaken, which can lead to premature aging. But stand-alone wine fridges can be perfectly acceptable even for the most discriminating of collectors: I know a couple who live in Manhattan and house a 1,500-bottle collection in six large EuroCave coolers in their building's basement. Under lock and key.

But if (or when) you start collecting more wine than you can easily drink in the near term, it's time to think about more serious storage. Some wine writers and collectors store their wine in a closet in their apartment. There's no temperature control so it will be on the warm side, but at least it is dark and vibration free.

But who can really give up closet space in the city? Consider heading offsite if your collection grows beyond the cozy confines. In most big cities you can find professional wine storage facilities. Such places keep your wine in a cool dark place, and either you can access it yourself in a locker, or they will fetch your bottles for you from a big storeroom. Insurance is optional.

It's worth noting that 98 percent of wine made today does not improve with age. So maybe the best solution is to order a case and then drink it. But if you have a few age-worthy bottles, maybe you need to find a friend with a mansion (or better yet, buy your own) and create your own cool storage area. . . .

Tips for Storing Wine in a Mansion

So now you're in your mansion. Sure, you have a driveway to shovel and a lawn to mow, but aren't you glad your apartment days are behind you? Now you've got space to build that wine cellar you've been dreaming about!

The cellars of Champagne are cool, dark, and humid, buried deep in the chalky soil. In Napa, wineries have excavated caves to achieve similar conditions. What wine enthusiasts outside of these regions try to do—sometimes in vain and sometimes at great expense—is replicate those surroundings.

Temperature is the greatest issue to consider when constructing a wine cellar, since the warmer the temperature is, the faster the wine ages. Some people don't have a problem with that since they don't have thirty years to wait around for specific wines to mature. I once visited a sixty-year-old gentleman's cellar at his spectacular house and was surprised to find no cooling system. But his entire collection was for his personal consumption, and he was fine with the faster aging tempo. His son, by contrast, had put in a cooling unit in his own wine cellar. It really is up to personal preference. But if you are seeking to make an investment in wine, it's best to have your cellar cooled to somewhere between 55 and 60 degrees all year round.

So find the coolest corner of your basement (usually on the northeast side) and store your wine there. Gradual changes in temperature won't affect aging too much as long as it doesn't get too warm. Sharper Image sells a digital thermometer that can record the high–low range; L.L.Bean has one too, that even has a remote device so it can be read upstairs in the kitchen. In terms of storage vessels, the downside of storing your wine in the original boxes, which is what I did for many years, is that once you start to accumulate a few cases, it can cause much delay in trying to find a specific bottle, much to the amusement and subsequent frustration of several friends, as I learned. Standing racks are pretty affordable, especially if you are willing to do some assembly, so I'd recommend investing in a couple.

If you decide to trick out your basement and put in a full-on cellar, be sure to consult *Tuscan Design Weekly*. Just kidding—I don't know if that publication really exists nor do I know why so many private cellars in America evoke Tuscany, but it's not mandatory. Park B. Smith, one of the greatest collectors in the world, has an Asian-themed eight-thousand-square-foot cellar (yes, that's just the size of the cellar, not including the house).

It's a good idea to wonk out on Richard M. Gold's no-frills, self-published book, *How and Why to Build a Wine Cellar*, if you're planning on going all out for your wine cellar. Be prepared to consider such details as vapor barriers, insulation, and drywall. An architect of high-end homes in Greenwich, Connecticut, told me that he likes to use energy-efficient spray-on foam insulation and drywall with mildicide in it to prevent mold in the wine cellars he designs. You'll also want good racking material made of a hardwood that won't warp and is moisture resistant—redwood is available in many rack kits, but some custom cellar builders use cherry, walnut, or quarter-sawn white oak, which can be stained with a water-soluble stain. Gravel is the flooring of choice in Bordeaux since it can provide humidity from the earth below and hide spills, but limestone is a more practical choice when the floor is going on a concrete slab.

Whether or not you get a cooling unit and whether that has a humidification function depends entirely on your basement conditions and budget. Bear in mind that low humidity may cause corks to dry out, but keeping bottles stacked horizontally will help reduce that problem. High humidity will keep the corks in good shape (but may cause the labels to deteriorate). While I know one collector who modified two air-conditioning units to cool his cellar, a final element to consider with any cooling unit is noise—think twice before situating it next to the meditation room.

Light is an issue, but the potential damage will mostly result from artificial lights, such as spotlights on magnums that cause heat. The dark glass of most bottles offers some protection from ultraviolet lights, but be sure to turn the lights off behind you so that the cooling unit doesn't work overtime.

A final consideration to the cellar is layout. While not every cellar is going to be as big as Park B. Smith's, with rooms dedicated to different regions, a big cellar provides space so that you don't have to be fumbling around in your cardboard boxes the way I did, and you can quickly and easily put your hands on the bottles you are looking for. One rack might be dedicated to a region or grape variety. And within that, the older bottles that are closer to being ready to drink might be at the bottom, presumably the coldest part of the cellar, with the youngest toward the top of the rack. It's a good idea to vary the racking and not have all single-bottle coves since some trophy bottles won't fit—nor will half-bottles or magnums. And don't forget a value rack so that if someone in the family wants to raid the cellar, they'll know which rack they can raid without suffering the most dire consequences.

On that note, if there are teenagers in the house, consider adding a lock to the door.

And remember that 98 percent of wine is not meant to be aged! Mature wine is not everyone's idea of a great time so you might want to experiment and taste it a bit before devoting your life's savings to it.

While we're on the subject of wine collecting, how do you determine whether mature wine is something you'd like to drink a lot of? You'll have to taste it. But that can be an expensive pursuit in and of itself. Here are a few tips for tasting mature wine without breaking the bank.

The best tip is to have generous friends who are collectors. This may sound like a joke, but wine geeks love talking about their wines and many times are extremely generous. I've often observed a wonderful disjuncture between captains of industry who collect wine: All day they must be thinking about net profits and returns on investment, yet in the evenings with friends, they can easily blow through hundreds or thousands of dollars of wine. I'm not suggesting that you abuse this generosity and invite yourself over every weekend; rather, collectors often just really love to talk and to taste. And you can always find a rare bottle to bring to the tasting too, in case you feel it is too one-sided.

Carrying this logic one step further, try to set up a tasting dinner or regular group with some friends who are seriously interested in wine. If there are four couples and each brings a really nice bottle around a certain theme, then you get to taste four bottles for the price of one. Not to mention enjoying fine wine in a great context, with food and friends.

So what about other options to taste mature wine? The most expensive way to taste mature wine is, clearly, to order it in restaurants with their high markups. The advantage here is that if the wine is corked, you may be able to send it back for another bottle, as Russell Crowe did with a bottle of Penfold's Grange from 1964, his birth year, while dining at a high-end restaurant in London (no, he didn't throw the bottle).

But the cheapest way to taste mature wine while still paying is to attend a preauction tasting. Auction houses often have tastings the night before or the morning of the auction. The general idea is to vouch for the collection and get buyers more interested in bidding. They also happen to be rooms full of mature wine ready for tasting, open to anyone willing to fork over the cash for the entry fee, which can be as low as $75. What such tastings lack in intimacy (the best ones are often packed), they often make up for in breadth and opportunity. A word of caution: Champagne can lose its fizz and mature wines can change quickly once opened, so be prepared, arrive early, and know where to go. Who knows, the experience might just make you want to grab a paddle and start bidding.

Check with your local specialty wine shops to find out if they arrange themed tasting dinners at a local restaurant. After all, tasting top wines is crucial to knowing good wine (one of the great travesties of the wine world today is the escalation in the price of the top wines, as demand outstrips the often-limited supply), and you just might meet some interesting people!

A final option to consider: many regions have festivals (see July for details on a great one in Oregon), where producers pour their current releases and sometimes include selections from their cellars. The festivals can be a good way to double up on tourism and tasting, so long as the crowds are not overwhelming. Ask a friend in the know, or read up on which wines to taste if time is an issue at a big tasting.

Spring Cleaning: Managing Your Wine Cellar Inventory

Before the weather improves too much and you want to spend your spare time outside, take a few hours to put a system in place for cellar inventory. Consider it a spring cleaning for the cellar so that you don't let bottles languish in the back of the cooling unit until they are past their prime. And I say, when in doubt, turn to software.

CellarTracker! is a fantastic, free online service. Eric LeVine, formerly of Microsoft, developed the platform for managing wine inventory and comparing notes. He is such a technology-loving wine geek, that he will import your data into his system regardless of the original electronic format. Once your data is in

HOW TO SELL GRANDMA'S BOTTLE

So you're helping your grandma clean out her basement this spring and you find some wine. It looks old, but how can you tell if it's still good? Or how much is it worth? And how can you sell it?

First off, shame on you! Trying to sell Grandma's wine collection out from under her. At least have the courtesy to drink it with her!

Seriously, if you wonder if it's still good, consult a resource, such as Robert Parker's vintage chart (online) or Michael Broadbent's book, *Vintage Wine*. And remember that the warmer the storage conditions, the faster the aging of the wine. So if you found the wine in the attic, chances are slim that it is still good. But really, there's only one way to see if it is good and that's to pull the cork.

If you really want to sell it, however, you can get a rough valuation for the wine from Wine-Searcher.com. Or check Wine Commune.com, which is a person-to-person auction site, like eBay for wine. You can sell it there too, though you'll do better if you have a favorable history of selling on the site. Finally, some stores will sell wine on consignment but, again, it helps if you've done business there in the past.

the system, you can track your consumption history and keep your own tasting notes. With over 500,000 tasting notes logged, currently the most distinguishing feature of CellarTracker! is the ability to share notes with others. This is particularly useful when you are thinking about spring cleaning, since you can see if a wine is starting to decline based on the recent tasting notes.

Sometimes data entry can be so time-consuming that it prevents wine enthusiasts from managing their cellars. Some savvy retailers have seen that gap and in a bid for customer loyalty now offer free cellar management software. One such retailer is Vinfolio, an Internet-only retailer based in California that has developed a hugely streamlined and handsomely designed system, VinCellar. What's more, if you buy wine from them, then it is automatically entered into your profile, erasing at least one step of the data entry process (which is great because then you can spend more time uncorking bottles).

Holy Wine and Wine for Holy Holidays: Passover and Easter

Every spring, as the tulips and daffodils push up through the thawing earth, wine-loving Jews and gentiles will face the question of which wine to pour on their holy holidays. Granted, the problems for each group are different—nay, as antithetical as finding a wine to pair with ham for the gentiles and a good kosher wine for the Jews—but the good news is that each problem is getting easier to solve.

First up, kosher wines. The four cups of wine are a staple of the Passover seder. Many wine-loving Jews of a certain age have not-so-sweet memories of Manischewitz, one of a few kosher wines that held the four cups in a vicelike grip. But lately kosher wines have been winning praise from many critics for their much improved quality.

Why the sudden improvement? Changes in winemaking are the main reason. Kosher wines must be made and handled from grape to glass exclusively by Sabbath-observant Jews, and all substances used in the winemaking must also be kosher. An additional optional step calls for boiling the wine to make it *mevushal*, which makes it so that a kosher wine can subsequently be handled and poured by non-Jews. But boiling is not a step of traditional winemaking, since it is a fast path to transforming good wine into bad. The introduction of flash pasteurization to produce *mevushal* wine has managed to preserve a greater range of flavors, although not as many as in kosher wines that aren't *mevushal*.

Further, winemakers are paying more attention to kosher wines. When I visited Cathy Corison in Napa Valley, she was clearing a portion of the winery for someone renting the space to make a kosher wine. In Bordeaux, several leading châteaus such as Léoville Poyferré, Pontet-Canet, Smith Haut Lafitte, and even the trendy Valandraud now offer kosher versions of their regular cuvées. Kosher wines are now made around the world, from New Zealand to Spain to Beaujolais and many places in between, and the diversity of kosher wine styles reflects the different places the wines are now made.

Another factor contributing to the improvement of kosher wine is that winemaking in Israel has taken off in the past couple of decades. While not all Israeli wines are kosher, many of them are actually quite good, and they have also received accolades. The Golan Heights Winery makes commendable reds and particularly whites under the Yarden label, according to Elin McCoy of Bloomberg.

Some Catholics have also gotten the memo that holy wines don't have to be choked down. The owners of Wine Authorities, a wine-shop in Durham, North Carolina, have made it their goal to improve the quality of the wine in the Eucharist at Catholic churches in the area. Craig Heffley told me that he was disappointed that the Eucharist is made with "industrial wine from California that is heavily manipulated." So he and his business partner have sourced various "honest," country wines from France, Spain, and Italy to sell in a three-liter bag-in-box format in their store. He said the explicit goal was to offer a compelling value wine to local customers (it comes out to the equivalent of $4.50 per bottle). But they also had the local churches, including the Duke Chapel, in mind since they thought the sacrament wine could do with an upgrading.

Finally, the Easter meal is the last of our holy holiday wine conundrums. Without any of the religious strictures of the Passover seder, the Easter lunch or dinner comes down to a simple food-wine pairing. So which wine *do* you pair with the cream-filled chocolate Easter eggs and bunny cookies?

Well, it's probably safest to stick with pairing wine with the main courses, traditionally ham or lamb. Although pork is, in general, wildly wine-friendly (the magazine *Wine & Spirits* once dedicated an entire issue to it), the hams at Easter and at Christmas are often spiral-cut honey hams, quite salty and also sweet. My first choice would be a low-alcohol Riesling from, say, the Mosel, since the low alcohol content won't make the salt stand out any more than it already does and an off-dry wine will work with the saltiness of the meat. Gewürztraminer has a lot of richness but often not enough acidity to balance it out. One that does have good acidity is the Abbazia di Novacella, a wine made at an abbey (how apt for Easter) in the northern Italian village of Alto Adige. A Pinot Noir would be good too, as would perhaps a decent Cava or Prosecco to get some bubble magic working. And if it's a warm Easter, maybe even a rosé would pair nicely with ham.

The lamb is a sign of spring, but its richer meat makes me want to look back to the heavier wines of winter, rather than forward to the lighter wines of the season to come. Try a Châteauneuf-du-Pape for a compelling pairing—Domaine du Vieux Télégraphe and Château de Beaucastel are two excellent producers. A compelling Syrah, particularly one from the Northern Rhône, perhaps with some age on it, would go well too. Leave the Easter baskets for the kids; take the nice wines to the table.

Travel to: Mendoza, Argentina—
Malbec, Meat, and Mountains

With the seasons flipped in the southern hemisphere, a trip to Mendoza, Argentina makes a great midwinter break from the U.S. If you want to see extravagant shows of gauchos and a parade with a ceremonial blessing of the grapes, and have a tolerance for crowds, then the annual harvest festival on the first Saturday of March is the time to go.

Crossing the high altitude desert, with vineyards on one side and the rising sun painting the snow-capped mountains pink on the other, I could have been in a modern day Western. But I wasn't riding a trusty steed across the dramatic South American landscape. Instead, I was in a van heading an hour and a half south from the bustling city of Mendoza, where I was staying, to the Uco Valley. This new favorite spot for winemakers has seen a boom in vineyard development (the local culture glorifies horses, praises grilled meat, and is the home to many great estates). My destination that day was Clos de los Siete, a 1,500-acre vineyard development that was scrub brush a mere five years before. Seven well-known families from Bordeaux started the project under the leadership of the globetrotting winemaking consultant, Michel Rolland. Indeed, Mendoza is one of the most cosmopolitan winemaking communities in the world today. Why? In part, it has to do with money, but also the *terroir* and the people.

In December 2001, the Argentine peso collapsed. One peso had bought one dollar in a fixed exchange rate for the previous decade, but this system unraveled swiftly, and within a few weeks, it took four pesos to buy one dollar. While this caused some painful adjustments within the country, for foreigners, Argentina was having a 75-percent-off sale.

Foreign capital started to flow in, particularly from France and Chile. The distinctive growing areas, with some of the highest altitude vineyards in the world, attracted the foreign vintners, many of whom feel that the wines from the area have a distinctive character and that they are not simply carbon copies of wines from the rest of the world.

Malbec, the grape that creates leading wines for the export market, was largely off the world's radar screen; previously its only real prominence was in Cahors, an interior region of France. But the match with the grape and the Argentine soil proved a good one, making fruit-forward wines that can have pleasant minerality. The grape has paved the way for Argentina on the world stage. And some of my favorite examples of Argentine Malbec are often the cheapest since they are unoaked, which preserves more of the sense of grape and the place where it was grown, rather than the oak barrel the wine was aged in. Many winemakers in Argentina—and beyond—feel compelled to add lavish oak treatments to justify higher prices.

But the relaxed people, who have been producing wine for generations, matter too in making the place a good one to visit and for winemaking. They love their *asado* (barbecue) almost as much as they love talking about the weather, local politics, wine, and soccer. The culture starts to rub off on even high-profile foreigners. Michel Rolland told me that "California may be the best place in the world to make wine, but it is a little bit boring. Argentina is fun and the people are great."

All of this interest from overseas has meant huge demand for deluxe accommodations in Mendoza. (The original luxury hotel, the Park Hyatt, was so full that two other five-star hotels were built in the city.) The city is a good place to stay, given its central location among the growing areas to the north, south, and east. But staying among the vines may be too tempting, and several of the bodegas offer accommodations sometimes along with other activities such as trekking, white-water rafting, and horseback riding.

✽ *Wineries*

BODEGA CATENA ZAPATA: This is a must stop. One of the early exporters, Nicolás Catena, built an enormous and glamorous winery in the structure of a neo-Mayan temple. The wines are often fruit-forward with new oak. Be sure to try some wines from the high-altitude experimental vineyards. The wines are widely available in the U.S.

ALTA VISTA: Owned by the Sansonnet family who has holdings in Bordeaux and Champagne, this winery architecturally blends old and new with a rehabbed barrel room and a swanky tasting room. Try some of the single-vineyard Malbecs, which are not easily available outside Argentina. They make an excellent rosé, but sadly have been having distribution problems in the U.S.

DOMINIO DEL PLATA: Susana Balbo, winemaker, and Pedro Marchevsky, vineyard manager extraordinaire, are Argentina's unofficial head wine couple. The winery is understated and utilitarian compared to some other flashy ones, but has family-run charm. Call ahead for visits.

FAMILIA ZUCCARDI: Inveterate experimenter José Alberto Zuccardi makes wines from grape varieties beyond Malbec. Many vineyards are farmed organically, and the wines are often available at Whole Foods in the U.S.

Getting there: Direct flights from several U.S. hubs make this an easy getaway. For example, take a flight from JFK that departs at 10 P.M., and you'll arrive in Buenos Aires at 11 A.M. Even though it's a long flight, there's only one hour time change so say good-bye to jet lag!

You'll get the chance to see some of Buenos Aires if you have a connecting flight directly to a wine-growing region because Buenos Aires has two airports, one for international flights and one for domestic. Given that you have to get in a taxi already, why not stay a night or two in Buenos Aires to take in the sights, sounds, and flavors of the capital city? The burgeoning wine bar scene is a great vantage point to survey the wines from all of the exciting regions.

Christie Dufault,

Wine Director, Quince Restaurant, San Francisco, California

How does context matter for enjoying wine?

Context matters a lot. Fresh air, fine food, the right stemware, and above all, an exemplary companion to share a great wine with, make a profound difference on how a wine shows.

What is one of your favorite food-wine pairings?

Lobster bisque and rosé Champagne.

How important is pairing wine with the seasons?

Very important. Can you imagine having a heavy red wine on a hot summer day?

If you had to have one wine per season, what would it be?

Winter: Champagne
Spring: Champagne
Summer: Champagne
Fall: Champagne

If you had to pick one season for drinking wine, what would it be? And why?

That is why I live in San Francisco. There are no seasons, so I drink my favorite wines all year round.

What's one of your most memorable food-wine occasions where the location or company really mattered?

Going on a challenging hike up Mount Tamalpais and stopping for a little picnic. To my surprise and delight my husband packed a perfect French lunch—pâté de campagne, crusty baguette, Fallot mustard, cornichons, vegetables, olives, a piece of Gruyère. There was also a half-bottle of Puligny-Montrachet Clavoillon, Domaine Leflaive 2002. I could not have been happier. The magnificent natural setting, the delicious food and wine, and my favorite person in the world.

APRIL

April is a good time to think about the earth—and how natural you want your wine to be, both in the vineyard and getting it to you from the vineyard (the carbon footprint). I really enjoy aromatic whites in the springtime, maybe because they remind me of the blossoms, so it is a good opportunity to discuss the role of oak and the backlash against it, since oak generally masks the aromas of the grape. It's also a time for us to render unto Caesar, which might make us start looking for some good value vino. Finally, it's a great time to get away to the Rioja region of Spain, particularly for wine enthusiasts who live in areas where spring weather isn't all sunshine and daffodils.

April Fool's! Smell the Cork and Look at the Legs (Ahem!)

When the wine waiter uncorks the wine and puts the cork on the table, you are supposed to pick up the cork, look at it, sniff it, cradle it in your arms, then ask the waiter if you can take it home. And when the wine lands in your glass, hold it up and exclaim, "Whoa! Look at those legs!"

Actually, in case you hadn't guessed by now, this is an April Fool's prank. Doing either of those things will get you severely demoted in your efforts to achieve wine geekdom.

Regarding the cork, there's no need to sniff it or pick it up. The cork might tell you some things about your wine, such as the probable storage conditions the wine was kept under (if the wine has seeped all the way to the top or if it is dry and crumbly, those are red flags, but those details are visible to the eye—no nose required), but it can also lead you astray. Better to sample what's in the glass to make your judgment about the wine. But you *are* allowed to take the cork home with you if you want. You bought it!

As to the legs, I'm not sure how the theory of their supposed importance ever gained such prominence. "Legs" refer to the tears that stream down the inside of the glass as you tilt it to one side. Technically, it is possible tell how much alcohol there is in the wine by looking at the legs. But there's a better way to do that too, and it involves swirling, sniffing, and sipping, which is much more fun than simply looking.

Growing Green for Earth Day

At Whole Foods, there are organic heirloom tomatoes and free-range turkeys—but where is the green wine? Even though restrictions make it hard to put "organic" on the label, natural winemaking is one of the hottest trends in winemaking today. And it's worth searching out the organic bottles since a "green" wine is likely to be more reflective of the *terroir* than of the hand of the winemaker.

Roughly speaking, there are two contrasting ways of making wine: Either make a wine that the consumer demands or make the wine that the vineyard can provide. The first approach goes like this: Start with what the consumer wants, which, for low-priced, high-volume wines, is frequently determined through focus groups. Higher-end wines that adopt this approach often substitute the palate of one consumer, the wine critic Robert Parker, for the whole focus group, and make a wine in a style that he rates highly. (There's even a consulting company in California that promises its winery clients that the wines it advises on will achieve a certain score from critics, plus or minus a point or two.) If the consumer or critic wants an oaky, buttery Chardonnay, for example, then harvest the fruit (mostly by machine for lower priced wines), put it in oak (or, more likely, put the oak in it—see "Walk the Plank: Does Oak Float Your Boat?" on page 88), and do a malolactic fermentation to soften the wine. When it comes to yeasts, this more end-driven approach almost always inoculates the natural yeast and introduces a commercial strain to provide greater consistency in the desired style.

The opposite approach is to make wine in a more traditional, pre-agrichemical way. Practitioners of this method don't use pesticides or chemical fertilizers in the vineyards, they harvest the fruit by hand, and they don't use commercial yeasts, a point of controversy. This is riskier: Ideally, the yeast that naturally occurs on the outside of the grape comes into contact with the sugars on the inside and they ferment into alcohol. But if the yeast gives out before consuming all of the sugars then the fermentation is "stuck," leaving residual sugar, making the wine taste sweet. This is how white Zinfandel came to be. Many wineries eliminate that risk (since who really wants to end up with white Zinfandel?) by killing the natural yeast and adding yeasts cultured in a lab that can finish the job and ferment the natural sugar into alcohol, leaving a dry wine. But this is anathema to the natural winemakers, since it breeds similarity rather than celebrating the diversity of wine.

I've had bad wines and good wines from both styles and, somehow to me, the greatest ones tend to be natural. The bad wines from the first category tend to be bad in a bland, innocuous sort of way, like Muzak, while the bad ones from a natural winemaking perspective tend to really be clunkers. I guess that's why there's still latent hostility to organic and natural winemaking among some wine critics and winemakers. Either that or a cabal of agrichemical salespeople is out to denigrate organic winemaking at every turn. The wines are sometimes distinctive and a drinker new to them may need a period of acclimatization, a sort of palate recalibration away from the gobs of fruit and toward more minerality and subtlety that speak of place and grape.

You may be wondering why I'm parsing my words when it comes to "green" or natural wines—why not just say "organic" wine, the way we talk about organic tomatoes? Well, the bugbear issue is sulfites, or sulfur dioxide, which are added to the wine in small quantities before bottling to preserve and stabilize the wine during transport. Even though they actually occur naturally in wine, the threshold level for them in wine is actually so low that virtually no wine can be called "organic." Instead, producers can state "made with organically grown grapes" on the label. But since only 70 percent of those grapes need to actually be organic to earn that distinction, this is a case of truthiness that would make Stephen Colbert arch an eyebrow.

Currently, having any mention of "organic" on a label is so difficult that really only the big producers can do it. Consider Bonterra, a 600,000-case brand from the drinks conglomerate Brown-Forman that makes wines from organically grown grapes. While there's no doubt that that is a lot of fertilizer not spilled into local waterways by virtue of their organic farming, there seems to be more than a whiff of marketing benefits driving the decision, since Fetzer spent $1 million in a recent advertising campaign to tell the world about the organic program.

But even those who can use the terminology often eschew it. Consider the case of Porter Creek, a family-run winery in Sonoma's Russian River Valley. They make a lovely Pinot Noir from Fiona Hill Vineyard, certified organic. But they don't put it on the label. Why? Many small natural producers want to be known first for their great wines and then second, if at all, as organic, sustainable, or whatever. But while their motivations may be more pure, they do make it much more difficult for green consumers to be able to tell that the wine is from organically grown grapes at a glance. Fortunately, many clever wine shops are now doing the coding on the shelf.

If this subject has caught your fancy, check out my book *Wine Politics: How Governments, Environmentalists, Mobsters, and Critics Influence the Wines We Drink* for a full discussion of the rules and regs.

❖ Seven Great "Green" Wine Producers

Again, many of the best tasting or most natural wines do not put any mention of "organic" on the label for a variety of mostly bureaucratic reasons. For imported wines, checking the importer can offer an insight into how natural it is: The importer Louis/Dressner has built an almost unrivaled portfolio entirely around winemakers of a natural philosophy; Kermit Lynch also prizes natural winemaking. Here are seven producers who make great natural wines.

CLOS ROCHE BLANCHE: Owners Catherine Roussel and Didier Barrouillet make extremely tasty and affordable organic wines from the Loire.

GEORGES DESCOMBES: Hypernatural and very tasty cru Beaujolais from Morgon.

CLEMENS BUSCH: Uses low-yields in the vineyard, organic farming, wild yeasts and hand harvesting to craft excellent Riesling from the Lower Mosel in Germany.

MOVIA: This Slovenian producer makes wines in a traditional way using biodynamics from many indigenous grapes. The white Ribolla Gialla is fascinating; the value Vila Marija Merlot is a steal.

PORTER CREEK: A family-run winery in Sonoma's Russian River Valley that makes particularly good yet reasonably priced Pinot Noir.

BRICK HOUSE VINEYARDS: Doug Tunnell has used an organic viticulture since 1991 when he left broadcasting and started his winery in Oregon's Willamette Valley. Biodynamic.

OCONE: This producer in Campania makes solid and affordable wine from Italy's indigenous grape varieties, Aglianico, Falanghina, and Greco di Tufo, among others.

Since sulfur is often the item that prevents a natural wine from being called "organic," will organic wines eliminate headaches? Unlikely.

Some people don't drink red wine because it gives them headaches. But is it the sulfites that are causing unease? Probably not. If someone has an allergy to sulfites, the symptoms will be severe and involve much more than a headache. If you're still not convinced, there are a few wines that are bottled without sulfur, so you can try to seek those out for the sake of comparison. A word of caution, though: Sulfites are a preservative, so exercise care when buying an unsulfured wine and give it a little more TLC, such as monitoring the storage climate when you get it home, than you would give a normal bottle.

A better test for a sulfite allergy is to see if you have a reaction when you eat dried fruits, particularly dried apricots. The sulfites on a few apricots are typically many times higher than what is used in a whole bottle of wine.

The fact of the matter is that nobody's quite sure why some people get headaches from red wine. The best guess is that it has to do with natural histamines in the wine. And since taking antihistamines and alcohol are not recommended, it's a tough balance. Maybe try moderation?

Going Green: The Carbon Footprint of Wine

Is that a whiff of dark cherries and leather you get from that red wine—or a whiff of petroleum? With some premium wines consuming three times their weight in petroleum, don't be surprised if it is the latter. If you're looking to turn over a green leaf this Earth Day, it's time to think about the carbon footprint of wine.

As I sipped an Argentine Malbec from a bottle that was half empty but so heavy it weighed as much as a regular full one, I wondered about the path it took to my table. So I called the importer and found out. The big bottle had gone over the Andes to a port in Chile, then headed by boat to Oakland, California, where it was loaded onto a truck and driven to me in New York. Yikes. That's quite a carbon footprint!

In an effort to learn more about which wines are the most "green," I collaborated with Pablo Päster, a sustainability metrics engineer. We developed a calculator to determine the carbon footprint of various different wine bottles, taking into account activity in the vineyard, the winery, and transportation. Surprisingly, we didn't find that much of a difference between organic grape cultivation and the conventional method—but we were studying strictly the carbon footprint (or, more precisely, the greenhouse gas emissions), not the effects on vineyard workers or the local habitat, which can be affected by synthetic fertilizers and pesticides. What we found was that the distance traveled, how those miles are traveled, and the packaging methods, were what mattered.

Consider a bottle of Napa wine going to a shop in Berkeley. The total footprint of the wine—from growing the grapes, to making the wine, to trucking it to the store—is about 2.6 pounds of carbon dioxide emissions. But send that same bottle to New York by truck, and the same wine would emit 5.7 pounds of carbon dioxide in total. Ship it to New York by air and the figure would quadruple since it takes so much fuel to keep a plane aloft.

Why? Glass. A forty-pound case of wine has about twenty pounds of glass in it—just feel your recycling bin on Monday morning if you have any doubts. So when a bottle of wine comes from California or France, it's primarily glass with a bit of wine in it. Buying half-bottles worsens the ratio of glass per ounce of wine, whereas buying magnums improves it. Alternative packaging such as Tetra Pak (think: juice box) and bag-in-box (think: Franzia) greatly reduce the mass, thus the carbon footprint of the wine. While we'll never see Château Lafite Rothschild in a box, it's a pity that, to date, such packaging has been reserved for such bad wines.

Because of the efficiency of shipping wine by sea, the wine with the lowest carbon footprint may actually come from far away. Consider a wine consumer living in New York. The wine from California trucked across the country actually emits 50 percent more carbon dioxide than a wine farmed the same way and in a bottle weighing the same amount from Bordeaux be-

TIPS: HOW TO SHRINK
THE CARBON FOOTPRINT
OF YOUR WINE

✻ Avoid wines shipped via
air freight.

✻ Avoid ridiculously heavy
bottles.

✻ Try to go local or go light
(packaging). How easy it
is to find good local wines
depends on your locality. If
you live on the West Coast,
you're in luck, but it could be
hard to find good local wines
if you live elsewhere. But
with wine made in all fifty
states, there's no excuse!
You have until August to find
one near you (see page 154).
For box wine picks, skip
ahead to July.

cause the ship is so much more efficient than the truck, from the perspective of greenhouse gas emissions.

If the French wine were loaded onto a truck and then driven all the way to Ohio, the two bottles would finally reach a break-even point. That makes a "green line" for wine: For wine consumers in Ohio and the East Coast, a bottle from Bordeaux actually creates less carbon dioxide emission; to the west, California has the edge.

But even if wine is worth more than its weight in carbon, it remains an hors d'oeuvre in our overall carbon diet, and we wine consumers can do more to offset our overall consumption. Purchasing a carbon offset is one option, as is turning down the thermostat in winter, riding a bicycle to work, giving up bottled water, and eating less meat, since one cheeseburger has a bigger carbon footprint than a bottle of California wine consumed in New York.

So this Earth Day, raise a glass to being aware of wine's carbon footprint and how you're going to offset it. Just make sure that the glass is poured from a six-liter bottle—and be sure to drink it completely, with friends, for maximum efficiency!

Walk the Plank:
Does Oak Float Your Boat?

If wintry weather is still lingering into April where you live and you're eager to break out a bottle of white wine, you could consider popping open a heavier, oaky white. Though this introduces a point of current controversy—are new oak barrels a part of natural winemaking? Many traditionalists think not, as is evidenced by the following story.

"No *barriques*!" said the seemingly mild-mannered man that I was sitting next to at a lunch. "No *barriques*!" he repeated, raising his hands and crossing his forearms in an "X." He was Italian.

What on earth was he getting all worked up about? In a word: oak. Or in two words: oak barrels, or *barriques*. If you ever want to see some fur fly with a bunch of wine enthusiasts just ask how they feel about hedonistic oak bombs. That should get the conversation off to an explosive start.

What's at stake is best summed up in Chardonnay. (Of course, wood is important and easily discernable in red wines too, but we already discussed that when we talked about "rustic" in January, page 31.) A neutral grape, Chardonnay has become the main delivery vehicle for foisting oak on unsuspecting masses at country clubs, beaches, and backyards around America. The oak gets layered on and the wine becomes rich and creamy (in part through malolactic fermentation). The resulting notes of butterscotch, toffee, coconut, and caramel make some people say "Mmm, home sweet home" and make other people gag and run for the nearest spit bucket.

Oak comes in several flavors. The classic is the *barrique*, the 225-liter barrel made most often from French oak. Since French oak happens to grow in the euro zone, these barrels can easily cost $1,000 in America. So what kind of wine is going to be found in those barrels? With two dollars worth of oak per regular bottle (the barrels can be used about two times and each barrel holds about three hundred bottles of finished wine), this sure isn't the raw material for building Two Buck Chuck! So a lot of midrange winemakers use American oak, which tends to have a wider grain and costs about $400 a barrel. Both kinds of barrels can have the insides burned to a greater or lesser extent depending on tastes and winemakers meet with barrel makers and order just what kind of a "toast" they want, which can lead to a greater oak taste. (When you order a lot of wines labeled "Chardonnay," you're often tasting variations in oak, not place.) The third option for real skinflints who want the taste without the price tag is to use oak chips. Essentially the producer is taking a giant tea bag full of oak shards and steeping it in the fermenting wine. Oak flavor at a fraction of the price and in a fraction of the time! Sometimes they also hang staves—planks of oak—inside the tank to increase the wine's contact area with oak.

Currently there's a backlash against oak in many white wines. Riesling, Pinot Grigio, Sauvignon Blanc from New Zealand, and Albariño have all benefited from the backlash since they see no oak, aging instead in massive stainless steel tanks that are as low on taste as they are on charm. Even Chardonnay is now proclaiming on the label when it is "unoaked" or "unwooded." All of a sudden, wine drinkers want to taste grapes, not barrels in their wine! This is a good thing, since so much wood has been applied in such a heavy-handed manner. In fact, the backlash has gone so far now that there's a backlash to the backlash. But it hasn't gathered much steam yet, and hopefully it will die out soon since I prefer to taste grapes that are expressive of where they were grown, not necessarily which barrels they were aged in.

Putting white wine in oak should not be dismissed out of hand. Old barrels are natural vessels for aging wines that allow a delicate interplay of oxygen and wine. Whites of Burgundy are often made with new oak, but can also be overdone. And, the white wines of Bordeaux have an assiduous oak treatment on the blend of racy Sauvignon Blanc and aromatic Sémillon grapes and can be outstanding, rich, and complex yet balanced. Compare this style to a New Zealand Sauvignon Blanc, unoaked and admittedly without the Sémillon, for two styles that are, aptly, at opposite ends of the scale.

So put some wood in your tasting glass and see where you stand. Several producers of Australian Chardonnay make both oaked and unoaked versions of the same wine for your easy comparison. You could also try a white Burgundy from France versus an American Chardonnay for about the same price, say $20. In the first, the oak will not have much of an influence since it was probably aged in large, old vats. The wine will probably have a pleasant core of acidity, a bit of stony mineral character, and maybe some green apple. But the American one will probably have those aromas of butterscotch and coconut and will probably have higher alcohol too.

You can even taste chips in your comparative tasting. Although most producers are reluctant to admit this shortcut, the winemaker at McManis has admitted to using chips. So throw that in your tasting! Just don't throw it in the cellar since McManis's wines are meant to be consumed right away.

Chacun a son goût, or "to each their own taste," as they say. But at least now, after trying this tasting exercise, you have a better idea of what your *goût* is and whether oak floats your boat. Convey this important finding to store clerks and sommeliers to find more wines in a style you like!

❈ *April 15: Ten Wines Under $10*

Tax day! No doubt we all feel a little lighter in the wallet on April fifteenth after we have rendered unto Caesar. But in the wake of all those nights trying to get Quicken to reconcile, what's left of the wine budget? Has it been left in tatters, shredded faster than an internal memo at Enron? Probably, so here's a list of great wines under ten dollars.

CHÂTEAU DU TARIQUET (GASCON, FRANCE): If you move off the beaten path, it's amazing how much value you can get. In Gascony, an overlooked part of southwestern France, Yves Grassa takes such care that he refrigerates his grapes as they are being harvested in the vineyard to maximize freshness heading back to the winery (on the same property). His Sauvignon Blanc at Tariquet is particularly delicious—try pairing it with Asian spices. He also owns Domaine de Pouy, another Gascon property that makes value wine.

DOMAINES LES HAUTES NOELLES, MUSCADET (LOIRE, FRANCE): People always say Muscadet goes great with oysters. Well, I have oysters once every five years and this wine is too good to wait that long between bottles. The *sur-lie* aging, or "on the lees" (lees are the spent yeast cells), gives some of the best Muscadet a richer mouthfeel but retains the characteristic crisp acidity, faint melon note, and gentle briny and almost nervy quality.

HUGUES BEAULIEU, PICPOUL DE PINET (LANGUEDOC, FRANCE): Known as the Muscadet of the south, this wine is an absolute crowd pleaser with its zingy acidity and zesty citrus aromas. And at this price, you can afford to slake the thirst of a crowd too. Stock up on this wine for summer outdoor entertaining.

BODEGAS CVNE (RIOJA, SPAIN): Dry rosé used to be an absolute bargain since it was out of favor with wine drinkers. But when that changed, the prices went up. It's still possible to find some excellent ones for under $10, start with this light and refreshing offering from Bodegas CVNE.

FONTE DA SERRANA (ALENTEJO, PORTUGAL): Alentejo is a hot, dry part of Southern Portugal that, when it comes to wine, traditionally has been more known for making closures—corks—rather than what goes in the bottle. But this wine will make them consider planting more vines. The alluring nose of dried herbs precedes the all-berry attack, which, in turn, is followed by a surprising degree of bright acidity and gentle tannins. A great summer quaffer.

VIÑA MONTGRAS (CHILE): Chile produces dependable values, especially in the "big red" category. Viña MontGras makes a rich wine from the Carménère grape variety that has a lot of gusto and a lingering finish. Montes is another reliable producer.

SUR DE LOS ANDES, MALBEC (ARGENTINA): Argentina also produces lots of good value wines, in part because their currency has fared even worse than the U.S. dollar lately. Another reason is that oak barrels are expensive so most of the wines under $10, particularly from the Malbec grape, are unoaked, which makes them less like wine cocktails and more pleasant with food. The Sur malbec is classy and sure to please a crowd. Also of note is the unoaked Ique from Enrique Foster; I have poured the wine as a ringer in blind tastings.

COLONIA LAS LIEBRES (MENDOZA, ARGENTINA): This winery (whose name means "rabbit colony") bears mentioning as a particularly ridiculous value that I have bought for as low as $4.49 with a case discount (come on, less than $60 a case? How could you say no?). This unoaked, unfiltered old vine Bonarda from importer Marco de Grazia's project in Mendoza has light and lively acidity and tart cherry notes. It's now my official burrito wine.

BODEGAS CASTAÑO, MONASTRELL (YECLA, SPAIN): More intriguing *aromatically* than many Cabernets, Monastrell (see November) generally offers great bang for the buck in the big red department. It's also one of the rare potentially age-worthy wines under ten dollars. Try with grilled meat.

SOBON ESTATE ZINFANDEL (AMADOR COUNTY, CALIFORNIA): A lighter style Zin, farmed organically and made at a family-run winery, this wine has dark cherry notes up front and a nice grind of spicy pepper on the finish. Try it with cured meats.

Feeling Grü Vee in the Springtime:
Get to Know Grüner Veltliner

Try the ultimate "green" wine for spring: Grüner Veltliner from Austria.

After tasting some of his excellent wines from the 2005 vintage, I asked Rudi Pichler, a winemaker in Austria's Wachau region, if the vintage was the best he'd ever had. His reply was simple: "Yes. Until 2006." And 2007 may have been even better.

There's never been a better time to try Grüner Veltliner from Austria. At the high end, the wines are incredibly good: I tasted through forty-one whites from the prestigious Wachau region, vintage 2006, and I found thirty-six of them recommendable. As befits Mozart's homeland, the recent story of Austrian wine has been of operatic proportions. What little credibility the wines had overseas was shattered in the 1980s by a self-imposed injury (some wines had antifreeze in them; cue joke from *The Simpsons*). But the Austrians overcame this adversity with a reform in winemaking and winemaking law, and a qualitative upswing that has brought them to the current highs (in 2002, Grüner Veltliner decisively beat white Burgundy in a blind tasting).

This is because of the flavor profile, which, despite the Germanic name, is not sweet like Riesling but instead is dry, Chardonnay-like, though with greater aromatics and a faint, enticing spiciness. And in more ripe vintages such as 2005 and 2006, there's a sweet fruit aroma of white peaches or even mangoes that layers seamlessly on the sprightly, fresh green (Grüner), minerally notes on the palate. Pair some lighter Grüner with your spring greens; some heavier Grüners with wintry crustaceans.

The only downside to Grü Vee, as it is sometimes known, is that the best wines cost as much as white Burgundy, so they're not exactly a bargain. The general vicinity of the Danube around Vienna happens to be a high-rent area so it's hard for Grüner to compete on price with wines from the southern hemisphere. But Grüner Veltliner, indigenous to Austria, has hardly been planted at all outside the country so they don't have anything to fear from imitators. And it is a favorite of sommeliers: a $30 bottle at a store has a terrible habit of becoming a $90 bottle in a restaurant. So you might want to pour quality Grü Vee at home, with an Austrian dish of spaetzle, cheese, fish, or grilled spring veggies.

✳ *Taste Grü Vee*

FRANZ HIRTZBERGER: An excellent producer starting at the *Federspiel* level (particularly Rotes Tor) right up to *Smaragd*. Wonderful depth yet also delicate. $$–$$$$

WEINGUT KNOLL: Another top producer, I particularly enjoy the Loibenberg *Smaragd,* which tends to be like a finely tuned sports car—a lot of power, yet it handles corners fantastically well. $$$

A NOTE ON AUSTRIAN LABELS

Falconry was once popular in the Wachau region, and the designation *Federspiel* (literally, "falcon play") on the label indicates a lighter style, from 11 to 12.5 percent alcohol. The *Smaragd* ("emerald") level, higher in quality and more age-worthy, starts at 12.5 percent alcohol and is a richer style thanks to coming from the best sites and the ripest harvest. And no, it's not named after the gemstone but after a lizard that basks in the glow of the sun on the stone terraces along the Danube.

RUDI PICHLER: The less famous Pichler (F.X. Pichler is legendary and also expensive), Rudi Pichler uses only natural yeasts and contact with the skins during fermentation to achieve a fuller, richer style. These are compelling wines that start at $30. $$$

NIKOLAIHOF: Christine Saahs presides over Im Weingebirge, the first biodynamic vineyard in Europe, having made the transition in the 1970s. (In fact, the Im Weingebirge land has seen a lot of history and transition during its existence—a vineyard on this site dates back to the fifth century. Amazing!) The wines from the Im Weingebirge vineyard, particularly the *Smaragd* level, are very impressive, with depth and minerality. This particular bottling is a keeper for the cellar. $$–$$$$

RAINER WESS: In his thirties, Rainer Wess makes very solid Grüner at reasonable prices, particularly for the Wachau. $$

SALOMON UNDHOF: A very good producer who makes excellent value Grüner from Kremstal. $$–$$$$

WEINGUT HOFER FREIBERG: Rich, with notes of tropical fruits but with a precise finish, this is a bargain at under $20. Somehow they also make a one-liter jug of Grüner Veltliner that sells for $9.99. The ultimate quaffer Grü Vee. $–$$$

Travel to: Rioja, Spain—Blending "Starchitects" and Tradition in Rioja

April is a great time to visit Rioja since it's beautiful there in the springtime, there are few tourists to contend with, and you'll beat the heat of summer (though June and September have wine festivals, so those are good times to visit as well).

Rioja is the grande dame of Spain. Producers in the region had hoped to become "the winery to the world" in the late nineteenth century when the vineyards of France succumbed to phylloxera, a vineyard pest. Those aspirations were short-lived, however, since the pest traversed the Pyrenees and ravaged Spanish vineyards as well.

Today, Rioja may seem the mature voice in the exuberant, young chorus of Spanish wine regions. The old-school producers still cling to old methods of making wine. But there's a new generation coming to the fore, shaking old traditions by building striking wineries and making modern-style wines.

Although the administrative seat is the largely ho-hum town of Logroño, the real wine action happens on the road from Logroño to Haro. That's the direction the Oja River flows, eventually meeting the Bay of Biscay, and it's a natural direction for wine travel. It also takes us from modern back to traditional.

Frank Gehry, an icon of modernism, has certainly left his mark in northern

Spain by making major contributions to the modern-style landscape and modern-day Spain as we know it. His design for the Guggenheim museum in Bilbao opened up the neighboring Basque Country to foreign visitors like no other achievement since the pilgrimage route of the Camino de Santiago de Compostela. And at Marqués de Riscal, a winery just outside Logorño, Gehry unfurled the waves of titanium sheeting again (reputedly after the Riscal management broke out a wine from his birth year, 1929, to get him to sign on).

The 150-year-old winery was transformed by Gehry into a four-story "City of Wine." It now boasts a five-star hotel, complete with forty-three luxurious guest rooms and a spa with vinotherapy treatments, a process where stuff from the bottom of the fermentation tank gets scraped out and placed on your back. Well, there may be more to it than that. Amazingly, all of this bling is on the back of the Marqués de Riscal winery, whose entry-level wine is a compelling value, retailing for about $10.

If that's not your style, visit Bodegas Ysios, which backs up to the craggy Cantabrian Mountains, and has more orderly undulations than Riscal. The striking winery was designed by the globetrotting architect Santiago Calatrava and is owned by Domecq, a subsidiary of the French Pernod Ricard. Be sure to book ahead if you want to tour or to taste.

On to the wine town of Haro, which has many of the old-school producers gathered around the train station. None should be higher on your list than R. López de Heredia. Even though the charming María José and her two siblings now run the family firm, their winemaking has changed little since 1877 when their ancestors founded the winery. Everything is done by hand, from the harvesting to moving the grapes into the 125-year-old oak fermentation casks, to the bottling and labeling. The only apparent nod to the twenty-first century is a swanky tasting room outside the winery designed by architect Zaha Hadid.

Orson Welles, who once told Americans in a TV ad to have no wine before its time, would love the bottle cellar at R. López de Heredia. Unlike other regions where producers move the wine out of the winery soon after it leaves the tanks, wineries in Rioja preage it for you. At López de Heredia, bottles age silently in the cellar while growing covered in mold from the humid conditions. It's not uncommon for their current releases to have seven years of age on them. For the top-of-the-line wines, the aging process is doubled since they age about seven years in barrel before moving to the bottle.

López de Heredia's distinctive white wines have been called the best white wine in the world. They take on a faint nuttiness yet remain absolutely vital. I tried some vintages dating back to the 1960s, and they were showing beautifully. The rosés are so mature (the current release often has 10 years of age on it) and complex that they take some acclimatization if you're used to last year's vintage from Provence. And the reds have a beautiful delicacy and poise.

But if this traditionalism earns your respect more than your actual enjoyment, head across the Haro Station District to Bodegas Muga. There, another traditional producer blends old and new, but in the line of wines, not with architecture. Muga uses lots of new oak, which makes the wines bigger and sometimes, in my view, overdone. The Prado Enea beautifully integrates wood tannin and oak tannin, but the Torre Muga (Muga Tower) wine is relentlessly modern, more akin to a new world wine than a Rioja. Two worlds, under one old-fashioned *torre*.

Practical tip: Many of the bigger wineries won't offer much to the drop-in visitor. Plan ahead and get on one of the scheduled tours; usually there's one in the morning and one in the afternoon.

When to go: A visit in April can beat the heat and give you a jump on the tourists (watch out for Easter, though); head for the second half of September and you may hit the harvest festival during traditional feasts of San Mateo.

Getting there: Connections from many U.S. hubs are available through London, Frankfurt or Madrid to the Calatrava-designed airport at Bilbao. It's almost impossible to resist tacking on a stopover there and hitting some of the Basque Country's great tapas (*pintxos*) bars and outstanding restaurants, such as Arzak in San Sebastian or Mugaritz just outside.

SOMMELIER SURVEY

Erik Leidholm,

Wine Director, Seastar Restaurant and Raw Bar, Seattle, Washington

How does context matter for enjoying wine?

It's quite important to me. In some instances the context itself can transform the wine to a higher station.

What is one of your favorite food-wine pairings?

Hot-and-sour soup with Vin de Bugey from Renardat-Fâche. Heat-n-sweet!

How important is pairing wine with the seasons?

For my guests' sake I try to stay with the seasons: heartier wine in the cold months and more crisp and refreshing wine in the warmer months. It also helps that our menus change with the seasons, which makes it easier. If I ruled the world it would be Champagne all year.

If you had to have one wine per season, what would it be?

Winter: Champagne
Spring: Riesling
Summer: Rosé
Fall: Chenin Blanc

If you had to pick one season for drinking wine, what would it be? And why?

Summer. I don't feel guilty drinking rosé. To me a young, fresh rosé IS summer. Talk about context!

What's one of your most memorable food-wine occasions where the location or company really mattered?

I was fifteen and sitting in a little village perched above the Lauterbrunnen Valley in Switzerland with my father and grandfather. We had been hiking for a few hours in the mountains and stopped to have our lunch at this idyllic spot on a beautiful summer day. My grandfather pulled out a chilled flask full of Fendant. It was so crisp, refreshing, and satisfying. We had it with cheese sandwiches that we had made with fresh local bread and local Gruyère cheese. Perfect! Tasting the wine today in my restaurant I am confident that it would be the innocuous wine that most people think it is, but twenty-two years ago it was a life-changing event.

MAY

While March is a transitional month mainly because of the weather, May is a transitional month due to the numerous life changes that take place from the first through the thirty-first. Graduation brings an end to the beer-drenched days of college and thrusts graduates into jobs where they might have to entertain clients at restaurants and order wine. And as the weather warms up to summer levels, pool covers come off across the northern hemisphere. The sense of anticipation and excitement about good things to come is highlighted as many wine producers, particularly in Bordeaux, offer wines available as "futures" to buy now and collect in two years.

Putting Down the Crystal Glasses and Picking Up the Crystal Ball: Futures

As spring gives way to summer, fine wine consumers ponder the future. It's not that we're becoming increasingly contemplative with the carefree days of summer approaching. It's rather that our in-boxes are filled with solicitations from retailers urging us to put down our money now for wine that will be delivered two years hence. Should you do it?

The ideal strategy is to prebuy in a rising market. Consider the 2005 vintage from Bordeaux, widely regarded as spectacular. Prices started high with futures (not physical bottles yet) of the celebrated Château Pétrus available for $24,000 for a twelve-bottle case—if you could find one. Specialty wine store managers from London to Los Angeles reported not having enough inventory to sell. Compare this with a Volkswagen Jetta, sticker price $23,975 with immediate availability and in other colors besides red. The winner, from a strictly investment standpoint, was the Pétrus, which was worth about $40,000 when it was finally delivered in the summer of 2008. Most of the other top three hundred or so wines from Bordeaux had tremendous run-ups in price too, driven by fierce demand upon release and the subsequent sagging dollar. The Jetta, by contrast, lost monetary value but presumably would have had tremendous use value, for doing things like driving to work. You can take a Pétrus for a swirl, but not for a spin.

Contrast that with the 2007 vintage, which got a critical reception almost as cool (though not as damp) as the weather during that year's growing season. Couple that with a softening economy, and there's not a lot of reason to rush into the market unless you absolutely must have a first growth or can't miss having a vintage of a certain producer in your collection.

To grow, make, and subsequently presell Bordeaux takes about a year for the top three hundred or so wines. The grapes grow on the vines throughout the summer. Orley Ashenfelter, an economist at Princeton, used to collect weather data from around the harvest and made his predictions about vintage quality solely on temperature and rainfall. But the more traditional measure of quality is the report from a vanguard of tasters who descend on the region in March, after the wines have been harvested. Although there are thousands of buyers from around the world and critics from many publications, the Bordeaux wine trade and the world have, to date, only really listened to the opinion of one man: Robert Parker.

Robert Parker swirls, sniffs, and spits his way from one château to the next every March during "primeurs." He tastes many of the inky-purple, tooth-staining, tannic barrel samples that have not yet been blended on the premises of each château. Then he flies home, pounds out his tasting notes, attaches a preliminary score, and publishes them in his newsletter, the *Wine Advocate* (how much longer he will be doing this remains to be seen since he has hired several other critics and has had health problems). The scores then get e-mailed around Bordeaux and, eventually, one château steps forward and sets a price. Then the others dither and wait, as the process can stretch into June before the top producers set their offering prices and presell the wine (oftentimes they hold back a good portion of production).

Although it might seem as if the producers would relish this situation—free media attention, getting paid for wine still in the barrel—some, in fact, object to it. Jean-Claude Berrouet, the winemaker for over forty years at Château Pétrus, has called the selling of futures "madness" since it requires that the wines must be made "seductive" at such an early point in their evolution. British wine writer Stephen Brook has gone so far as to call the process a "con" because consumers have to put down the money so early.

So if you want to play the futures game, be sure to buy from an established or well-capitalized retailer since you want to make sure they are going to still be around in two years so you can collect the wine. Shopping around on a price comparison site, such as Wine-Searcher.com or WineZap.com, can help you find the best price among reputable retailers.

In sum, buy futures only if you like the producer, absolutely must have a top wine for a special year in your life, have an indication that the vintage is quite good, and think that the prevailing economic backdrop will support higher prices when the wines arrive a couple of years later.

Otherwise, you might just make more money with less risk and get beautiful mature wine by buying at auction. Ask yourself: Would you prefer to spend $150 for a bottle of wine that won't be available for two years and then requires another decade in the cellar, or for something with fifteen years of age on it now? (More on buying mature wines in September.)

Tyra and Tannins: Why Moscato d'Asti Is the Ultimate Wine for Newbies, Pools, and Tyra Banks, and Is a Great Wine for This Time of Year

As college grads move on from hanging out by the keg and everyone starts to think about hanging out by the pool, wine newbies can hardly find a better start to their wine education than a Moscato d'Asti. Consider the curious case of Tyra Banks who doesn't like wine, but orders it to look sexy.

After a tasting trip to Napa Valley, America's former top model was quoted saying that she only takes a couple of sips of wine but continues to hold the glass " 'cause it makes me feel sexy, but I still don't drink it because it tastes kind of nasty to me."

Help Tyra like wine! I take no issue with her calling wine sexy. But with such diversity in wine, there's no way to categorically say wine is nasty—unless you're fundamentally opposed to alcohol, which is fine, but then you probably wouldn't think it's very sexy.

Big red wine, which Tyra had, can be tough for newbies. Tannins, which give red wine intensity and come from both the grape skins and oak barrels, can make you chew and chomp. As a result, many California wines, like top models, have been airbrushed. The winemaker's tool for softening tannins is often a process that involves running tiny bubbles through the tank of fermenting wine, a process known as micro-oxygenation that makes the wines more drinkable in their youth. Unlike a cosmetic surgeon, the winemaker's nip and tuck makes the wines appear older and removes the harsh vigor of the tannins in young wine. It's not illegal, although it is controversial and the wines may not last as long as a result. I find such wines a mixed bag, but many people enjoy the plush, smooth wines that emerge from such a treatment.

So if Tyra doesn't like reds, tannic or not, she needs to think sweet, and there's no better newbie wine than Moscato d'Asti. I'm still trying to find a newbie who doesn't like a good Moscato. Why? It's slightly sweet, low in alcohol, and lightly sparkling. It's tempting to say that it's the soda of wine, but that's really an insult to Moscato.

Where does this newbie wine hail from? Asti is a town in Piedmont, the northern Italian region known more for serious reds, and many of the large producers in the region make Asti Spumante, a generic bubbly sometimes known to its detractors as "Nasty" Spumante (but is it sexy?). But the small producers of Moscato d'Asti have gotten the memo about upgrading quality, and there are some beautiful ones out there. With the light fizz, notes of white peach, and 5 percent alcohol level, a good Moscato is also the ultimate wine to have in the sun by the pool. I brought a bottle of La Spinetta Moscato d'Asti to a poolside lunch with friends, and it was gone in a hurry despite protestations about it being midday. Elio Perrone also makes a brilliant Moscato—try it with prosciutto and melon. Or biscotti. Or ice cream.

Beyond Moscato, off-dry wines, particularly Riesling, are a great place to start when introducing someone to wine. You remember the riddle the Sphinx posed to Oedipus: What walks on four legs in the morning, two at noon, and three in the afternoon? (The answer isn't "wine enthusiasts after a long night.") Well, the equivalent wine riddle might be: Who drinks Riesling in the morning, Syrah (or a big red) at noon, and Riesling in the evening? Done right, Riesling is a great, approachable wine that often gets unfortunately relegated to the beginning and end of a wine enthusiast's arc of life.

Hopefully Tyra Banks and wine newbies everywhere will give one of these a shot and find wine to be sexy *and* tasty.

My Mom, Brunch, and the Oak Bomb:
Mother's Day Wines and Wine Spas

A quick note about my mom and her wine preferences before we tackle Mother's Day picks: Although my mom has a predilection for oaky Chardonnay, it's just a fallback position, her comfort zone. Since she is willing to experiment, I'm always trying to present her with some other wines to broaden said comfort zone.

One summer, after (not before!) my mom had completed a stint of midday babysitting for my son, I brought her back a Soave. Before you gasp in horror that I gave my mom an industrial wine from the north of Italy, it's worth noting that in Soave, as with so many regions in the wine world, some producers have gotten the memo about upgrading quality. Strategically, the Soave that I brought her, from the producer Prà, was chilled, so she offered to uncork it then and there. The wine's aromas of honeysuckle followed by a full, rich mouthfeel and gentle acidity made her a fan despite the fact that it is unoaked. Pieropan also makes an excellent Soave. Perfect as the weather is warming up, it's the sort of wine that nobody has ever heard of but instantly likes.

Now, on to What to Drink to Celebrate Mother's Day

Although mothers deserve respect and admiration every day, Hallmark tells us that there is one particular Sunday in May when we should glorify them. And the cornerstone of the celebration is brunch. And brunch may seem at first glance to be an impossible food-wine pairing, but, in fact, the many savory dishes pair well with some wines.

A little bubbly always makes the occasion more festive. And if you're looking to pair something with pancakes and maple syrup, just douse the bubbly (preferably a nice Cava or Prosecco) with orange juice and make it a mimosa. Pairing wine and eggs is a tad tricky, but Champagne is always a reliable choice, especially in this celebratory occasion. Prosecco can also work, and I can see some Riesling being a beautiful pairing. But one of my ultimate brunch combos is an "everything" bagel with cream cheese and smoked salmon. So much flavor! So much salt! I love it with a glass of grower Champagne (see February).

Another way to pamper Mom with wine is to encourage her to snuggle up—with grapes. Pioneered as "vinotherapy" at Château Smith Haut Lafitte in Bordeaux, naked bodies are wrapped, massaged, and smothered with grape extracts all in the name of reducing wrinkles and shifting cellulite. The concept of paying people to heap their grape waste on you has now become possible at spas as far afield as Tribeca in New York City and Salta, Argentina. Since independent research questions the effective uptake of antioxidants through the skin, it's probably best to apply them internally as well by having a tannic red wine after the treatment. I'll have to give my wife a spa gift certificate to try this theory out next Mother's Day. After I finish cooking her brunch, that is.

Congratulations, New Hire, Here's the Wine List! (Gulp)

So you graduated from college and got a job. That's the good news. But now you're entertaining clients and trying to impress dates in restaurants. Time to bone up on how to navigate a wine list.

Perhaps the most important thing you can do to ensure that you'll have a good wine experience in a restaurant is something you should consider before you even arrive: You greatly increase your chances of having great wine if you choose a restaurant with a great wine program. If you're stuck at an Afghan place with a bunch of cheap Shiraz and oaky Chardonnay, it's impossible to pull a rabbit out of your hat and make good wine appear. However, you can pull good wine out of a brown paper bag if it is BYOB—a topic covered later in this chapter. And note: Not all restaurants that have good wine lists are expensive.

Once you've selected a wine-friendly restaurant, check out the wine list beforehand. It's laughable how little time we actually get with the wine list before we're called upon to make a decision. And when a thick wine list lands in my hands, I want to spend time studying it. Fortunately that can be done in the comfort of your office since many restaurants now put their wine lists online, or you can ask them to e-mail it to you. Then you won't get bogged down at the table and have to keep asking for "one more minute" before placing your drink order, which everyone wants to get in right at the beginning of the evening anyway. If you need to buy some time, order a glass of bubbly, even if it is a rip-off.

If you're not the advance-planning kind of person, engage in a dialogue with the server. This is really key if you're overwhelmed, since the server can presumably offer you some inside information and steer you in a good direction. Except, that is, when the server can't. I asked an accomplished sommelier once about the lamentable state of wine knowledge among some waitstaff, and he suggested to ask for the wine director or "whoever wrote this list" if you are underwhelmed with the service. It's a ballsy move, to be sure, since that same server will later be bringing out your entrées; consider it the nuclear option. Again, at a restaurant with a good wine program, the staff should have a good knowledge of the wines on the list.

If you do need to ask for a recommendation, try to convey as much information as you can about what you want in the brief exchange with the server. If you had a great wine recently and want to try something like that again, tell what it was that you had, and if it is not on the list, ask if the server could perhaps recommend something similar. Or convey the style of wine you'd like: Saying that you'd like a light and fruit-forward white might get you a Sauvignon Blanc or a Pinot Grigio whereas asking for something medium-bodied and minerally might get you a Chablis.

If you have decided on your food but are still unsure about the wine, tell the server what you're having and ask which wine he or she would recommend, within price parameters, either subtly or in the open. Wine directors love this sort of a challenge. If you want to establish some hard-core credibility in the blink of an eye, tell the server that you like Zweigelt or Zierfandler, respectively obscure red and white grapes from Austria. Of course, you need to have tried this before to see if that is indeed what you want, but the point remains that if you need to prove instant credibility in an exchange with a sommelier, talking about something obscure can give you some great street cred.

Unless you are out to dinner with your rich uncle who's picking up the tab, feel free to be open about price with your server when asking for a recommendation. It is a common misperception that sommeliers don't want to talk about price, but in fact they are very open to working within a budget. If you're with your spouse or partner whom you can easily talk about price in front of without worrying about looking like a cheapazoid, then just say you're looking for a red wine to match the squab that's under $50. You fill in the blanks.

But if you're on a business dinner or a hot date and you don't want to mention price, there are other ways of conveying the point. One of my favorites is to say, "I'm looking for a medium-bodied red wine like THIS," pointing to the price, not the name. The sommelier will get the point instantly and will cooperate nine times out of ten. If the dreaded up-sell happens then you can reiterate that you really were looking for something more like *this*! Ahem.

If you want to go beyond the basic set of questions when seeking a recommendation, you can ask further questions that will sometimes lead to more interesting wines. For instance, ask the wine director if there is a wine in your price range that's a little off the beaten path that offers compelling value. There's usually a region that's difficult to pronounce that the sommelier is fired up about that nobody ever orders because it doesn't say "Chardonnay" on the label. Or ask the wine director what she is having at the end of the night. Or which wine is the chef having? This line of questioning usually yields great finds, sometimes even off-the-list steals.

One final point bears mentioning. When you are in charge of ordering the wine for clients or dates, just bear in mind that your main goal is to make them happy. Ask them if they have any preferences, likes or dislikes, since you don't want to order a big and expensive Cabernet, only to find out that they only like Pinot Noir, or order some hipster grape like Ribolla Gialla only to find that they like buttery Chardonnay. And you don't want to buy a bottle of 1996 Cristal Champagne if your date doesn't like bubbly. This may seem obvious, but it's important. The client/date is always right. Aim to please.

How to Use Wine by the Glass to Your Advantage

As you expand your knowledge of wine, remember this tip: Wine by the glass is a huge rip-off. The restaurant can cover the costs of the whole bottle by selling only one glass. Remember that while a wine shop might mark up a wine it buys from the distributor by 50 percent, the restaurateur might mark up that same wine bought from the same distributor by 300 percent or more. And by-the-glass mark-ups are even higher. (That, in part, explains the wine bar phenomenon since wine bars have stripped-down kitchens and pour mostly wine by the glass—pure profit.) Given these dire economic realities, approach wine by the glass with caution. But there are ways to make it work for you.

For instance, if you don't like red and your date doesn't like white, then go your own ways from a wine perspective and order by the glass. Also, some restaurants are now offering wine pairings with each course. While I would generally approach these with trepidation—are all the wines really good? what could you buy off the list for the same amount of money?—sometimes they can be a fun way to explore new wines. Use wine by the glass to experiment. A lot of times the bottle is open behind the bar, and if you ask and smile sweetly, the server will pour you a taste to see if you really like Falanghina or not.

Wine flights can also be a good way to use wine by the glass to your advantage. Some wine bars and restaurants offer flights of three or four wines in smallish pours, selected based on a certain theme, such as Italian reds. Again, I suspect that there's going to be one clunker in the bunch, but if the restaurant I'm in generally knows what they're doing, then I'm game to jump on board their flight. I'm always especially eager to try a flight at a good wine bar that's in or near a wine region, say a flight of Pinots in Portland or Zinfandels in Sonoma. A lot of times the smaller producers don't send their wines too far afield, so a flight of local wines can yield some good discoveries that aren't available elsewhere.

Feel free to insist on a fresh pour. Wine-by-the-glass bottles are generally fast moving so spoilage shouldn't be an issue, but sometimes if you're at a place in the afternoon or early evening, you can get a less-than-best pour off a bottle opened the previous night (or worse). If something tastes off to you, don't hesitate to ask for another glass immediately.

After all, with those kind of profit margins, they can afford to open a new bottle for you.

Yes, you might be faced with this decision at some point. And even if you don't want to do it, sometimes—hopefully rarely—it has to happen. Generally, there are two reasons for sending a wine back: It's corked or it's cooked.

For a wine to be corked (a euphemism for "spoiled," rather than meaning simply "closed with a piece of cork"), somewhere along the way, whether in the barrels, the winery, or most likely in contact with the cork, the noxious chemical known as TCA (or 2,4,6-trichloroanisole if you want to be wonky) entered the wine.

It's so easy to sniff out TCA that a caveman could do it. In fact, it smells like a musty cave, or like a stack of wet newspapers that have been in a damp basement for three weeks. Or a dirty pool. You can smell it without ever tasting it—and you're certainly better off not putting corked wine in your mouth, as I have done in the name of experimentation. The taste ruins a perfectly good evening, haunting any wine to follow. If you believe your wine is corked, bring it to the attention of the waiter immediately, and he or she will duly bring another bottle.

Cooked wine, the other bottle ruiner, may necessitate actual tasting to identify. This sort of wine is prematurely aged, as if someone left it sitting out in a loading bay all last August. The colors will be more mature, the nose will have more ripe fruits rather than fresh, and the wine will seem old beyond its years. This doesn't happen too often, but if you thought you were getting the most recent vintage and you receive something that seems to have been made when you were in high school, bring it to the attention of the waiter.

BYOB (Bring Your Own Bottle): The Wine Geek's Way
to Getting Good Wine in Restaurants on the Cheap

One way to really impress someone is to *bring* the perfect bottle of wine. I once saw a bottle of wine at a store for $15 only to see it a few days later on a wine list for $90. With restaurant wine prices all too often marked up to astronomical levels, it's small wonder that diners who are either into wine or into not getting ripped off like to bring their own.

But improving the quality of wine enjoyed with your meal while lowering the total price of your restaurant visit does come with some protocol. If the restaurant has no liquor license and allows patrons to BYOB, then you have carte blanche. In this case, some cities may not even allow restaurants that don't have a liquor license to charge a corkage fee since then they would be profiting from the sale of liquor without a license. So if you feel a corkage fee is unduly burdensome and you want to take action, then inquire with local authorities. (In general, I don't mind paying a small fee since I want the restaurant to stick around if I like it.) Norms vary across the country on BYOB protocol, so if you're moving or traveling, check out the local situation. And if the restaurant has a liquor license, then they can decide their own BYOB policy. Ideally the place in question will have great food and a gentle corkage fee. But I've been to nice restaurants that charge $75 *and* limit the number of bottles you can bring in.

At the ideal restaurant they won't mind what you bring in, and they'll just charge you the corkage and move on. But at a high-end restaurant, the management may insist that the only wine that can be brought in is something that is not on the list, and you'll probably get a significant corkage fee added to your bill. If it is a mature wine, you may want to drop it by the restaurant a day or two before so that they can stand it up and let the sediment settle to the bottom, and when you consume the wine it's polite to offer the wine director a taste. In some cases, such a gesture can lead to the corkage fee being waived or the arrival of a bonus dessert. If you happen to be a regular, this is a particularly prudent thing to do.

Travel to: Douro, Portugal—*Blending Grapes and Charm in the New Douro*

If you saw a chain of six men bobbing up and down, arms interlocked over each other's shoulders, singing, wearing short-shorts, and with legs stained red from grapes crushed beneath their feet, where would you be? The only surefire answer would be Portugal, in the Douro region, and this is the perfect place for wine lovers who are interested in beating the early summer heat by visiting in May.

The heart of this area is the Douro River, which meanders for some six hundred miles across Spain and Portugal before dumping into the Atlantic Ocean at the city of Porto. While the houses that store port, that sweet, ruby to tawny nectar, are in the city, the vineyards that grow the grapes are up river, in a quasi-hinterland by the Spanish border. The region is a must visit for the curious wine enthusiast, with its beautiful vistas, compelling wines, and great food.

The Upper Douro was for many decades a backward part of a backward country. Many winemaking facilities in the region ran on generators as late as the 1980s because consistent power was not available. Dams provided electricity and turned the rushing, narrow river into a languid, wide one. Be sure to take a boat ride up the twisting and turning river—it will help you to avoid some of the small roads, which often provide great vistas, but are far from straight. And if you think the roads are treacherous, don't even try driving in the vineyards. On a recent trip one winemaker gave me a ride to the top of his vineyard in an old jeep. He floored it hard up the loose, dry dirt of the hill, and I was thrown toward the back of the vehicle due to the acceleration and the steep grade. On the corners, I thought we would roll over. Fortunately, we made it to the top unscathed, but it was a ride I'll never forget.

The wines are unforgettable as well. As with so many wine regions in the world, a qualitative revolution is underway. But instead of exchanging quantity for quality as is the usual story, the Douro's change is from sweet to dry. For three centuries or more, the grapes of the Douro have gone into port, a sweet fortified wine (see January for more information on port). But port wine is no longer as in demand as it was back in the eighteenth century. The market for port is declining while the market for dry table wines is growing in countries like the U.K. and the U.S. Grape growers and port winemakers have seen the market shift and have started to adjust accordingly. The resulting table wines are often rich and concentrated reds that avoid the global trap of simply being replicas of the world's great wines, thanks to the vineyards, which have a seductive, lush quality to them but also a local distinctiveness, because of the arid growing area and the distinctive local grapes.

Some of the best table wines in the region are made by a group who call themselves "the Douro Boys." The group actually includes "boys" ranging from about thirty-five to seventy years of age from five *quintas*, plus one woman. They all descended from, or worked for, the major port houses but now are leading the charge for making dry table wines worthy of the world's attention, even if some of them do still make some port as well.

While all five *quintas* are impressive, the Quinta de Nápoles stands out for blending old and new. Dirk Niepoort, an owner of the estate, oversaw the building of a new winery in a time frame hard to imagine in New York let alone Pinhão. Started in February 2007 and completed by that August, the stunning concrete-and-rock structure designed by Austrian architect Andreas Burghardt is perched on a hilltop. The stonework mimics the terraces so it blends in with the landscape. Dirk, in his early forties, has a mop of curly blond hair and is rarely seen without his Crocs. He is a wine lover and a winemaker, and his wines encompass a full range of wines, from his stunning white Tiara, to the Burgundian Charme, and the more full-bodied Redoma.

But the building and growth of the region aren't limited to the Quinta de Nápoles. Summer 2007 saw the transformation of the Douro into sparkling modernity. Two new luxury hotels opened: the Aquapura, a fifty-room, Asian-inspired hotel built onto one of the region's precipitous slopes; and Quinta da Romaneira, which was built on almost one thousand acres of vine-covered terraced hillsides, and features a riverside spa. Rooms start at about $400 and $1,000 a night, respectively.

In addition to the great wine and accommodations, the food is a big draw as well. Portuguese food has traditionally been hearty fare, meat and potatoes to fuel the workers making their way up and down the vertiginous hillsides. Be sure to try the wonderful local cheeses, particularly the bica de queijo sheep cheese, which, paired with quince paste, is completely addictive. But joining the shift to the modern, some top chefs have started to leave their mark on the region. The menu at Redondo, the top restaurant at Romaneira, has won acclaim, as has the Douro Inn, a modernist restaurant perched on stilts above the river filled with furniture by Philippe Starck.

❋ Wineries

QUINTA DE NÁPOLES: Impressive winery built in 2007 for making Niepoort wines. The stylistic range of wines is broad and excellent. Be sure to try the white Tiara, which is quite possibly the best white wine in Portugal.

QUINTA DO VALE MEÃO: This quinta up the Douro toward Spain, run by the Olazbal family, used to make only port, but in the early nineties shifted to table wines. They make powerful yet refined wines from the traditional grape varieties.

QUINTA DO CRASTO: A truly spectacular hilltop site at a bend in the river. Jorge Roquette and company make one of the best Touriga Nacional varietal wines in the region.

QUINTA DO VALE D. MARIA: Cristiano van Zeller's family sold the esteemed Quinta do Noval in 1993 to AXA Millésimes, the fine wine division of the French insurance group AXA. Then in 1996 Cristiano, a former rugby player with a mellifluous baritone, acquired and started making serious table wines at the small historic Quinta do Vale D. Maria.

QUINTA DO VALLADO: This quinta makes a charming white that pairs perfectly with the shrimp fritters that are popular in the area. The house also has renovated guest rooms at a reasonable price.

When to go: May will likely beat the searing heat of summer; September and October are fun times to see the traditional foot treading.

Getting there: While TAP Air Portugal runs a direct flight from Newark to Porto, most visitors will have to go via Lisbon or connect elsewhere in Europe. Lisbon is worth a stopover to enjoy the great restaurants, if time permits.

SOMMELIER SURVEY

Tysan Pierce,

Sommelier, The Herbfarm, Woodinville, Washington

How does context matter for enjoying wine?

It matters a great deal. *Vin de Pays* wine while you're lounging in the south of France on vacation is going to taste a lot better than the same bottle at a trade tasting in a warehouse! There are transcendental wines . . . but they are rare. I always try to remind people that the company at the table matters as much as the food and wine!

What is one of your favorite food-wine pairings?

Ah . . . that's like asking a parent to pick a favorite child. There are so many! The classics are classics for a reason—caviar and Champagne, seared foie gras and Sauternes, oysters and classic Chablis can be tough to beat. But one of my favorite new pairings we did recently at The Herbfarm was Washington Gewürztraminer from Canoe Ridge with a buttermilk and sorrel panna cotta and Dungeness crab. The minerality of the wine pulled out all the great flavors of the sorrel, and the sweetness of the crab showed off all the fruit in the wine. It was like tasting and drinking springtime!

How important is pairing wine with the seasons?

I feel that it's very important. At my restaurant, we only work with seasonal ingredients since everything is sourced from our farm and local farmers. Nature hands us a wonderfully varied menu throughout the seasons, and the wine pairings follow along with the food. Other than bubbles—which I feel are *perfect* in any season—I think that certain wines tend to gravitate to certain seasons. Big hearty reds in the winter, and crisp Sauvignon Blanc in the summer. Luckily, that seems to be the way nature wants it too, as everything we get during those seasons seems to compliment those wines!

If you had to have one wine per season, what would it be?

Winter: Southwest French reds, Cahors, or big rustic reds like that.
Spring: German Riesling, preferably with some age on them.
Summer: Rosé. I'm a big fan of the Pinot Noir rosés that have been coming out of the Willamette Valley.
Fall: Burgundy—Chambolle-Musigny

is my favorite commune, but I usually stick to Volnay because it's got a more reasonable price tag.

If you had to pick one season for drinking wine, what would it be? And why?

What season is it? This one . . . whatever it is! I think it's a shame that American culture doesn't assume wine to be a part of the dining experience. Food and wine play off each other—it's like hearing the orchestra, instead of just the one instrument. Both benefit and are brought to a higher level when they work together.

What's one of your most memorable food-wine occasions where the location or company really mattered?

My very best friend and I splurged once and bought a whole tin of sevruga caviar and ate it with a bottle of Pol Roger Winston Churchill 1990. That was the most decadent food and wine moment of my life, and it was *totally* worth every penny!

PART THREE

Summer

As the temperatures soar, the asphalt sizzles, and the smell of grilled meat hangs in the air, summer is upon us. Because much of the delight of summer is being outdoors—whether at the beach, on the deck, or on a mountaintop—the wines need to be light and thirst quenching rather than serious. So much about enjoying summer wines is about the context, and that means being outdoors, whether it is daytime or evening. Would you really want a fine wine in a plastic cup by the pool? Or what if a nephew's beach ball knocked over your glass of Bollinger La Grande Année Champagne? You might be miffed. But if it were Prosecco, you'd just pour another round. So much of summer wine is about enjoying summer, and the wine becomes a component of the whole experience, rather than the main attraction. But that doesn't mean it has to be boring!

Beyond the mood, the food of summer also dictates pairings. And there's lots of grilling. Grilled meat and wine are the food-wine equivalent of a slam dunk since so many big reds today need that fat and protein to rein them in. But leave the summer blockbusters for the silver screen: The heat of summer necessitates that those cult Cabs be kept inside for the winter months while you indulge in some lighter wines. If it's too much of a hardship to leave your cult Cabs behind, you can always seek solace in the fact that lighter wines are easier on the wallet. Or you can retreat into the air-conditioning.

In pairing wine with grilled foods a key rule of thumb is to focus on what the wine is working with: the meat or the sauce? With a grilled steak, it's clearly the meat. But when the barbecue sauce starts getting slathered on, then it's the sauce that's worth paying attention to. This is a time when the "big with big, light with light" suggestion really should shine. Below are some wines for the summer that sizzle.

�֎ *Summer Whites*

PROSECCO: From northeastern Italy, the lightness and fruitiness of this bubbly is great for outside. Try matching with salty hors d'oeuvres but could go with a wide range of foods. And it's just so refreshing that it can also be great after a hike or cutting the lawn. Good producers are Bisol, Col Vetoraz, and Zardetto. All under $15 a bottle.

VINHO VERDE: This is the ultimate "not serious" wine. It's harvested in high yields and bottled quickly—there's often a refreshing spritz still in the bottle. And at five dollars a bottle, it's something you can stock by the case by the pool or on the boat. Try the Fâmega from Caves de Cerca.

CRISP, HIGHER ACIDITY UNOAKED WHITES: Albariño and Godello from Spain bring a welcome freshness to the summer table. Picpoul from the Languedoc is deliciously refreshing. Gaujal makes a nice one for under $10.

PIEROPAN SOAVE: Soave is an often-maligned Italian white. But the Pieropan Soave is just excellent—summer in a glass. Beautiful aromas of white flowers and peaches, the lushness on the palate is extremely enticing. And a relative bargain too, since the Classico is about $17.

A STUDY IN SAUVIGNON BLANC: Try a wine from Sancerre, a New Zealand Sauvignon Blanc, and one from California to see the grape as it changes from place to place and winemaker to winemaker. One such lineup would be a Sancerre from the Thomas-Labaille or another producer from the Monts Damnés ("damned mountains"), a Sauvignon Blanc from Craggy Range in New Zealand, and the Honig Sauvignon blanc from Napa. It's fun and is about as much of a homework assignment as you want in the summer. Pair with light fish or grilled veggies.

KICKIN' ASSYRTIKO!: The white Assyrtiko from Santorini works since there's certainly plenty of heat in a Greek summer! The island, formerly a volcano, may be known today for the sparks flying in its bustling nightclub scene. But for wine enthusiasts, the Assyrtiko grape creates wines that have surprisingly refreshing acidity and almost a saline quality to them—great for summer weather and seafood. Try Hatzidakis and Sigalas, two of the leading producers.

❊ *Barbecue Reds*

TRY A MALBEC WITH MEAT: The *asado,* or grilled food, is a staple of life in Mendoza, Argentina, at the foot of the towering Andes. So is Malbec, often had with the wonderful meats off the grill. So defer to local custom and try a Malbec and meat. Terrazas de los Andes Malbec Reserva has been throttling back on their oak in recent vintages of this wine, which has a particularly attractive quality-to-price ratio. The Terra Rosa is also a compelling value offering that is made by American Patrick Campbell in Argentina.

LAMBRUSCO: This is another good summer wine that craves unadorned meat. As with so many wine regions, there is a sea of insipid, mass-produced Lambrusco; one brand went so far as to proclaim in TV ads that it was "so nice, on ice." Um, okay! Now, smaller producers are aiming at quality and doing a great job with the purple fizzy wine from Emilia-Romagna. Try one from Lini, Francesco Vezzelli, or Vittorio Graziano, particularly with cold appetizer meats (mortadella is the regional perfect pairing).

ZINFANDEL: If you are going to try a Zinfandel—and I'm not a fan of the pairing given that high alcohol and high heat are not my favorite together—try the entry-level Zins from Rosenblum and Sobon, which are both around $10.

EXOTIC ITALIANS: SANGUE DI GIUDA: For barbecue sauce, try a recherché (but only around $15) Sangue di giuda. Slightly sweet, this "blood of Judas" is a great match for the sweetness of many barbecue sauces—drink it chilled. Bruno Verdi is a very good example. Also for big exotic points, try a Frappato from Sicily, a light red sometimes called Italy's answer to cru Beaujolais (Valle dell' Acate is a good producer).

And for more details on essential rosés, cru Beaujolais, chilled reds, Moscato, see those sections, on pages 102, 140, and 148.

JUNE

find that people seem particularly energized in June—summer has officially arrived and everyone's trying to plan picnics and parties, get together with friends at an outdoor café for a glass of wine, and cut out of work early to catch a baseball game. In this section, I'll give you tips for what to sip outside and drink with your hot dog so you'll be ready to go post–Memorial Day. June is also the most popular month for weddings, and if you're involved with planning one such happy occasion I'll offer you some tips for saving a fortune on celebratory bubbly. It's a great month to travel to the Loire (a wonderful potential honeymoon destination for those getting hitched in June!), and you'll find tips for planning a getaway there this month. And don't forget Father's Day . . . I offer some wine-related gift options in this chapter as well.

Weddings: When the Champagne Toast Shouldn't Be Champagne

Good Champagne is often wasted. As a general rule, the larger the group, the truer this maxim is.

It's not as if the group can't drink all the Champagne; it's rather that Champagne is expensive and the crowd often doesn't really appreciate it since there's just too much else going on to sip and savor the wine. As a charismatic Champagne buyer at a major wine store often says, "Don't give a hug when a handshake will do."

A wedding is perhaps the biggest party that some people will throw in their lives. The guests aren't there to drink wine—they're there to celebrate the couple. The "Champagne" toast to them is often prepoured and many guests take a sip and don't touch the rest. Moreover, many reception facilities insist on buying all of the wines, which allows them to mark up, thus a $10 bubbly becomes a $40 bubbly without improving the quality. Not fun.

Weddings are a perfect example of where context almost entirely trumps the wine in the glass. So I say spend the budget on the flowers, the dress, or the decorations and downgrade the bubbly. It may seem like I'm raining on the bride's parade, but for grooms, suggesting cheaper bubbly is a quick path to getting on the good side of the father of the bride or a great way to economize if you are paying for the wedding yourselves.

That doesn't mean that you have to gag on your bubbly. There are plenty of good alternatives. Try these picks or flip back to February for recommendations for the real deal, if you must.

❈ *Party Hearty: Sparklers Under $20*

ROEDERER ESTATE ANDERSON VALLEY BRUT: This nonvintage bubbly is one of California's best. It's made by Champagne house Roederer, who also make the superb Cristal ($250) and a very good nonvintage Champagne ($40). Rather than the chalky minerality of those wines, this bubbly has more fruit but still good acidity. $$

BISOL CREDE PROSECCO: A killer Prosecco, dry and crisp. Super value bubbly that I often pour for big groups. $$

NINO FRANCO RUSTICO PROSECCO: A very nice apéritif and a perfect wine to raise and toast a couple. It has a lighter bead than most Champagne, and more fruit, but the bubbles are there and people will get the idea. $$

SAVIA VIVA CAVA BRUT: A very pleasant sparkler from Spain. Good for toasting, and it's food-friendly too. Little will your guests know, it's also organically grown! $

DOMAINE CHANDON: One couple asked me for a $10 bubbly recommendation for their (self-funded) wedding, and we tried this California one together. They liked it and went with it. As far as I know, they are still married. I include it here because it is widely available at wedding reception–type facilities and is better than other domestic choices at this price. $

Wine with Baseball: The Juice, Dogs, and Kraut

The weather's heating up and it's time to head to the ballpark. So what do wine-loving fans at sporting events consume to quench their thirst and console themselves as the Cubs melt down in their patented June swoon?

Much to the dismay of many wine enthusiasts, the bubbly of choice at the ballpark does not come with a cork. Adding insult to injury, beer at ballparks is often of miserable quality and is more overpriced than a glass of Pinot at a hipster wine bar, which leads us to contemplate the burning question of June: Which wine goes with baseball?

You might want to go with something American, since baseball *is* America's pastime. But the trouble is that too many American wines are more juiced than the players mentioned in the Mitchell Report. They've been amped up on new oak, left on the vine to get maximum richness and extraction, and roll in with low acidity and high alcohol. Sound like fun in the sun? Not to me.

So rather than go for a national pairing, let's refocus on the food: hot dogs with sauerkraut. A difficult minefield of meatlike product, nitrites, and pickled cabbage. Is it an impossible food-wine pairing? No way! You can spin it at least four ways.

1. A higher-acid red like a Barbera. The acidity helps cut through fat and kraut. Some Oregon Pinot Noirs could be good too, for these same reasons.

2. A brut zero Champagne. How sweet it isn't! With no dosage (a dollop of added sugar), brut zero has crackling acidity. But with most examples rolling in north of $30, it's not one for spraying around the locker room after a big win.

3. Rosé. Some nice red berry fruit complemented by good acidity could make this the one to beat. Try one from Provence or Spain.

4. Off-dry Riesling: This pick introduces good acidity as well as a dollop of sweetness. Riesling rides to the rescue!

These pairings should knock the ball out of the park. Try them all! And hopefully soon you'll be seeing the wine equivalent of those beer hats with straws at a ballpark near you.

Bling Dad, Frugal Dad:
Wine and Winelike Gifts for Father's Day

Forget buying your dad a tie for Father's Day: We all know what he really wants is wine and wine related paraphernalia. This June, try out these wine-themed gifts.

If you want to splurge on a handsome gift, a corkscrew is a stately way to go. Some might suggest the Rabbit, a big fancy corkscrew, as a gift, but after a particularly bad experience with one of these contraptions, I'm not a fan. (If you must know, I brought a nice bottle of red as a housewarming gift for some friends' new and freshly painted house. They gave me their Rabbit to open the bottle and instead of levering out the cork I drove it down with such force that wine splattered all over the counter and the walls. Doh! Fortunately, they still invite me over, but they do keep me away from the Rabbit.)

So go with the Laguiole. Only someone in a cave in the south of France, where these are made, actually knows how to pronounce this: Opinions vary (*la-GHEE-yole* or *lah-YOLE*). But no matter how you say it, their corkscrews make a great gift. It's the kind of thing you'll want to hold on to for a long time: One of my friends got one for his twenty-first birthday and still uses it to open most wine bottles almost twenty years later. Made by a knife specialist, the design resembles the classic "waiter's friend." But the handle comes in various exotic woods, including, yes, wood from a 224-year-old tree planted by Marie Antoinette. The top-of-the-line Château series ranges from about $130 to $300. Not cheap, but they're easy to use—no smushing the cork down with these beauties!

As I mentioned in the Basics, I'm a fan of the Tritan "impact resistant" line of titanium-infused crystal glasses (see pages 7–8). A six-pack of the Forte line is a great gift for everyday use. Ravenscroft also makes a good, affordable line of lead-free crystal. For ostentatious displays, Riedel and Bottega del Vino make hand-blown crystal glasses for $50 a stem (and up). They tower above other glasses—and as a party trick, can fit a whole 750 ml bottle in one glass. No matter which brand, crystal glasses always make a great gift for Dad since whenever you return home to visit, you can be assured you'll have some nice stemware to drink the nice wine you bring, being the good child that you are.

A decanter is always a good way to go when it comes to wine-related presents. As a gift, you might want to get one that favors style over function, and those generally start at $50. Experimenting with decanting one wine and not another is a fun activity to do with Dad—it sure beats splitting wood!

Books always make good gifts. Wine books used to only come in one format: weighty tomes bound for the shelf where they remain unread. Fortunately, many wine reference books are now both reader-friendly and absolutely worth reading, not just for resting your crystal glass on. Consider Jancis Robinson's two excellent reference books, the authoritative *Oxford Companion to Wine,* which should be on every serious wine lover's shelf, and her *The World Atlas of Wine,* which merits detailed perusing in front of the fire (I'm a sucker for maps). As the wine world becomes more specialized, there are other regional references that may make good gifts if your dad is hooked on the Rhône or wines of the Pacific Northwest, for example. And what about *A Year of Wine*? I'll bet Dad doesn't have this one in his collection!

In addition, as America's thirst for wine grows, wine is appearing in more books featuring narrative arcs that you might actually want to take to the beach. Wine-fueled voyages of discovery, epic family and business tales, explorations of the local politics of environmentalism, struggles against globalization and standardization, and combating fraud in a quest for the rarest bottles have all served as themes of books that will have you turning the pages as if reading a novel. Check out *The Billionaire's Vinegar* and *The House of Mondavi.*

And finally, wine itself is a wonderful gift. I find there are two ways to make an impression—either go for quality or quantity. You could get a bottle of Krug Champagne for $125, for example, or you could get a mixed case of $10 wine (for impressive gift wines, check December; for value vino, check April). The former route might lead to an epiphany, revelation of hidden truths, or other such monumental occasions, while the latter could educate, inform, and provide enjoyment for a couple of weeks to a couple of months. They're both impressive gifts and you'll have to judge which kind of dad you have, a bling dad or a frugal dad, before making your purchase. Either way try to pull the cork together since that's the best way to enjoy such a gift. Consider it bonding with your male progenitor.

Do You Need a $300 Decanter?

There's a beautiful crystal decanter out there that's shaped like a "U" pushed thirty degrees off center. There's another one shaped vaguely like a duck. And another one that is so sloped that it looks as if the wine might spill out of it if the corner of a cashmere sport coat grazed it.

Do you *really* need any of these decanters, which are priced between $100 and $300? Well, while a little style is always nice, it's not always necessary. But having a decanter of some sort is.

One veteran wine writer told me that he decants almost every bottle of wine into a plastic pitcher. Then he takes another pitcher and pours the wine back and forth between them over the kitchen sink for five minutes. Then he puts the wine back into the original bottle and serves it. And Eric Asimov wrote in *The New York Times* about his satisfactory experience using lab beakers of differing sizes as decanters. So the term "decanter" can be broadly defined, but it definitely doesn't mean a $300 piece of designer glass.

What's crucial in decanting is exposing the wine to the air rather than to the actual style of the vessel itself. That's why simply uncorking a bottle of wine and leaving it on the counter for an hour doesn't do a whole lot: The exposed surface of the wine is less than an inch. Pour it into a decanter and you greatly expand the surface. Pour it back and forth between two, and you can achieve an hour's worth of decanting in five minutes.

Decanting a wine serves a few purposes: First, it exposes the wine to oxygen thereby softening the tannins. The writer who decanted with vigor must really not like harsh tannins and, in fact, most consumers don't like them either these days. Young tannic wines become a lot softer with air. Some whites gain greater aromas with air.

Second, decanting helps keep older wines free of sediment. Have you ever been in an old-school restaurant where they decant the bottle with a candle under the neck? They're not trying to heat the wine; they're adding a light source so that the sommelier can pour the wine slowly into the decanter while keeping the sediment in the bottle. In this case, it's not about letting the wine breathe. Since many mature wines can collapse quickly when exposed to air, it's about not pouring a glassful of thirty-year-old grit.

Third, some wines bottled under screw cap can be especially closed and reticent in their aromas. These in particular may need some air.

Loire Reds to the Rescue: How to Not OD on Whites and Rosés During the First Few Weeks of Summer

Although the whites and pinks of summer have tremendous appeal, don't forget some reds. Lighter bodied reds from the Loire make an excellent choice because of their versatility with food, lower alcohol level, tremendous character, and relative value.

When I told a friend that I had just blind tasted forty-one red wines from the Loire, he responded with, "What are you, a pleasure-hating wine Nazi? Don't you know that Loire reds are all thin, weedy, and deeply antihedonistic?" Fortunately, he was kidding.

Contrary to this belief that my friend jokingly espoused, and that some people in all seriousness adhere to, Loire reds are some of the most delicious red wines out there, with tart red fruits, lip-smacking acidity, refreshingly low alcohol levels, and some tannins that make them relatively age-worthy.

The main grape that gives us these great reds is Cabernet Franc. The Loire Valley, in northern France, has proven a hospitable climate for this grape. Although the grape is grown elsewhere in warmer climes, wines made from grapes in warmer regions can lack the superb acidity of the Loire. Cabernet Franc has to meet its detractors' cries of "Vegetal! Stemmy!" head-on, and the Loire reds have a main weapon in their arsenal: global warming. As the region has longer, warmer summers, the wines are becoming slightly easier to enjoy while retaining their intrigue and allure.

Moreover, the wines remain some of my favorite bargains in the wine world, with many rolling in between $13 and $19. And the best are often natural, as with the whites, since many producers in the region make wines as their grandparents made them, using organic (certified or not) methods that favor hand-harvesting and the eschewing of synthetic fertilizers and biocides.

Another wonderful attribute of the Loire reds is that food pairing is a no-brainer. A local Loire specialty is rillettes, a fatty pork dish. Paired with rillettes, as well as other fatty pork or fried chicken, the acidity cuts through the fat and makes you want more of each, food and wine. And pairing these wines with Loire chevre is a great way to get your evening started right.

In addition, the versatility of the wine carries over to the way you serve it. I've decanted young Loire reds with success to soften the young tannins. I've also had it slightly chilled on a warm day, which made it just that much more appealing—so before you reach for that bottle of rosé, give this a try.

❋ *Six Essential Producers of Loire Reds*

DOMAINE BERNARD BAUDRY: A top producer of Loire red, this estate in Chinon is hitting its stride. In the blind tasting of Loire reds that I mentioned above, the 2005 wines stood out for their superlative quality, especially the single-vineyard offerings, with ample tannic structure and acidity for aging. These are serious wines that I am aging in my cellar. The top wine is priced under $30. $$

DOMAINE CHARLES JOGUET: The other top producer in Chinon, Joguet makes excellent wines in the regional style. Decanting is often a good thing with the younger wines. $$

CLOS DU TUE-BOEUF: The name (*"tue boeuf* means "kill cow" in English) might sound more Native American than French, but such is the name of this vineyard estate belonging to the Puzelat brothers. The purity of their wines is impressive and I have been impressed with their wines, which are often bottled as humble *vin de table* instead of with the usual appellation. $$

PUZELAT: Thierry Puzelat buys grapes from respected and natural vineyards to bottle under this Puzelat label. The KO in particular is worth seeking out, chilling slightly, decanting, and serving with a goat cheese salad and some crusty baguette while dining outdoors. Mmmm . . . $$

CLOS ROCHE BLANCHE: Naturalists Catherine Roussel and Didier Barrouillet make bargain reds and whites from their certified organic vineyards. I tried their 2004 Cabernet (Franc and Sauvignon) with four years of age on it, and it was still drinking beautifully. The wines crave food—try chevre or roast chicken. $–$$

CATHERINE & PIERRE BRETON: Catherine and Pierre are leaders in the organic viticulture movement. One of their wines, Nuits d'Ivresse, is bottled without sulfur, so if you have always wanted to try an unsulfured wine, here's your chance! It's quirky but worth trying. (As always, buy one bottle before rushing into a full-case purchase to make sure it's a style you like.) In addition, the Beaumont is an excellent example of Chinon, with gentle red fruit, a hint of smoky intrigue, and delicate, invigorating tannins. $$

Travel to: The Loire—*How Everyone Can Win the Battle of the Châteaus*

I was locked in the middle of an epic sword fight on the formal grounds of the sixteenth-century Château Cheverny. As I battled my opponent, first under the June sun and then in the shade as I pushed him back to the mature oaks and toward the pen of hunting hounds, I thought I had him on the ropes. Then I heard the sound of metal hitting metal, and my opponent struck me in the leg. I was done for.

This loss was, in fact, how I won a victory in the battle of the châteaus. You see, after my hard work covering a wine trade show in Bordeaux, I met up with my family in the Loire. My opponent was my four-year-old son, and his battle garb consisted of a new toy suit of armor, complete with a plastic sword that makes a classic "swordfight" sound whenever it touches anything, worn throughout the trip (even on the castle tour). I had only a cardboard poster tube to defend myself. But by losing the encounter at the handsome castle, I set the stage for my turn to choose the next destination. In our battle of the châteaus, my son favored the castles, while I favored the wineries, often known by the more humble term *domaine* in the Loire rather than *château,* as they're referred to in Bordeaux. With so many exciting winemakers in the Loire and only limited time, I was hard-pressed to decide which one I wanted to visit. So I picked Huet in Vouvray.

Vouvray is a postage stamp–size town, and the grape of renown there is Chenin Blanc. One of the world's great white grapes with wonderful aromatic intensity, capable of tremendous aging, it is made into four styles of wine: dry, off-dry, sweet, and sparkling. All are on display in Vouvray and we tasted them all at Huet, a family-run estate that practices biodynamic viticulture. Huet has several single-vineyard wines, and some are even bottled as *premier trie* ("first pass") indicating the attention to detail as the workers select only the best grapes on their first pass through the vineyard.

There's a small tasting room at the property, and the staff obligingly pulls sample bottles out of a low horizontal fridge with a sliding glass top that, at closer glance, resembles something from Coldstone Creamery rather than the Sub-Zero wine fridge line. The vintages and tastes kept coming: We tasted some fifteen wines in all dating back to 1990. I later heard from friends that if I had asked, the friendly staff might have even dug up some even older vintages. I bought several bottles since they were much cheaper than in the U.S. even with the poor exchange rate.

June is a particularly great time to visit the Loire since the castles and wine would make this a romantic spot for a honeymoon, and the days are long and warm but the summer crowds have yet to build since the French school holidays don't arrive until later. The vibrant reds and whites also offer vibrant summer alternatives to an all rosé regime. The Loire is also the ideal family vacation destination for wine enthusiasts in so many ways. There are castles, towns, and historical relics such as the magnificent tapestry at Angers and the Da Vinci museum in Amboise that everyone—including kids—can enjoy. There's even a mushroom museum in Saumur! (The French take their food seriously.) For the grown-up wine lover, there are wonderful, food-friendly wines that are reasonably priced and often naturally made, and for the green-minded wine fans the Loire is a hotbed of organic and otherwise "natural" winemaking.

Setting up a base: The Loire is a vast area so it is best to divide and conquer it. The east end has Sancerre and the west has Nantes and Muscadet. Given its central location, perhaps the best place to stay is around Tours. To the west lie Saumur and Chinon; just to the east lie Montlouis and Vouvray. Spectacular castles also abound.

Wineries to visit: While almost all of the producers in the Loire are happy to receive visitors, it's best to call ahead if only to confirm the hours.

In the Savennières, Coulée de Serrant has perhaps the best vineyard site. Domaine du Closel has wonderful grounds, charming owners, and very good wines. The domaines Bernard Baudry, Catherine & Pierre Breton, and Charles Joguet in Chinon stand out as does François Chidaine in Montlouis. In Vouvray, Huet is a must-stop.

When to go: June is ideal for the good weather; in the cold month of February, there is a big wine expo called the Salon des Vins de Loire. Although it's officially a trade-only show, there are some other off-premises events.

Getting there: Fly to Paris and then take a one-and-a-half hour TGV ride to Tours or Orleans, where car rentals are available.

Shelley Lindgren,

Wine Director, A16, San Francisco, California

How does context matter for enjoying wine?

Context is incredibly important and can really be an integral part of enjoying wine. The time of day, daily weather forecast, place, company, occasion, and atmosphere for wine enjoyment (e.g., list/wines available, glassware, temperature) all impact and allow for optimal flavor of any wine. I personally like a simple combination of flavors and surroundings. But from home, to a taqueria, to the finest dining in town, wine should be approached with what is appropriate and heartfelt.

What is one of your favorite food-wine pairings?

Champagne and oysters, Ribolla Gialla from Friuli and white beans with extra-virgin olive oil, and fried cauliflower, Margherita pizza with Nero d'Avola from Sicily.

How important is pairing wine with the seasons?

Even though we don't have too many changes in weather in California, vegetables and fruits are very seasonal. The weather can also dictate the mood for a wine.

White wines that are best drunk young like Falanghina and most *rosatos* are perfect for sunny days and warmer weather, offering a refreshing start to meals. These wines are great in cooler weather to start a meal and go with lighter, high acid food or seafood (like oysters and crab, which are best enjoyed in the winter). So, I offer at least one *rosato* by the glass all year round.

If you had to have one wine per season, what would it be?

Winter: Syrah
Spring: Champagne
Summer: Fiano di Avellino
Fall: Nerello Mascalese

If you had to pick one season for drinking wine, what would it be? And why?

Summer. I am crazy about tomatoes and have had so many wonderful preparations of them that I can only eat them in season . . . I'm ruined for life!

What's one of your most memorable food-wine occasions where the location or company really mattered?

I'll never forget being in Perugia, Umbria, during truffle season in 2001, not realizing that Umbria had its own black truffles. A simple umbricelli pasta with extra-virgin olive oil and shavings of local, Umbrian truffles with a bottle of Sagrantino do Montefalco from Arnaldo Caprai, transcended my senses and taught me how simply and ideally some flavors can match.

JULY

By the time July arrives, summer is in full swing, with lots of picnics and splashing time in the pool or at the beach. Refreshment is key and practically no wine is as refreshing as rosé. But we're also looking for mobility, so don't be afraid to drink inside the box. Also, prepare to celebrate the Fourth of July with a toast to independent winemakers in America, and travel to Oregon for the annual Pinot Noir festivities.

Independence Day: Unusual American Winemakers That Are Worth Seeking Out

There are now over five thousand wineries in the United States, according to *Wine Business Monthly,* a trade publication. The top thirty of those make about 90 percent of American wine by volume. This Independence Day, why not try a wine from one of the 4,970 small American wineries? Here are some of my favorite independent American winemakers who make Chardonnay, Sauvignon Blanc, a white blend, Syrah, Cabernet Sauvignon, and Pinot Noir:

STONY HILL VINEYARD: In a land of oaky, high-alcohol Chardonnays, Stony Hill Chardonnay stands apart. The wines express the grape and the place, not the barrel, since the barrels are old and thus neutral vessels for fermenting the wine. When I visited the Napa property, I asked Peter McCrea, the second-generation owner, if he ever gets new barrels. "Yeah, when one gets a hole in it," he deadpanned. But he might actually have been serious. The Chardonnay is the main reason the winery has over two thousand fervent fans on the mailing list. With only 13 percent alcohol, lively acidity, and an underlying note of crushed stones, and retailing for about $35, the wine has more in common with Chablis than with so many of the toasty oak, high-alcohol, expensive Chardonnay made nearby. The winery offers free visits by appointment. $$–$$$

SCHOLIUM PROJECT: Abe Schoener's passion for wine and pursuit of making unusual but compelling wines led him away from his academic job—and has brought him to the brink of bankruptcy at least once. A burly man with thick-framed glasses, he explained to me "You can't make skin-fermented Sauvignon Blanc if you have kids." It's just too risky. Good thing he is single and lives in a rented house and doesn't own a physical winery (he rents space). Try the "Prince in His Caves" from the rocky Farina Vineyard ($$$) in Sonoma as a good example, and the Naucratis ($$) for a compelling Verdelho.

Schoener makes perhaps America's most thought-provoking Sauvignon Blancs, sourced from out-of-the way vineyards that he often scouts by driving around Northern California. Some of them are made like red wine with extended contact with the skins—as much as nine months. The resulting wines are not summer sippers but are profound, contemplative wines that are particularly well paired with seafood in the winter and comparable to the best Sancerre and whites from northern Italy. Beginning with the 2008 vintage, Schoener started making wines from New York State as well in an old warehouse in Red Hook, Brooklyn. $$–$$$$

CHANNING DAUGHTERS: If you got lost and happened upon the property of Channing Daughters in Bridgehampton, New York, you would be forgiven for thinking that it was an art museum since it is strewn with almost more sculptures than vines. But it's not the work of one of the owners, sculptor William Channing, which makes this place in the Hamptons shine: It's the indefatigable curiosity of winemaker Christopher Tracy. While some winemakers are content with making a red and a white, Tracy makes twenty-three different wines from his Long Island *terroir*; rare red grapes such as Blaufränkisch and Dornfelder; skin-fermented Sauvignon Blanc; three rosés; wild-yeast fermentation Chardonnay; and some Tocai Friulano among others. Raised in the San Francisco Bay area, he trained as a chef but his thirst for wine ultimately prevailed. With several selections for the heat of summer, reach for the aromatically intense blend, Mosaico, for fish, a rosé for salads, and perhaps the Rosso Fresco for grilled meats. With such fascinating wines, it would be easy to paint a seasonal arc just with these wines. Even though some of the wines are hard to come by (the mailing list might be the best option), the wines remain reasonably priced at $15 to $40. $$–$$$

CAYUSE: No list of independent spirits in the American wine world would be complete without a winery from Walla Walla. And perhaps no spirit is more independent in this Washington-Oregon growing area than Christophe Baron. With sunglasses on, curly flop of hair blowing in the breeze, and his black Lab almost eating the low-hanging grapes off the vine, he explained to me he could have continued making Champagne at his family property in Champagne, or he could come to the great American viticultural frontier that was Walla Walla. So in 1996 when an old apple orchard on savagely rocky soil became available, he bought it and began the arduous task of replanting it to vines. The winery is called Cayuse, after a Native American people in the area, but there is also the double entendre with Baron's native French, *cailloux*, which means "rocks." Inside his "wine studio" (he doesn't call it a winery), the canary-yellow walls practically pulse with energy. Baron stands in front of an egg-shaped concrete fermentation vessel. He explains that the egg is a natural form for adding vitality, which his wines certainly have. All of the discussion of energy is because Baron practices biodynamics, a sort of feng shui for the vineyard and winery. And his Syrah really hops, particularly the whimsically named Bionic Frog. American wine, made by a Frenchman. $$$–$$$$

CORISON: On a cool February morning, Cathy Corison reaches down and plucks me a small pod of winter peas from her vineyard. Peas in a vineyard? Yes, it's true. The eight-acre Kronos Vineyard around her Napa winery in Rutherford has been farmed organically since 1995, and winter peas are one type of cover crop that she plants annually to restore nitrogen to the soil. Even though Corison has worked at some of the leading wineries in the valley, she started her own winery in 1987 and went her own way. The current trend is to harvest Cabernet Sauvignon late, which means that the grapes have high sugars and the resulting wines have high alcohol. But Corison is proud to tell me that she picks early and the wines have about 13 percent alcohol, below the norm. The result, she says, is that she is able to make wines that grace the table and have a long life. After tasting three of her wines with between ten and twelve years of age on them, I'd have to agree that she is making some of the most delicate, poised, and food-friendly Cabernet in the valley—very much worth seeking out. $$$$

AU BON CLIMAT: Jim Clendenen makes quite an impression: tall, stocky, wearing a loud Hawaiian shirt, and a mullet hairstyle that is worthy of an eighties metal band. He is something of a living legend in American Pinot Noir. He got bitten by the wine bug early in life, gave up prelaw, and lived in Bordeaux and later Burgundy where he worked for renowned American wine importer, Becky Wasserman, building his enthusiasm for and knowledge of the wines of Burgundy. At his no-frills winery outside of Santa Barbara, Clendenen and his business partner Bob Lindquist are legendary for the fine wines that they pour at lunch for the winery staff. Indeed, Clendenen needs six labels to contain his enthusiasm for wine, including the Burgundy inspired lineup at Au Bon Climat. He doesn't have time for concentrators and spinning cones that are common parts of the California winemaker's tool kit, and, for his Pinot Noir, he favors picking early. He's not shy about oak aging (he even owns part of a cooperage). The Pinots are more Burgundian than they are Californian with higher acidity, but not Burgundian in pricing since they are about $15 to $50. $$–$$$

Don't Be Afraid to Drink Inside the Box at Your Next Picnic

Affordable and portable (no need to worry about bottles clunking around in your backseat and getting broken!), boxed wine is the perfect picnic companion.

In general, boxed wines have yet to escape the stigma that haunts them in America. But they're popular overseas: In Australia, boxed wine is as common as Fosters (almost); in France, practically no fridge south of Lyons is considered stocked in the summertime without a box of rosé in it.

The box is incredibly convenient and brings the price of a glass of wine down to chump change. As a result, it makes you generous too. When my wife and I spent a summer in France we kept the obligatory box in the fridge, and anybody who came within fifty yards of our kitchen was offered a nicely chilled glass of rosé. That will make you quite popular.

The technology of bag-in-box is great for wine that is ready to be consumed now, which includes approximately 98 percent of all wine produced, because, as you draw a pour, the plastic bag inside the cardboard box collapses and prevents any exposure of the wine to oxygen. The wine can stay fresh for a month or perhaps even longer. With a decent three-liter box (the equivalent of four bottles) going for $20 and no spoilage, that's a value proposition that bargain hunters can't ignore. Keep your wine box on the counter or in the fridge for Sunday to Thursday convenience, and splurge on the weekends. Take it with you on a picnic or on backpacking trips. Don't be afraid to drink inside the box. The only unfortunate characteristic of boxed wine thus far in America has been the quality of wine put in the box. Sadly, California producers by and large see the format as a way to drain surplus wine out of the state. But they should pay heed to overseas producers who are putting good wine in these new wineskins.

One final reason to reach for a box is that it can make your red, white, and rosé a little greener. The packaging is so light that it produces only half of the carbon dioxide emissions put forth from a regular bottle. Now that's something everyone can raise a glass to! (And if everyone did, it would be the equivalent of taking 250,000 cars a year out of circulation.)

✤ *Four Box Wines to Try*

DTOUR: The restaurateur Daniel Boulud, his wine director Daniel Johnnes, and excellent Burgundian winemaker Dominique Lafon collaborated on this wine. Three connoisseurs putting their names on wine in a box is a huge endorsement for the format. One launched in 2005 to great acclaim. However, the wine had to be withdrawn because of problems with the stylish cardboard tube. Value wine enthusiasts eagerly await its return. $$$

YELLOW AND BLUE MALBEC: Matthew Cain launched this wine in 2008 with the environment in mind (Yellow + Blue = Green, get it?). In order to reduce the carbon footprint, the wine is imported from Argentina in bulk tanks and the packaged in North America in one-liter Tetra Pak containers. It's a fantastic, robust, unoaked Malbec from organically grown grapes. Throw it in your picnic basket. $

THREE THIEVES BANDIT: These three collaborators from California, aka the Three Thieves, have gotten the message. Their first wine was a one-liter jug; later they introduced a wine in a Tetra Pak, a kind of juice box for adults (straw not included). These packs come in a one-liter brick or four 250 ml boxes sold together. It sounds like a gimmick, but fortunately the wine inside is, well, decent. The Trebbiano and Pinot Grigio are great to take on picnics or to the park. $

FRENCH RABBIT: The winemaker Boisset developed this Tetra Pak packaging specifically for the keen environmental awareness of the authorities' Liquor Control Board of Ontario who liked it because of its ultralight weight. While there's no mistaking the Pinot Noir for a Gevrey-Chambertin, it's serviceable, especially when chilled. $

Rosé on a Sunny Day

What do a six-foot-seven basketball coach, a macho architect who designs mega-mansions for hedge fund managers, and my Chardonnay-loving mom have in common? I poured them all their first glass of dry rosé, and they all came back for more.

That's right, on a hot summer day, there are few things more satisfying than a nice dry rosé. Simply seeing it being poured at a table induces salivating: bright pink chilled wine, with condensation on the outside of the glass. Add some food enhanced with garlic or simple grilled fish, some good friends, a grassy view, and you are in business! Or, more likely, on vacation relaxing, and life is good.

I've poured rosé for friends and people I've just met. I've poured it at my classes and at private events. And I've washed down plenty of summer meals with this refreshing and carefree wine. It's a great halfway wine, particularly for mid to late summer when whites seem to have lost their refreshment value and you're looking for something modestly more substantial.

For a long time, Americans remained leery of pink wines, and rightfully so. Almost all rosés are made from juice that is "bled" off red wine. In the curious case of white Zinfandel, while making a standard dry rosé from Zinfandel grapes, the yeasts gave out before fermenting all the sugars into alcohol, leaving a sweet pink wine behind. When this wine sold out quickly, Bob Trinchero and his brother decided to do it again the following year. It's now ubiquitous but often lacks acidity (and is simply cloying and boring). The only option available in the U.S. for a substantial amount of time, it gave pink-hued wine a bad name. And then a few years ago, dry rosé jumped out of the heart-shaped tub and captured the hearts of writers, sommeliers, and diners across the land. Ever since, dry rosés from Europe, America, and beyond have been flowing freely.

In fact, too freely for some! Now, some of the very writers who helped stir up the rosé tsunami are running for cover. What's a wine drinker to do? Have rosés jumped the shark? Tune out the backlash, I say, the same way you might have tuned out the critics' scorn for rosé a few years ago. But the backlash does raise an important point: As rosé has become more popular, more producers have started to see it as a destination for the fruit of their young and inferior vines and some rosés have lost that alluring acidity. This is definitely something to watch out for, but there are still plenty of good ones—particularly from the Mediterranean—to have with salty, garlic-drenched foods or by the pool all summer long. And into the fall, since their food-friendliness is irresistible.

But wait! I almost forgot the most important thing about rosés: They're a final bastion of value in a world of ever-escalating wine prices. I just can't wait until we get a good one in a box.

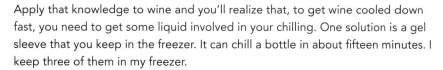

HOW TO CHILL A WINE BOTTLE IN FIVE MINUTES

Water cools faster than air. Think about it: Walking through a park on a seventy-five degree sunny day feels great, but swimming in a 75-degree pool is bracing.

Apply that knowledge to wine and you'll realize that, to get wine cooled down fast, you need to get some liquid involved in your chilling. One solution is a gel sleeve that you keep in the freezer. It can chill a bottle in about fifteen minutes. I keep three of them in my freezer.

If you're in a hurry, fill a bucket with ice, dump in a generous amount of salt, and fill three-quarters of the way with cold water. Submerge the bottle in this Arctic environment and it will be ready to go in less than five minutes. The trick here is the salt, which allows the water to lower its freezing point by a few degrees. Spinning the bottle will help get the warmer wine from the middle of the bottle toward the cool glass.

But a word of caution—don't overchill wine since doing so closes down the aromas. Wine at thirty-eight degrees (fridge temp) doesn't have the aromatic intensity of wine at cellar temperature (fifty-five degrees) or room temperature (70 degrees). While an icy cold wine may excel in refreshment value on a hot day, aromas also help wines express their individuality and add to the enjoyment.

❉ *Ten Great Rosés That Will Make You Think Pink*

Once a rosé goes over $15, I find some of the summertime fun starts to dissipate, so pricier rosés have to be pretty incredible. Also, rosé is a carefree wine for quaffing so you should try to find one from the previous vintage.

DOMAINE TEMPIER, BANDOL: This storied winery from Bandol, Provence, makes a superlative, light-colored, and delicate rosé with a satisfying, long finish. Definitely worth the price based on taste alone. Plus, it's farmed organically and, because of the high proportion of the age-worthy Mourvèdre grape, it is one of the rare rosés that can age—but who can wait? $$$

DOMAINE SORIN, TERRA AMATA, CÔTES DE PROVENCE: Sustainably grown, this pale pink rosé goes wonderfully with fried calamari. I've seen it in a box in France and would love to see it here in that format. Instead, they have handsome bottles with a wax seal. The upshot is this is a good gift wine for summer hosts! $$

CHÂTEAU PEYRASSOL, CÔTES DE PROVENCE: At this slightly higher price, this wine is in my grump-zone, but it's still a very nice, light, Provençal-style rosé. $$

COMMANDERIE DE LA BARGEMONE, CÔTEAUX D'AIX EN PROVENCE: Fresh strawberry notes, good acidity, and under $15. I had it one time at a crowded, un-air-conditioned, midsummer dinner, and this wine is just about the only reason I made it through the dinner. Since then, I've had it many times since its delicate balance and low price make it a to-go.

DOMAINE HOUCHART, CÔTES DE PROVENCE: Vibrant, electric pink, very berry notes, this wine just makes me daydream about having lunch outside under an umbrella. $$

BODEGAS MUGA RIOJA ROSADO: This one is easy to find and a huge value. I introduced my mom to rosé with this one and she now asks about Muga all summer long. $

CVNE RIOJA ROSADO: Light as a feather, but with good acidity and fruit, this wine is a steal. $

COPAIN, LE PRINTEMPS, MENDOCINO COUNTY: This rosé of mostly Pinot Noir comes from Wells Guthrie, a top California winemaker. It has a light pink hue, aromas of strawberries, and a rich but balanced mouthfeel with a finish that is smooth as satin. A hugely impressive rosé at a very reasonable price. Bravo! $$

HAMACHER, ROSÉ FROM PINOT NOIR, WILLAMETTE VALLEY, OREGON: Eric Hamacher, one of my favorite Oregon winemakers, makes this rosé with a salmon-colored hue and mouthwatering acidity that makes it wildly food friendly. $$

R. LÓPEZ DE HEREDIA ROSADO, $30: I put this one last because although it is quirky (and on the expensive side), it is complex, rewarding, and demonstrates that some of the best rosés can age, since this is usually released about ten years after the vintage. The resulting wine is slightly oxidative and nutty but, in my view, utterly delicious. A wine geek's rosé. See April, page 96, for more information about this traditional producer. $$$

Travel to: Oregon—*Pinot Noir Finds a Great Home in Oregon*

With the Fourth of July this month, check out some of America's greatest Pinot Noir in Oregon wine country. Celebrate independence with your fellow wine-loving compatriots.

From the landscaping farms that feature hundred-yard rows of boxwood bushes, to the long rows of hops, and finally the vineyards and their undulating rows of grape vines, practically everything seems planted in rows in the Willamette Valley. Driving through this expansive area, plenty of green stripes of vines score the hillsides. And there are a growing number of stellar wines to go with those stripes, especially during the flag-waving month of July when the weather is at its best, and stars and Pinot-philes converge on the region for the International Pinot Noir Celebration.

If the unofficial shoe of the Napa Valley vintner is the loafer, in Oregon wine country it is the slip-on Merrell. But the differences don't stop at footwear: While Napa is dominated by the late-ripening Cabernet Sauvignon grape that basks under the California sun, Oregon has come to specialize in the fickle Pinot Noir grape, which requires a more temperate climate to produce wines that have sparked such rhapsodic adoration. Although Burgundy is the ancestral home for Pinot Noir, Oregon's climate may well give it the advantage over rival Pinot Noir producers in California's Central Coast.

Given their differences today, it might come as a surprise that the pioneer of Oregon wine, David Lett, studied enology at the University of California at Davis. Lured by a climate he saw as similar to Burgundy, he planted the first Pinot vines in Oregon in 1966 and was soon followed by others, including Dick Erath and Dick Ponzi, both also Californians. By the 1970 vintage, Lett had 115 cases of his "Oregon Spring Wine" made from Pinot Noir at his Eyrie Vineyards and sold them with difficulty at $2.65 a bottle, according to Pinot Noir researcher John Hager. However, Lett's 1975 South Block Reserve showed so well at a blind tasting Paris in 1979 that it beat all but one of the red Burgundies.

This triumph in international circles put Oregon on the map. One attendee who paid particularly close attention was Robert Drouhin, a vineyard owner and *négociant* from Burgundy who had actually organized the 1979 tasting. So impressed was he with the Pinot Noir from Oregon that instead of simply being beaten, he decided to join. His charming daughter Véronique had studied enology in France but was drawn to Oregon and, in 1987, her father bought a hundred-acre property next to Eyrie and she was put in charge. Other international figures were drawn to the region to complement the local talent and soils: several more from California; Brian Croser of Petaluma, Australia; and even wine critic Robert Parker owns half the property at Beaux Frères with his brother-in-law, Michael Etzel. And despite this influx of attention, Oregon remains down-to-earth and as green as a wardrobe of fleece and flannel shirts would imply. Despite a climate that can pose difficulties for organic viticulture, one-third of all vineyards are certified some shade of green (sustainable, organic, biodynamic).

This lush country is a wonderful place to visit, particularly in the summer. Although the Pacific Northwest may be known for its rain, the summer months are relatively dry and cool. (Thanksgiving also makes a good time to visit, as many wineries that don't usually open their doors welcome visitors. And the wines go so well with the foods on the Thanksgiving table.) Proximity to Portland and its great restaurants and wine shops is a plus, though most of the wine action lies in the Willamette Valley about an hour's drive to the southwest.

You can knock off (and knock back) ten wineries with one stop in the tiny town of Carlton. Eric Hamacher founded the Carlton Winemakers Studio in 2002 so that producers could reduce their costs and wouldn't have to build a physical winery. Up to ten vintners can make wines in the cutting-edge, gravity-driven winery that was the first winery to be registered with the U.S. Green Building Council. The tasting room offers visitors a chance to taste and buy many of the excellent value wines produced in the facility. Ken Wright Cellars, another of the industry's first movers, is also located in Carlton, as are several other tasting rooms: consider the Scott Paul tasting room a "must stop" as well since the proprietor, the amiable Scott Paul Wright, not only makes a line of toothsome Pinot Noirs but also imports some delicious artisanal Burgundies that are available for tasting. I vote Carlton the biggest little town in Oregon wine country!

But no trip to the area would be complete without hitting the Red Hills of Dundee. There, Domaine Drouhin, Domaine Serene, The Eyrie Vineyards, and Sokol Blosser, to name but a few, could easily fill an action-packed weekend.

The real summer draw of the area is the International Pinot Noir Celebration. Started in 1987, the three-day annual festival of all things Pinot lets Pinot-philes discuss the grape, visit vineyards, and attend tastings and dinners with local winemakers, as well as those from Burgundy, New Zealand, and beyond. The grand finale is the salmon bake on the final evening, where salmon are baked on stakes suspended over an enormous bonfire. Many collectors bring fine Pinots from their cellar to share at the open-air dinner. Choose your seat wisely.

When to go: The summer months are best since the region's rain falls mostly in the fall, winter, and spring. At Thanksgiving, many wineries that are closed to the public open their doors.

Getting there: Portland has many flights; instruct your private jet to fly to McMinnville Municipal Airport.

Shayn Bjornholm,

Master Sommelier, Director of Education, Washington Wine Commision

How does context matter for enjoying wine?

Of course it means an incredible amount! The same wine can taste twenty different ways in twenty different situations. Why, when, where, who . . . mood, fatigue, event, nature . . . all of it creates an environment of sorts that will affect your perception of a bottle of wine. Even an amazing producer like Coche-Dury is going to taste that much better sharing it with your fiancée while admiring her new Tiffany diamond than it would at an industry tasting with five hundred people milling around you. The key is recognizing the context you are in before making decisions, and letting the drinkers' space help inform your choice. Why waste $500 on a rare Champagne in a national chain country buffet–style restaurant with one type of glass "stemware" for a table of angry in-laws squabbling over who gets the last square of jalapeño corn bread and honey? Or miss one of life's great opportunities by ordering the cheapest glass of oxidized, maderized, industrial plonk while celebrating your daughter's recent acceptance to an Ivy League college?

What is one of your favorite food-wine pairings?

I am a big fan of the "simple wine with complex food, complex wine with simple food" principle. Nothing thrills me more than red wine and herb-braised leg of lamb with an aged Côte Rotie—the straightforward gamey, iron nature of the meat with the multilayered, savory, floral, peppery, smoked meat, iodine, tar scents of aged Syrah to provide complexity to the dish—like an extension of the sauce. Too many cuisines these days have fifteen flavors on a dish—why would I order a wine with fifteen more? The chances of them marrying are much lower than them clashing.

How important is pairing wine with the seasons?

I am not one to follow that particular theory. Yes, rosé and sparkling wine are better on a covered porch in Georgia at noon in August than a Barossa Shiraz, but I am driven more by what is on the plate in front of me. As that is usually driven by the seasons, so perhaps it is an extension. However, I never go into spring thinking I have to think lighter wines now . . . or winter thinking I have to drink heavier wines.

If you had to have one wine per season, what would it be?

Since I have to . . .
Winter: Rhône Valley—Syrah, Grenache, or Viognier
Spring: Vouvray—Chenin Blanc
Summer: Red Burgundy—Pinot Noir
Fall: Piedmont—Nebbiolo

If you had to pick one season for drinking wine, what would it be? And why?

I would go with early fall. The fresh foodstuffs of summer that I enjoy so much are on their last dances while the earthier, tarter flavors of fall are coming in. I love wines that combine fresh fruit and earth for heightened complexity (German Riesling, Barolo, white and red Burgundy, Rhône reds, Champagne), and these tend to go really well with the foods of fall. And yes, there is that melancholy that encourages a bit of retrospection/introspection during the fall—which makes it a perfect time to drink something deep, profound, and delicious while warming your insides against that nip in the air.

What's one of your most memorable food-wine occasions where the location or company really mattered?

The most memorable for me was the night after I passed my Master Sommelier examination. It was 7:30 P.M. on a Saturday, and I was working the floor at Canlis Restaurant. All of a sudden, the entire kitchen team filed onto the floor. I thought, How strange . . . must be some form of training method to connect the front and back of the house, make the kitchen better understand service. Then, amazingly, everyone on the floor had a glass of sparkling wine. This is a restaurant that seats 160 people at once. I was actively working the floor and serving guests, and somehow I did not catch 160 flutes being set up in the back, poured, and distributed. I thought, What the *&^% is going on here???

Then, Chris Canlis, the owner of twenty-eight years, was on a microphone. I was busy pouring Pinot Noir for table ten, and I was in the middle of my schpiel. He stopped service. At 7:30 on a Saturday night. For the second time in the history of a fifty-eight-year-old restaurant. And he, as eloquent a speaker as breathes on this planet, toasted my passing of the exam with 160 guests and another sixty employees, many of whom I had grown to think of as family over my five years there. I was speechless. I looked around the room, saw faces full of pride and joy, and my entire insides went to pudding. At every table a glass was raised in celebration over something I had done!

Then, for the first time in my tenure there, Chris Canlis pulled me off the floor . . . to dine with him, one on one. No one gets pulled off the floor on a Saturday night at Canlis—ever!

As if that were not enough, he handed me the 2,200-bottle wine list we had built together with love, sweat, tears, and a lot of his money, and said, "This is yours. You built this. Order any bottle you want—and don't shortchange me!" This coming from a man who once rented a Bobcat to get the snow off his own parking lot rather than pay another $75 to a plowing company! He meant it, so I did not shortchange him. I selected a 1985 Leroy Musigny for $1,500.

Now, the wine was spectacular. The meal was delicious. Canlis is a stunning restaurant. But it was the feeling of love I felt from the 220 people on that night, the inclusion into the Canlis family on a level I had never considered, and the knowledge that I had reached one of the highest personal peaks of my life just the day before, which made a legendary wine better than it will ever be, perhaps better than any wine will ever be.

AUGUST

These dog days of summer are not the most inspiring for wine lovers: The heat can sap the desire for serious wines, yet there may be some fatigue from the carefree wines of summer. So it's time to try cru Beaujolais, gulpable red wines that can be served chilled. It's also the time of year when people skip town for vacation destinations, eager to beat the heat, so I'll offer some tips for transporting wine back home from foreign destinations as well as a great location for a final summer getaway: South Africa.

Get Your Bojo Working: Cru Beaujolais for the Height of Summer

In 1395, Philip the Bold, Duke of Burgundy, was so afraid of Gamay that he banned it, calling it "wicked and disloyal." That's right: A man named "the Bold" feared a grape. Why? Philip was afraid that Gamay would move northward and encroach on the turf of Pinot Noir, the native red grape of his homeland. And indeed it might have;

Gamay yields Beaujolais—food-friendly wines high in acidity with red fruit notes. You could easily see why the Duke of Burgundy might be running scared.

In August, you should quell whatever inner Duke of Burgundy lives inside you and embrace Beaujolais. But before you run to the wine store, take note: There's a key word to add to requesting a Beaujolais in a shop, "cru." Unfortunately, the name "Beaujolais" has come to be inextricably linked to one of the ultimate "not serious" wines, Beaujolais Nouveau (see November for more). Essentially, "cru" means that you're asking for serious Beaujolais, a real wine, as opposed to something winelike. Just to keep you on your toes, it doesn't say "cru" anywhere on the label. Instead, there are ten small appellations, or growing areas in the region, each with its own subtleties and style, that range from the more robust Morgon to the more elegant Fleurie.

One August evening, Michelle and I had some friends over to the Dr. Vino World Headquarters. I explicitly invited one couple because I knew the husband *loved* cru Beaujolais while I knew that his wife *hated* Beaujolais. I wasn't trying to cause marital strife for them; I was trying to help them overcome this point of difference by helping her silence her inner Duke of Burgundy! (Dr. Ruth meets Dr. Vino?)

Fortunately, it worked. Confronted with a dozen excellent cru Beaujolais on the deck on a warm summer evening, some of which were slightly chilled, along with some cru Bojo–loving friends, and she was singing the praises of Gamay by the end of the evening. Six months later she told me she was still really enjoying cru Beaujolais. Our deck had been her road to Damascus.

Like Loire reds, the best crus Beaujolais have some nice fruit, balanced with acidity and tannins. The wines are less prone to stemminess and more prone to vivacious fruit, sometimes cherry and sometimes all the way to Jolly Rancher. Pair them with fatty meats (again, like Loire reds), or a fresh chèvre.

Beaujolais has a reputation for being "gulpable." With that in mind, the wines should be consumed, not aged. Sure, three years in the cellar shouldn't do any harm, but why wait that long before pulling the cork if you don't need to?

Some final general tips for getting your Bojo working in the height of summer:

✳ Chilling leads to thrilling. Some of the wines we drank on the night of our friend's conversion to cru Bojo were slightly chilled, and they were more pleasurable than their unchilled counterparts. Five minutes in an ice bucket should do the trick.

✳ Decanting actually helped one of the wines; another really opened up after some air. Maybe chilling and decanting is the ultimate Bojo experience?

✳ Jancis Robinson has called Beaujolais "the archetypal lubrication wine" and "gulpable" if served chilled. Keep in mind that it's really a wine for drinking, not for pondering, even if crus are the most ponderable.

✳ 2005 was a great vintage; the wines will keep for a decade or more in the best cases.

✳ The wines have typically been a great value, about $12 to $20. Unfortunately, a combination of word getting out about their quality and a declining dollar means that the price range has shifted higher, although there are still some great ones to be had at the low end of the range.

✳ Remember, this is NOT Beaujolais Nouveau, which is a whole different ball game (this point is so important, I just had to reiterate it!).

✳ *Six Great Cru Beaujolais Producers*

MARCEL LAPIERRE, MORGON: Lapierre is one of the leaders in the "gang of four," pushing for quality wines from the region. He also adheres to a natural winemaking philosophy using little if any sulfur. The resulting wines are wonderful expressions of Gamay; the wax cap is a nice touch (I'm a sucker for wax caps) to make it a handsome gift wine, too. $$

CHÂTEAU DES JACQUES: Louis Jadot, the Burgundy producer, acquired the Château des Jacques in Moulin-à-Vent in 1996. That meant that Jacques Lardière, the Jadot winemaker in Burgundy, would be making Gamay. I poured the 2005 Château des Jacques at our Beaujolais tasting and one guest quipped that it was "the best Pinot Noir of the tasting" because of its similarities to Burgundy. True, humble Gamay can make rewarding, impressionable, even concentrated wine, and Moulin-à-Vent is the most likely place to find them. Lardière would have made Philip the Bold issue another edict banning Burgundian winemakers from traveling south. $$

CHÂTEAU THIVIN: Another great producer, this time from the Côte de Brouilly, making seriously fun Bojo. Is that an oxymoron? No. $$

CLOS DE LA ROILETTE: This wine comes adorned with a bold yellow label with a horse's head on it. No, it's not a mafia-endorsed wine (Hey, better the head on the label than in the bed!). The image has something to do with an old racehorse that once lived at the estate. Or maybe it was a French answer to those "critter labels" from the New World that depict animals. Whatever the reason it's on there, look for the horse. The regular bottling is lip-smacking Bojo; the cuvée Tardive is a selection of the finest old vines and is meant for aging (I've got a magnum of the 2005 I'm planning on uncorking in 2015). $$

DOMAINE MICHEL TÈTE: Another good producer, and despite his last name meaning "head," he has no horse head on the label. But he's head and shoulders above most Beaujolais. The cuvée prestige is a fantastic wine that is particularly age-worthy. $$

> **TIP:** CHECK THE BACK LABEL
> Cru Beaujolais, though an affordable treat, can be confusing. Check the importer on the back label and if it is Louis/Dressner or Kermit Lynch, it's most likely excellent.
>
> It's not written "cru Beaujolais" so look for a wine from one of these ten appellations (from north to south). I've starred my faves:
>
> ❋ Saint-Amour
>
> ❋ Juliénas
>
> ❋ Chénas
>
> ❋ Moulin-à-Vent*
>
> ❋ Fleurie*
>
> ❋ Chiroubles
>
> ❋ Morgon*
>
> ❋ Régnié
>
> ❋ Brouilly
>
> ❋ Côte de Brouilly

DOMAINE DU VISSOUX: A family-run estate with several single-vineyard bottlings. The wines have good poise; the Fleurie Poncié is particularly tasty and is reminiscent of a lighter Burgundy. (It was acquired in 2008 by Henriot, the Champagne and Burgundy makers.) Serve it at a weekend lunch and amaze the guests. $$

Know Your Limits: Bringing Wine Back Home from Your Travels

August brings a chance for an extended break, often to wine country somewhere in the world. But you don't need to drink it all in situ since it is possible to bring some of the bounty back with you.

On a recent summer vacation in Paris, my family and I assumed a divide-and-conquer strategy one afternoon: My wife and son tackled the Luxembourg Gardens with its treasure trove of playgrounds, puppet shows, and pony rides while I went off to pillage the city's great wine shops.

Even though I was thrilled to discover wines that either couldn't be found in the U.S. or were available for greatly reduced prices thanks to cutting out the U.S. importer and distributor's markups, one thing took the spring from my step as I sprinted from store to store: the thought of figuring out whether I could bring it back home.

Back in the pre–liquids ban days, I would have packed cases of wine and carried them from taxi to concourse to aircraft until my fingers lost circulation. But the TSA intervened, so then I started checking wine in the hold of the plane. I have done this many times since with never a bottle breaking (knock on wooden wine case!) by wrapping bottles in T-shirts and putting them in the center of the luggage. (The safer choice is a styrofoam wine shipping box and some airlines insist on this now.) So logistics weren't a problem, but how much was I legally permitted to bring back? I recalled seeing a sign the last time I went through customs stating there was a two-bottle limit. Not wanting to forfeit fine wine to the customs agents, I decided to obey the laws and bought only enough wine that we could consume during our stay, plus two bottles each for myself and my wife to take home to New York. (Since I miscalculated and overbought, we had some pretty hedonistic dinners toward the end of our stay.)

But it turns out that my caution was entirely misplaced! After we had returned with precisely one bottle each of Vouvray, Condrieu, Burgundy, and Champagne, I consulted the U.S. Customs and Border Protection agency's "Know Before You Go" pamphlet—and only if I *had* known! Much to my chagrin, I learned that the limit I had remembered was, in fact, the *duty-free* limit! The *actual* limit is, in fact, governed more by practicality than by customs-imposed limitations, and is susceptible to tax beyond the duty-free limit. Two bottles of any value are allowed in free and the rest of the wine is taxed at the measly rate of 3 percent of the purchased value! And many wine enthusiasts report that when they enter wine in the "something to declare" line on the customs form, the customs officer just waves them through.

Furthermore, some of the more savvy wine retailers in Europe may even offer tax rebate forms for purchases over a certain amount (ask the clerk if the purchase qualifies for the refund). In those instances, a case of red Burgundy falls by about 20 percent in price after the value added tax (VAT) is reimbursed at the French airport. It just keeps getting better! (Just be sure to budget enough time at the airport to collect this tax rebate.)

So pack an empty suitcase or buy a Styrofoam wine shipping container from a store in Paris or wherever your wine itinerary takes you, inquire with the airline about baggage limits and extra baggage charges, and check the duty at the airport where you will be clearing customs back in the U.S., since states or municipalities may (or may not) impose a tax in addition to the 3 percent.

The next time I divide and conquer Paris with my family, I'll have a spring back in my step. Now if only the dollar would regain some of its lost luster.

HOW TO OPEN A BOTTLE WITHOUT A CORKSCREW

Who has more of my corkscrews than I do? Sadly, this is not a trick question. Transportation Security Administration agents have relieved me of many corkscrews that I've forgotten were in my laptop bag while going through security at various airports. Oddly enough, it's not the screw part of the contraptions they're worried about—it's the half-inch foil cutter!

So maybe you too will find yourself in a jam, without a corkscrew one day. Not a problem. Here's what to do:

1. Screw caps don't need a corkscrew. While out of town once, I was faced with buying a good $15 wine and the cheapest corkscrew in the store—$7. I applied my corkscrew budget to the wine and got a $20 bottle of wine with a screw cap. I was happy.

2. Champagne doesn't need a corkscrew. Stuck in a hotel with your partner or spouse and no corkscrew? Champagne, and sparkling wine in general, is the ultimate "screw the corkscrew" wine.

3. Get some hardware: Take a screw and a screwdriver from your hardware drawer. Delicately drill the screw half way into the cork, then use a hammer to gain leverage for removal. This process gets the job done but is best performed out of guests' sightlines since it's not the most elegant procedure.

Red, White and Blue Wines

November may appear a more political month than August since, after all, we cast our ballots in November. But every fourth year, a few good days of summer sports are bumped from TV screens to show well-choreographed political conventions. We can seize on this to reach across the proverbial aisle and look at wines made in red and blue states.

Consuming wines in the United States has long been a bipartisan affair. So much so, in fact, that the United States will soon become the largest wine-consuming country in the world—even though this largesse hides our diminutive per capita consumption, which still is about a quarter of that of France and Italy. This thirst has driven wine to be *made* in all fifty states. (Sometimes the fruit is actually imported, but each state now has a bonded winery and one count puts the total number at 5,000 in total.)

But when examined through the lens of voting behavior, American winemaking has a decidedly "blue" tint: California alone makes 90 percent of wine in the United States while blue states Washington, New York, and Oregon round out the top four. Beyond that, the vines can be thin on the ground.

It's not always for a lack of trying: King James and Thomas Jefferson both tried to plant vines in Virginia, to no avail. King James abhorred tobacco and saw developing the colonies as a wine producer to be a way to thwart dependence on adversaries France and Spain. But the wines sent back to England were unpalatable, and the colonists took to planting tobacco. In Jefferson's day, the vines still didn't yield worthwhile fruit. The phylloxera louse, the root of their problems, was ultimately defeated in the late nineteenth century.

Today in Virginia, there are ninety wineries, up from only six in 1979. Even the governor, Mark Warner, has a vineyard. The Zonin family of Italy has owned the Barboursville winery near Charlottesville since 1976, planting many Italian grape varieties. Norton, an indigenous grape, is also on the rise. Michel Rolland of Bordeaux also consults to a local winery. This reflects a growing trend across the south as tobacco fields are plowed under and grape vines are planted in Kentucky and North Carolina as well.

But America's thirst for the fruits of the vine has led to rapid growth in plantings everywhere: In Illinois, there are now seventy-two wineries up from twenty-seven in 2001, and even Arizona has twenty-eight wineries. Texas, where nothing is small, is home to the second largest federally recognized growing area (AVA), Texas Hill Country to the west of Austin, and even has other wineries around Dallas and the High Plains area near Lubbock. While the wave of new vintners in the 1970s included lots of investment bankers and doctors, colorful characters abound in this current expansion: Richard Childress, a former NASCAR driver and team owner, has a winery outside of Winston-Salem, North Carolina, and Maynard Keenan, lead singer for the alt-metal band Tool, started the Arizona Stronghold Vineyards to pursue his passion for wine.

Many of these have a strictly regional clientele thanks largely to the increased profits of direct sales but also that old bugbear, politics. It's not partisan politics in this case; instead, it is the politics of interstate shipping, since state legislators, often funded by local distributors, enact laws to make it difficult for smaller wineries to sell anywhere other than their home states.

So scout out a winery near you. And get ready for the third Thursday of November, when we can all raise a glass of local wine, be it red, white, or blue.

Beat the heat of August and escape to the Cape—the Winelands of the Western Cape, that is.

Hail can damage plump, juicy grapes in Argentina and Piedmont. Birds can ravage the berries just about anywhere. Glassy-winged sharpshooter can carry disease into the vineyards of California. But Chris Mullineux, a thirty-something South African winemaker with shaggy blond hair, told me that he encounters an entirely different pest: baboons.

The forty acres of Tulbagh Mountain Vineyards back up to a national park. Mullineux said they used to lose a quarter of the crop to marauding baboons that would swoop in and pluck the grapes off the vines just before harvest. They put up a fence and the baboons dug under it. They used patrols, but the baboons waited until the guards passed and then went in for their juicy plunder. But Mullineux found something that would scare the poop out of the primates: lion dung.

After fielding several suggestions, Mullienux got lion dung from a lion park in nearby Stellenbosch and sprinkled it around the periphery of the vineyard. It worked and the grape loss was cut in half.

Tulbagh Mountain Vineyards succinctly conveys the dynamism and creativity in South Africa's wine industry today. The vineyards were planted to mostly Syrah, Cabernet, and Mourvèdre in 2000, overlooking the local Pinotage. And according to the philosophy of the absentee British owners Jason Scott and George Austin, the vineyard has been farmed organically since day one, and they are now converting to biodynamics. Mullineux told the authoritative Platter guide to South African wines in 2005 that, "wine grown from fertilized soils mostly reflects the *terroir* of chemical companies." And true to the fluid situation that predominates today, Mullineux left Tulbagh to move westward to Swartland to make his own wines with his new American wife at Mullineux Family Wines.

This exciting wine country is 350 years young. When the Dutch settlers arrived in the seventeenth century, they planted vines in Constantia and in Stellenbosch, which makes South Africa lay claim to being the oldest producer of the New World. The nasty interregnum of apartheid set the wine industry back in the twentieth century when export markets and international capital dried up and the best talent left. In 1994, when the country reopened to the world, the vast vineyards (the country has more acres under vine than Australia) produced such insipid juice that much of it was distilled or sold as concentrate.

After a preliminary post-apartheid zig, the wine community in the Western Cape has now zagged back to the fast track. At first, the producers thought to continue to emphasize Pinotage, a local red grape that is an odd cross between the workhorse Cinsaut and the noble Pinot Noir. But the tepid reception overseas for Pinotage and its odd, musty, brambly aromas led the winemakers to start planting Syrah and Cabernet Sauvignon, as they did at Tulbagh. Globalization has served up an invigorating blend of interest and enthusiasm from international wine luminaries from Bordeaux such as Michel Rolland, May-Eliane de Lencquesaing (formerly of Château Pichon Longveville). Comtesse de Lalande, Bruno Prats (formerly of Cos d'Estournel), Alain Moueix, Hubert de Bouard (Château Angelus), and Zelma Long from Napa among others.

Of course it's easy to fall in love with what Jancis Robinson has called "the most dramatically beautiful wine country in the world." With a Mediterranean climate, the stunning city of Cape Town is dominated by the blue bulk of Table Mountain, often graced by artistic clouds on the top. The Winelands are within an easy hour or two and are extremely inviting to international tourists, offering many opportunities to stay at guesthouses among the vines. Although the summer really sparkles, the mild climate makes winter a good time to visit as well, when you'll be tempted to throw a log on the fire and enjoy a big, rich, red wine.

Under apartheid, Paarl was the center of winemaking with its large co-operatives. Although some good wines continue to be made in Paarl, today the restaurants of Franschnoek and the university town of Stellenbosch have all the buzz.

On the whole though, the country seems to be more sure-footed when it comes to white wines: Be sure to try some of the Chenin Blanc, the magnificent and multidimensional grape that has the Loire as an ancestral home (see June). Chenin Blanc in South Africa has been rescued from the nondescript bulk wines and fortified wines it went into and now is making some refreshing, dry wines that are great values. If you do make it to South Africa in the warm weather, there's no doubt you'll be raising a glass of Chenin Blanc while dining al fresco.

✱ *Wineries*

The Constantia wine route is the most convenient to Cape Town, a scant fifteen minutes away in affluent suburbs, with Table Mountain serving as a stunning backdrop, and on the way to the Cape of Good Hope. The historical importance of this wine is a draw since few wineries in the world can claim to have made wine as far back as 1689 as Constantia can (the original property was split up into Klein Constantia, Groot Constansia, and Buitenverwachting). Constantia Uitsig wine estate has a spectacular restaurant—reservations are essential.

VERGELEGEN: This stunning property in Somerset West has three-hundred-year-old camphor trees, includes handsome gardens, and makes some of the most highly acclaimed wines in the country. Consider it a must visit as Queen Elizabeth and the Clintons have done. In an odd mix of crossholdings, it is a part of the Anglo American group, one of the world's largest mining companies.

THELEMA MOUNTAIN VINEYARDS: A beautiful, family run winery in Stellenbosch that produces highly acclaimed reds and whites (there's even a Riesling!).

DE TRAFFORD: This acclaimed producer in Stellenbosch is open for visits midday Friday and Saturday.

TULBAGH MOUNTAIN VINEYARDS: Check out the latest in baboon prevention. Be sure to try the Syrah Mourvèdre and the Theta wines.

Good to know: Signs along the wine route scream *Wynverkope,* which means "wine for sale."

Essential reference: *John Platter South African Wines* is an essential annually updated guide. Its winery profiles provide historical details about the property and the key personnel, visiting hours, and addresses. Tasting notes of the key wines can help guide a tasting.

When to go: For such a long trip, plan to go for a good chunk of time; the August holidays offer a good opportunity. At the beginning of the month, there is the annual Stellenbash wine festival.

Getting there: Nonstop flights to Cape Town from the U.S. are rare, so expect to change in a European hub or Johannesburg.

Roger Morlock

Wine Director, Park Avenue Seasons, New York, New York

How does context matter for enjoying wine?

Basically it depends if somebody knows already what he or she would like to enjoy, if somebody wants to "explore" a wine they never tried, or if the wine should be paired with dinner. Recognize their intention! So the type of wine drinkers matters, which should not limit them to any selections at a certain time of the year.

What is one of your favorite food-wine pairings?

Chocolate and Syrah/Shiraz.

How important is pairing wine with the seasons?

A lot of wines reflect the seasons in their styles, which makes it essential for our restaurant since everything is based on current seasons. Certain types of meat, fish, and produce as well as types of preparation and cooking methods used each season allow a variety of wine selections.

If you had to have one wine per season, what would it be?

Winter: red Rhône-style blends (Australian or Californian)
Spring: Riesling (Rheingau)
Summer: Sauvignon Blanc (Argentinean)
Fall: White Châteauneuf-du-Pape

If you had to pick one season for drinking wine, what would it be? And why?

Autumn. This season is the most diverse. You can catch warmer days where the weather invites you to be outside. Harsher days might follow up that force you to get a little bit more cozy inside. This leaves us with many possibilities to enjoy wine (and food) and be creative with it.

What's one of your most memorable food-wine occasions where the location or company really mattered?

I hosted a Krug Champagne tasting dinner at Hotel Ermitage, Restaurant "Le Pavilion" in Kuesnacht (near Zurich) in Switzerland. The dinner was outside overlooking the Zurich Lake. The combination of this garden restaurant, outstanding Champagne, and great food gave the event a special flair.

PART FOUR

Fall

As the leaves start to fall and the temperature drops, my thoughts turn to serious wines, wines with more heft, both red and white. These match the back-to-school studiousness of the season as well as the cuisine, which turns more toward earthy mushrooms, squash, root vegetables, and game. Picking wines to match is not hard: Earthy and fuller whites fit the bill, as do a larger range of reds. Here are some fall picks that will hopefully make it a bit easier to say good-bye to summer.

CHAMPAGNE: With the weather cooling off, I prefer to move back to Champagne as opposed to other bubblies. That chalky minerality is just terrific and worth savoring. See February for picks from big and small producers.

WHITE BORDEAUX: This is a great transition to fall. The Sauvignon Blanc provides a core of acidity, and the Sémillon grapes provide wonderful aromas while the barrel aging provides richness. Try Château Carbonnieux and Smith Haut Lafite for some excellent examples.

THINK TEUTONIC: Fuller-bodied Grüner Veltliner goes well with richer foods, such as some game and spaetzle, a Germanic dish of tiny egg pasta. See April and select a *Smaragd*-level wine from one of those producers. Off-dry Riesling also provides ample food pairing options, particularly for spicy food.

SOME ITALIAN WHITES: More known for their carefree quaffing, many Italian whites are rewarding and even thought provoking. The region of Alto Adige is the home to the Abbazia di Novacella monastery and their superb Kerner, a cross between Riesling and Trollinger grapes, as well as the exceptional value Pinot Bianco from Alois Lageder. From Tuscany I also like the Il Corzanello, a value blend of unoaked Trebbiano and Chardonnay, from Corzano e Paterno (who also make excellent cheeses).

EXOTIC WHITES: Try an exotic white, such as a white made like a red wine with extended skin contact to provide greater heft and mouthfeel. The original wines of this kind are from a few producers in Sancerre (Daganeau) and Friuli (Gravner, Radikon) in northern Italy, but there are now some domestic producers as well, including Scholium Project (the Prince in His Caves) and Channing Daughters (the Meditazione).

RHÔNE WINES: These are a great transition to the fall. The whites, such as Marsanne, Roussane, and Viognier, often have wonderful aromas and a delicate, lanolin quality that pairs well with autumnal cuisine. The simple reds are a great transition too. In the Côtes du Rhône values abound, while in the north the appellations of St. Joseph and Crozes-Hermitage offer some excellent Syrah-based wines for prices a fraction of their neighbors, such as Hermitage.

PORTUGUESE REDS: Many of the Portuguese reds are from indigenous varieties that have a lot of charm and often have fantastic value. One such wine is the Crasto from the Douro, an unoaked red blend of mostly Tinta Roriz grapes. The Meia Encosta from the Dão has a Pinot Noir–like lightness for under $10.

OREGON PINOT NOIR: Oregon is perhaps the best of American Pinot Noir. It's food-friendly and fruit-forward so put it on your fall table. Some excellent producers are Domaine Drouhin, Cristom, Hamacher, Bethel Heights, and Domaine Serene. For an old-school choice, try Ken Wright Cellars or an excellent quasi-organic reserve Pinot Noir from The Eyrie Vineyards.

SEPTEMBER

September brings great excitement with the return to school and getting back into the groove at work—it's a time to get serious again and our wines tend to shed their carefree qualities. It's also time for unwinding on the couch with the new TV season. In the wine world, the harvest continues in earnest in the northern hemisphere. As a wine getaway, why not check out the easily accessible wineries of Long Island now that the summer crowds have tapered off?

Back to School: Learning by Tasting

"Without comparisons to make, the mind does not know how to proceed," wrote Alexis de Tocqueville. Even though he was talking about political systems, he might well have been talking about wine.

When it comes to learning about wine and expanding our knowledge, tasting is clearly the easiest and most pleasurable way to study. Tasting one new type of wine here and there to see if you like it is good, but a simultaneous tasting involving more than one wine is always better. Here are some affordable ways to taste many wines, which I'll follow with additional lesson plans.

1. Taste at shops. Many shops have free tastings on weekends. (Sadly, some states don't allow this.) But where available, always try all the wines being offered even if you think you won't like them—you might be pleasantly surprised. And, come on, it's free!

2. Taste at wine bars. Even though wine by the glass is a rip-off, wine bars do provide the chance to try something new, and the wine has already been approved by the establishment's wine director.

3. Taste with friends. Wine and friends go together as well as wine and food. So put together some themed tastings at your house and then rotate to another house the next time. Either the host can set the theme—a grape variety, a region, or different vintages of one producer in a vertical tasting—or it can be democratically decided. But either way, tasting around a certain theme really helps sharpen your knowledge and having everyone bring a bottle gives them a stake in the fun evening.

4. Set up a program with your local shop for giving and receiving feedback. Give them a budget, have them select a mixed case, then go home and drink through the wines and take notes. Bring the list back to the store and talk with the same clerk who put together the case about what worked and what didn't for you.

5. Attend wine events. There are an increasing number of mega-wine events. Although they can be packed, they also can offer great opportunities to taste wines side-by-side and to meet winemakers or winery owners. They can also be complete boondoggles, poorly organized with bad wine and people who appear to be trying out for a position at the right hand of Bacchus. Some of the best wine events are. The International Pinot Noir Celebration (July, McMinville, OR), Hospice du Rhône (May, Paso Robles), and Pinot Days (various, San Francicso, New York City, Chicago).

6. One resource to *skip*: wine of the month club by mail. With a mail-order wine club there's no forum for feedback, and they just send out whatever they have on hand, which all too often is not inspiring. A notable exception to this is if you get on the mailing list of a winery you like, as opposed to a retailer, since then they might send out limited production wines to their list of members that are not available elsewhere.

Back to School: Get Me a Formal Edumacation

If the unstructured, self-directed form of learning has not satisfied your thirst for wine knowledge, formal wine education has become a growth industry.

Attracted by high margins and the prospect of greater customer loyalty and wine sales, many stores offer classes and educational events. These can be great if the staff is made up of knowledgeable people from the wine trade and the classes are held in a suitable learning environment (e.g., students are not sitting on cases in the storeroom). They can also make for a fun date night.

Extension schools at colleges and universities are getting into the wine education business as well. Perhaps the most famous is the course offered at the University of California at Berkeley, which has a six-week, two-part "Fundamentals of Wine" course. I also teach a six-week class, "Becoming a Wine Expert," at New York University. (And, no, it's not a class undergrads can take to earn credits.) In addition, culinary schools across the country are starting to offer wine classes in degree and nondegree programs.

But if you decide that you want to throw in the towel on the rest of your life and start soaking up wine knowledge, you can strive for the titles of Master of Wine or the Master Sommelier, which require completion of wildly intensive and long programs (and therefore are really only appropriate for people interested in jobs in the trade). While both involve extensive blind tasting exams, a main difference between the two is that passing the final level of the Master Sommelier exam requires a knowledge of many elements of dining room service, including fortified wines, spirits, beer, cider, and cigars, particularly Havanas. Chew on that.

How to Save a Half-Bottle of Wine

$\mathcal{I}$t was with great pride one evening that I declared to my prim and proper ninety-year-old grandmother that I had found a new way to save a half a bottle of wine from one evening to the next. The item was a little rubber stopper that allows you to pump the oxygen out. My grandma just looked at me with a twinkle in her eye and said, "Tyler, I've got a better idea: How about you finish that bottle!" Go Grandma!

But if you're not in the same league as my grandma and you just want a glass or two from a bottle one night (say you are home alone and want to enjoy a glass of wine with your favorite TV show and some delicious take-out), you have probably wondered how best to save a bottle from day one to day two (or three).

The important thing to bear in mind is that wine is basically a way station between grapes and vinegar. The grapes ferment into alcohol (and carbon dioxide), which is then preserved away from oxygen, first in tanks, then in bottles. Pulling out the cork hastens the inevitable slide to vinegar—unless, of course, the wine is consumed promptly. The oxygen actually activates harmless bacteria that start to transform the wine, turning it sherrylike (oxidized) and eventually turning it into sour vinegar. (However, some, albeit rare, wines actually perform better on day two simply from being left open on the counter, since some wines need a lot of air.

But for normal wines that deteriorate rather than improve over the course of a day or two after being opened, what to do? Well, you can get some of those little rubber stoppers known as Vacu Vin ($15 for a pump and one stopper). Or you can get an argon gas dispenser and squirt some into the bottle ($100). The theory here is that argon is heavier than oxygen and therefore blankets the surface of the wine, keeping it removed from oxygen. Some winemakers use argon during winemaking to prevent the wine from having contact with oxygen.

Another option is to install an Enomatic machine in your home ($10,000). Housing eight bottles with tubes running out of each, behind glass and stainless steel, the Enomatic pumps oxygen out and puts inert gas in. While it'd be fun to have one around the house, the prohibitive cost means these are mostly used at wine bars and stores.

And finally, the best thing you can do to preserve wine overnight is also the simplest: seal it and put it in the fridge. Use the cork or a rubber stopper, whatever is your preference. The key is putting it in the fridge—be it red, white, or rosé—which slows down those bacteria.

One other trick is to pour the remaining wine from a normal-size bottle into a half-bottle and then stopper it. Reducing the bottle size is a tried-and-true way to reduce the amount of oxygen in the bottle. And you can find another use for the little bottles with a big carbon footprint!

Riesling: The Choice for Takeout and TV

We all know that the arrival of fall means three things: leaves crackling underfoot, harvested grapes fermenting in wineries, and the start of a new season of TV shows. And when you're hurrying to sit down on the couch in time to catch a new episode, who has time to cook? Clearly takeout is the answer. Great plan, but it can be foiled by a difficult food-wine pairing

Four times out of five, the answer to this dilemma is Riesling.

Some long-dead winemaker in Germany is probably spinning in his lederhosen over the fact that I pair his wine with Chinese food. Or Indian food. Or pad thai. Or Vietnamese summer rolls. But come on: Cabernet with chicken tikka masala? Shiraz with shu-mai? No thanks. Off-dry Riesling provides a gentle sweet blanket that softens spice, and the spice can also enliven the wine. A semisweet wine is not always what you want as an apéritif, but with the right food it really transforms, becoming wildly better than you thought it could be.

My grandmother used to order a glass of "Rhine wine" every time we went out to dinner. She was ahead of her time, sadly, as Riesling has gotten a lot better than it was back in her day. But fortunately for us, in place of the cloyingly sweet wines in tall blue bottles that she ordered, today there are many producers who take a lot of care crafting fantastic wines, sometimes completely bone dry and sometimes with a hint of sweetness, balanced with lively acidity. (However, it is still a mixed bag, so if the first Riesling doesn't grab you, try one from a different style or producer. In fact, Riesling is kind of like my sister-in-law: When it's great, it's really, really great . . .)

Just a few years ago, Riesling was the best-kept secret of chefs and sommeliers who would toss it back at every opportunity. But now it has broken through into almost the mainstream. Wine drinkers who are tired of Chardonnay, awkward oak, and high alcohol levels are now, more than ever, asking for Riesling, which is always unoaked and can have alcohol levels as low as 8 percent. If many people consider Pinot Grigio to be the anti-Chardonnay, then Riesling is the anti-Chardonnay for wine geeks and hipsters.

Germany is the homeland for Riesling (France's Alsace and Austria could also make a claim), and two important changes have happened there to make the wines more appealing. First, a new generation of winemakers—Thomas Haag (Schloss Lieber), Tim Fröhlich (Schäfer-Fröhlich), and Klaus-Peter Keller (Weingut Keller) to name a few, all in their thirties—is taking the reins and making serious, enjoyable, and sometimes sensational wines. Second, while it's hard to think of anything positive about climate change, the locals are reveling in it through their SPF 45 sunscreen in the Mosel Valley! Global warming has made the wines better, since Germany has some of the traditionally northernmost vineyards in Europe (although now, again, thanks to global warming, there are vineyards in England and even some grapes in Norway!). Climate change has led to rounder wines with more depth of flavor even in the dry wines.

And, yes, there are dry wines in the Riesling family. Riesling, like Chenin Blanc, is another one of those chameleon whites that can range from dry to very sweet. In Germany, labels can state dry or slightly off-dry (*trocken* or *halbtrocken*). But, confusingly, this rating only applies to the amount of sugar in the vat before fermentation, which means that it could have no bearing on the finished wine, which has led for some to call for a sweetness rating to appear on Riesling labels. Riesling from elsewhere in the world tends to be less sweet than some German examples; from Australia to New Zealand, from Austria to Alsace, it is almost always dry. And although Riesling has a good claim to being a wine for all seasons, you can still have a seasonal approach to it by having lighter, drier ones in summer and richer, heavier, sweeter styles in the winter.

Another benefit of Riesling is its incredible ability to age. In Germany, the sweeter wines become dry with age but are still incredibly rich—indeed, having thirty-year-old Riesling is the height of vinous accompaniment for venison in Germany. In Alsace, the mature Rieslings take on a note of petrol, which may sound like something you'd feel compelled to put in your car, but in actuality is phenomenally alluring and unforgettable for days afterward. In Australia, some of the Rieslings can be austere and unforgiving in their youth, but with age become much more expressive—and some twenty-year-old examples are sometimes even bottled in screw cap! Very progressive.

Despite all of these things that Riesling has going for it, it's still somewhat under the radar so it generally remains a good value. So when you see someone in the wine store turn away from those tall, fluted bottles, use that lingering prejudice to your advantage since there's hardly enough of the good stuff to go around anyway.

❋ *If These Seven Rieslings Don't Convince You, Then Give Up on Riesling*

TRIMBACH, CUVÉE FRÉDÉRIC-EMILE: Trimbach makes the greatest Riesling in Alsace, the Clos Sainte Hune. But it is expensive, about $150 on release. The Frédéric-Emile, aka CFE or "Freddy," is about three-quarters of the wine at one-quarter of the price. It is one of the best white wines in France, if not the world, and an absolute steal for $35 or so upon release, usually with six years of age on it. Wonderful petrol on the nose, it has a terrific weight in the mouth and a lingering finish. Try with food, try as an apéritif, just try it. $$$–$$$$

JOH. JOS. PRÜM: From the steep banks of the Mosel River come these revered Rieslings. The wines from the south-facing Sonnenuhr (sundial) vineyard are particularly sought-after. $$$–$$$$

DÖNNHOFF: This is another iconic name in German wine. These hail from along the banks of the Nahe River, farther south of where JJ Prüm is made. The wines are excellent though richer than the Mosel, and like Prüm, the wines start at $20 and move up from there. $$–$$$$

SCHÄFER-FRÖHLICH: This estate makes some amazing wines, including the *halbtrocken,* which for under $20 is an incredible value. It is the ultimate takeout pairing. Buy it with both hands. $$–$$$$

KELLER: Klaus-Peter Keller has inherited the responsibility of making the wines at this family estate in Rheinhessen, the home of the wine travesty known as Liebfraumilch. But don't worry: Even in this improbable location, Keller crafts one of the finest (and rarest) wines in Germany, the G-Max. The other wines are top-notch in their respective ranges (about $20, $40, and over $100). $$–$$$$

REINHARD & BEATE KNEBEL: Beatriz Knebel makes delicate Rieslings in the Middle Mosel. $$–$$$

LEEUWIN ESTATE: Located near the Margaret River and the Indian Ocean in western Australia, this is one of the country's top winemakers. The Rieslings are dry, long-lived, and don't break the bank. $$

Travel to: Long Island—*Looking Up in L.I.*

After the crush of tourists, a post–Labor Day trip to Long Island lets you see the crush of the grapes, up close and personal.

Even though New York is the third largest grape

grower in America, the wines have not received a lot of praise outside the state—heck, even inside the state thanks to some uninspiring blends of Concord grapes and even other fruits (gasp!). Despite having an open mind about wine from remote regions of the world, for some reason I had a mental block when it came to the wines of New York. So I piled the family in the car and drove to Long Island to find out for myself.

What we found was a growing industry with about seventy-five growers that is making some compelling wines. Louisa and Alex Hargrave planted the first vines on an old potato field in the North Fork in 1973. Most of the wineries still cluster on the North Fork of the East End but two worthwhile ones somehow eke out an existence in the expensive real estate of the Hamptons.

To get an idea of the seriousness of what's happening today, we dropped by and visited Eric Fry inside the large, vaulted tasting room at Lenz winery. Fry, who has made wine at Robert Mondavi and Dr. Konstantin Frank in the Finger Lakes prior to coming to Lenz, has strong opinions and speaks with the zeal of a convert about the wines and the area's potential. The large-framed man with a shaggy, graying beard and hair pulled back in a ponytail over his untucked denim shirt launched into a diatribe against critic Robert Parker right off the bat and peppered our discussion with swipes at California, and praise for Burgundy, Merlot, and consuming wine with meals. But even this last point we don't quite get right in America, according to Fry. "In Europe, you drink your grandfather's cellar and you buy wines for your grandchildren," he told me. "Here, people want to know what wine to have with pasta tonight."

So Fry's answer is to age his wines, often releasing his Merlot with seven years of age on it. The resulting wines are particularly good examples of the downtrodden (thanks to *Sideways*) grape: I bought two bottles of the Estate Selection Merlot and poured the wine blind to my NYU class later that week. Not only was the wine unanimously liked but the participants all practically fell out of their chairs when I revealed, first, that it was a Merlot, and second from Long Island. The top Merlot (about $50) has subtle and delicate notes of black raspberry with finely integrated oak. You're not going to mistake it for the $1,000 a bottle Château Pétrus—and I didn't when I later tasted them together in a blind flight—but it is a very good example of merlot that, indeed, has a food-friendly alcohol level of 12 percent. When you get home, round up some adventuresome friends and try blind tasting these Merlots against similarly priced ones from California and the Right Bank of Bordeaux.

Although many in the local industry favor red grapes such as Merlot and Cabernet Franc, tasting wines from a couple of other wineries made me wonder if white wines weren't at least as good an option.

Driving past the farms and farmstands down the flat Route 25, we headed back down past Jamesport to Paumanok. Charles and Ursula Massoud founded this winery in 1983 at first using earnings and later expanded with a buyout from IBM. If Fry looked like he would be at home in a VW van, Massoud looked every part the executive with his close-cropped hair, wire-rimmed glasses, and dapper V-neck sweater. The whites are appetizing and easygoing, but none more so than the dry Chenin Blanc, with lively acidity that would pair well with the local seafood.

Finally, we tried some whites and rosés from Channing Daughters and their winemaker Christopher Tracy (see the Fourth of July section on pages 134–137 for more details). The wines are wildly experimental and wonderfully tasty. A particular specialty is the Tocai Friulano, which finds its way into a varietal wine as well as the exciting Mosaico blend, which has six white grape varieties from one vineyard site, all fermented together.

And speaking of finding the way, now that we know the way to the East End, we'll be back.

✳ *Wineries*

LENZ WINERY: For the Merlot and the sprightly Gewürztraminer and a chat with Eric Fry, if possible.

PAUMANOK: A gorgeous setting (ideal for weddings), you can enjoy some very good wines at this family-run winery. Charles and Ursula Massoud are known for being generous hosts; their son Kareem is now the winemaker.

BEDELL CELLARS: Founded by Kip Bedell (aka Mr. Merlot) and subsequently bought by Michael Lynne, a CEO of New Line Cinema, some say the best days are behind this winery while others point to the new resources at their disposal. Sit on the spacious deck in Cutchogue, sip the wines, and decide for yourself.

CHANNING DAUGHTERS: Located near Bridgehampton, this beautiful winery makes a fascinating range of twenty-three wines. Although I haven't tasted them all, I have yet to find one that I don't like.

WÖLFFER ESTATE VINEYARD: Also in the high-rent district of the Hamptons, winemaker Roman Roth is making worthwhile wines from this stunning locale.

When to go: Some would suggest summer is best, but the crowds can be overwhelming. September still has good weather and there are things happening in the winery. Fall is also a good time to go as the farm stands continue to display local, autumnal produce.

Getting there: About 75 miles east of Manhattan, take the Long Island Expressway until the end. The Hampton Jitney also runs and biking is easy in this flat area.

Thomas Carter,

Sommelier, Blue Hill at Stone Barns, Pocantico Hills, New York

How does context matter for enjoying wine?

The charter of wine is greatly defined by the area and method in which it's grown. This is also true for enjoying it. Wine reaches its full potential when it is paired with the right food and company.

What is one of your favorite food-wine pairings?

Riesling and pork belly.

How important is pairing wine with the seasons?

Seasonality is of the utmost importance. If you have a summer tomato salad, you wouldn't pair it with a big jammy Zinfandel. The tomatoes would be lost.

If you had to have one wine per season, what would it be?

Burgundy all year!! There is a great deal of diversity in Burgundy, so much that it can be drunk all year. In the spring and summer months a steely Mâcon, Saint-Véran, or Sauvignon de Saint-Bris can do the trick. Red wine can even be an option during these warmer seasons such as a lean Monthélie or Rully, a Volnay can even work. During the fall and winter seasons whites such as Meursault or Puligny work great with fuller meats and root vegetables. With reds the options are endless, your biggest Gevrey from Claude Dugat will stand up to any duck or pork dish or even braised items. Other appellations are great in the winter as well such as Vosne-Romanée, Nuits-Saint-Georges, etc.

If you had to pick one season for drinking wine, what would it be? And why?

Fall: It's not too cold, not too hot, and the flavors are extremely conducive to pairing with red and white Burgundy.

What's one of your most memorable food-wine occasions where the location or company really mattered?

I had an epiphany at Louis XV Alain Ducasse in Monaco that involved a bottle of Château Beaucastel Hommage Jaques Perrin 1989 and spring lamb and early spring vegetables. The lamb, with all its flavors of herbs and farmland was echoed by the Châteauneuf-du-Pape. The wine with its aromas of southern Rhône herbs, cedar, dark fruit, and olives resembled so many components of the dish.

OCTOBER

The leaves are changing, the air is getting crisp. As the weather cools, the food on our plates turns to earthy mushrooms, game, squash, and root vegetables, and the wine in our glass tends to get red for good. Pinot Noir can help transition to the fuller bodied wines of winter. And since Halloween is approaching, it's a good time to learn more about biodynamics, a winemaking practice that involves skulls and bones—but also makes some of the world's most compelling wines. For collectors, it's time to buy and sell as the fall auction season reopens after a summer hiatus. October is also a good time to talk about looking for mature wine, as we're starting to become more introspective with the colder weather. It's also the best time of year to go to Piedmont in northwestern Italy for the glorious fall foods, truffles, and Barolo.

Give Miles Pinot Envy: Pinot Noir under $25

While it's a delicious red that can be enjoyed year-round, October is an excellent Pinot month. Just like the wine, the season is extremely versatile. And just as October can be sunny and warm one day and dreary and cold the next, Pinot Noir is a fickle grape.

In addition to being fickle, Pinot is a needy and transparent grape, much like the character Miles in *Sideways,* who lusted after it. The wines Miles pined for were from Burgundy and southern California and mostly cost hundreds if not thousands of dollars a bottle. Just how envious would he be if we found a fantastic Pinot for under $25? Very. Pinot Noir's ancestral home is, of course, Burgundy. But in an era when a Musigny costs a small fortune, the frugal Pinot-phile is forced to venture off the beaten path. The problem with this approach is that Pinot reflects the place where it is grown so well that, while Cabernet and Chardonnay exuberantly trotted the globe, Pinot Noir for a long time was considered a homebody, sticking around Burgundy. When Pinot Noir first hit the road and landed in California in the 1970s, some disparaged it as "not to be compared with Burgundy" and others wrote it off completely saying it tasted of "rubber boots."

While Pinot Noir has since then found a very good home in Oregon and parts of California and New Zealand have excelled in producing it as well, the same attitude toward Pinot Noir from emerging areas that prevailed in the 1970s remains today. Recently, when I mentioned to a usually good-natured wine collector that I was going to a tasting of Pinot Noir from areas not Burgundy, Oregon, or California (thus from New Zealand, Germany, Chile, Australia, and other places), he scoffed that there would be a lot of full spit buckets.

He was right. Pinot from nonestablished "Pinot" areas and Pinot under $25 is too often not worth pouring over yourself from a spit bucket let alone down your throat from a crystal glass. And *Sideways* is partly to blame since it sparked an interest in wine in general and Pinot in particular—as new consumers scooped up bottles marked Pinot Noir, the two percent of American plantings dedicated to the grape simply could not keep up. So in their haste to get more wine labeled "Pinot Noir" on the shelves, some producers took advantage of labeling requirements that stipulate only 75 percent of a wine must contain the grape on the label. While it's fine to blend Merlot with your Cabernet, blending a rich, heavy grape with Pinot Noir makes it look and taste like, well, Merlot, the object of Miles's wrath and derision.

The best wines are often ones that reflect the combination of the grape variety and where the grapes are grown. Pinot Noir certainly underscores this notion. When Pinot Noir under $25 is not being stretched or darkened with other grape varieties, it is often given too much oak, whether from a barrel or from a stave. So you have to tread carefully. But fortunately, defying the naysayers, it can be done, as evidenced by the wines on the following list.

❋ *Seven Super Pinots under $25*

STADLMANN (NIEDEROSTERREICH, AUSTRIA): Excellent varietal character and balance between fruit, tannin, and acidity. A terrific value to stock up for the approaching holidays too.

ST. MICHAEL-EPPAN (ALTO ADIGE, ITALY): This entry-level Pinot Noir is a steal—it made me crave food.

J. HOFSTÄTTER (ALTO ADIGE, ITALY): Another entry-level Pinot Noir from the foothills of the Dolomites.

NINTH ISLAND (TASMANIA, AUSTRALIA): Tart Bing-cherry note and good acidity make this a good choice from the distant island Down Under.

MAYSARA, JAMSHEED (WILLAMETTE VALLEY): Solid wine from this organic and biodynamic producer. Try the local pairing—with salmon!

AU BON CLIMAT (SANTA BARBARA COUNTY): A dollop of Burgundian funk provides the intrigue on some ripe red fruit.

LUCIE AND AUGUSTE LIGNIER BOURGOGNE PASSETOUTGRAIN (BURGUNDY, FRANCE): A value red Burgundy can be a difficult proposition—in the good years, it usually even trickles down to the basic Bourgogne rouge. But the subregion of Bourgogne-Passetoutgrain allows the blending of Pinot Noir with Gamay, which makes for a juicy, refreshing, and enjoyable spin on Pinot Noir.

Columbus Day: Go Native! From Aglianico to Zierfandler

We know that in 1492 Columbus sailed the ocean blue. The story we learned in school is that this man from Genoa, funded by the king and queen of Spain, "discovered" America. Of course, to the indigenous people already living there, this discovery was, well, news to them.

This Columbus Day, embark on your own voyage of discovery. One of the great paradoxes of globalization is that on the one hand it's easy to crank out a sea of look-alike wines from whichever country is the lowest-cost producer of the day. But on the other hand, globalization has made available all sorts of wines from grapes that were relatively unknown and certainly unavailable on our shores even as recently as a few years ago. While most Old World countries can claim at least a handful of grapes as their own, Italy is the undisputed champion with as many as two thousand indigenous grape varieties.

So this Columbus Day, go native! Try wines from off-the-beaten-path grapes, which have a doubly delicious reward: Because they are relatively unknown and relatively difficult to pronounce, they often sell at bargain prices. Here are seven from Italy and Spain, the two countries behind Columbus Day, as well as two from France and one from Austria to help get you started.

AGLIANICO: From the remote, landlocked region of Basilicata, located in the arch of the boot that is Italy, comes this brawny red. Although Greeks might dispute the claim to it being indigenous to Italy since the name comes from *ellenico* ("Greek"), others say that it is a wild vine. Today the vines cling to the sides of the extinct volcano Vulture and provide the dark, thick-skinned fruit that makes for wines that have notes of tar and tobacco. Pair with sausage. Producer to try: Viticoltori De Conciliis. $$

FIANO DI AVELLINO: Campania, the southern Italian region that is home to Naples and the Amalfi Coast, should be a top destination for those seeking indigenous grapes—almost all of them are native. Vineyard workers in Avellino toil in the shadow of still-active Mount Vesuvius while tending the Fiano di Avellino, the grape that produces smoky, almost nutty, serious, full-bodied and elegant whites. Try with white fish grilled with herbs. Producer to try: Mastroberardino, "Radici." $$

MENCIA: Bierzo, a bowl-shaped valley in northeastern Spain at the base of a dormant volcano, is attracting top winemakers from the country to the Mencia grape. The red wines vary with the amount of sun the grapes get during the day and the extent of oak treatment in the winery; the less expensive wines almost always come unoaked and are very food friendly. Producer to try: Abad Dom Bueno. $$

NERO D'AVOLA: This robust red from Sicily seems to be a popular choice for pizza. I, however, would prefer the elements of ripe black fruits to go with meat, such as lamb, since the grape is often compared to (and blended with) Syrah. Producer to try: Valle dell' Acate. $$

PICPOUL: This zingy fresh white grape is grown both in the Rhône (where it also comes in a red version, Picpoul Noir) and in the Languedoc, where it plays a starring role in Picpoul de Pinet. These crisp whites are also extremely good values, mostly selling for under $10—buy it by the case for the summer season. Producer to try: Hugues Beaulieu. $

CAZIN ROMORANTIN: From the Loire comes this rare white grape, a relative of Chardonnay that stylistically splits the difference between the aromatics of Chenin Blanc and the acidity of Sauvignon Blanc. The wines can be either dry wines or off-dry—try both with hard cheeses. Producer to try: Domaine François Cazin. $$

ZIERFANDLER: This grape from the Thermen region, south of Vienna, is grown only in a couple of hundred acres. The resulting wines are zippy and food friendly; from a top vineyard such as the Mandel-Höh, the wine is haunting in its intensity with citrus, spice and low alcohol. Producer to try: Stadlmann. $$

Do Skulls and Bones Make the Greatest Wines in the World?
A Lesson in Biodynamic Wines

By burying bones and working with the phases of the moon, biodynamics may seem to have a winemaking manual written for Halloween. But the wines are more treats than tricks as this natural winemaking method has attracted many prestigious adherents.

While I was visiting his one hundred acres of vines in Oregon's Willamette Valley, Moe Momtazi handed me a long, twisting cow horn. He then explained how he will fill it with manure and bury it in the vineyard on the autumnal equinox. The manure will ferment, and he will unearth it in the spring and add the resulting liquid to a "preparation" that he will apply to one acre of the vineyard to stimulate the life forces.

Momtazi practices a natural winemaking method known as "biodynamics." He told me that there are too many chemicals in the American food chain and the foods that he encountered when arriving here in the 1970s from his native Iran didn't have the same freshness he was used to. One year at the International Pinot Noir Celebration, an annual celebration of the grape in nearby McMinnville that attracts growers from around the world, he tried the wines of Domaine Leroy, a rare and supremely expensive red Burgundy, and he was blown away. When he found out that Lalou Bize-Leroy practices biodynamics, he became intrigued.

Biodynamics has captivated the attention of many of the world's great winemakers. And a lineup that includes Araujo in Napa Valley, Pingus in Spain, Domaine Leflaive in Burgundy, Jacques Selosse from Champagne also underscores that some of the most expensive wines in the world also follow biodynamics.

Biodynamics is like homeopathy with a dash of feng shui. Based on a series of lectures given by Rudolf Steiner in 1924, biodynamics tries to capture the "life energy" ("bio" from the Greek for life and "dynamics" from the Greek for power) inherent in the vineyard and make it a self-regulating eco-system. Ideally, all the manure and compost inputs come from animals on the farm itself. Instead of trying to eliminate pests and vine maladies with chemical treatments, biodynamics focuses on cultivating life in the vineyard, ranging from microbial activity to simple earthworms that can combat maladies naturally. It's like organic farming in that it prohibits chemical fertilizers and herbicides, but it goes further into the winemaking by preventing the addition of commercial yeasts (which, as discussed in April, can affect speed of fermentation and perhaps the taste of the resulting wine), adding various treatments, and timing its rhythms to the lunar calendar. Biodynamic farmers keep a calendar telling them whether it is a root day, leaf day, flower day, or fruit day to guide their activities in the vineyard and the winery. Some even extend this calendar to tasting, making the case that their wines might show better on one of the four days.

Back at Maysara, I'm standing underneath a fifteen-foot-high tower with a brown liquid cascading down each of the five tiers. Each tier looks like a sink and the liquid flows out what looks like the drain and then into the next sinklike vessel, where it cascades around the bowl in the other direction, and then out that drain. Once it gets to the bottom, it gets pumped up to the top again to run through the various tiers.

Momtazi urges me to drink it. With trepidation, I extend a glass and capture some of the liquid and raise it to my lips. It tastes vaguely like unsweetened iced tea. I didn't bother with a second sip and went in search of Pinot Noir.

The liquid is stinging nettle tea, used in part of a treatment that has the clinical name of "preparation 504." The tea must be "dynamized," a vigourous stirring that results in a vortex in the liquid, and should ideally be done manually over a period of hours: biodynamic practitioners believe that some part of the person enters the preparation. But because this stirring can make the person irritable, some practitioners, such as Momtazi, have chosen to perform the dynamization with a contraption such as the cascading tower that I stood under. Incidentally, the sinklike vessels were actually casts of a very pregnant woman's belly. Applying this tea to the compost is supposed to bring vigor to the vines.

So how do the wines taste? A reporter for *Fortune* magazine gathered several wine experts and poured analogous wines blind, changing almost only the fact whether they were biodynamic or not. In all but one case, the tasters preferred the biodynamic wines. Many observers noted there is a greater vitality to the wines, and I would tend to agree. And there's also likely to be more vintage variation since the wines are unadorned expressions of the places they have come from. If the wines do taste better than conventional, it's certainly not for a lack of tender loving care. Doug Tunnell, who practices biodynamics at his Brick House vineyards in Oregon, told me that he is in the vineyard so much, he probably knows each of his vines individually.

❋ *Four Biodynamic Leaders*

CLOS DE LA COULÉE DE SERRANT: Nicolas Joly, a biodynamic pioneer and author of two books on the subject, makes these white wines from his stunning, amphitheater-shaped vineyard overlooking the Loire. He recommends decanting them one day prior to consuming. The wines are polarizing with vociferous admirers and also detractors—they are an unusual expression of Chenin Blanc. $$$–$$$$

NIKOLAIHOF: Christine and Nikolaus Saahs were the first to apply biodynamics to vineyards in 1971. Their vineyard at a bend in the Danube makes excellent whites from the Grüner Veltliner grape. $$–$$$$

DOMAINE LEFLAIVE: Anne-Claude Leflaive makes these white wines from Puligny-Montrachet; she has observed that since changing to biodynamics in the early 1990s, her wines are more resistant to oxidation. $$$$

MOVIA: Ales Kristancic makes biodynamic wines often without sulfur in Slovenia, including a compelling sparkling wine Puro. $–$$$

Birth Year Wines

By the time October rolls around I've adjusted to fall pretty well. I'm comfortable. I don't have to worry about the holidays, or even which wines I'm going to serve with the Thanksgiving turkey yet. Which leaves me with plenty of time to dream up other wine challenges, such as birth year wines for my loved ones. October's a good time to do this, since if you're faced with a particularly difficult challenge (like I was when my son was born) you might have the solution in time to present the person in question with the perfect bottle by Christmas.

Finding Birth Year Wines: Newborn Edition

In 2003, the year our first son was born, Europe was suffering through a heat wave that was baking the grapes and making them ripen at unprecedented levels. This would make the wines they yielded freak wines, big and accessible only when young (if at all), but not worthy of prolonged aging. An unfortunate predicament for wine producers and enthusiasts, but the weather posed another problem for me: Which wine would I buy to share with my son and his mom on his twenty-first birthday?

This is a question that's on the minds of a lot of wine-loving parents these days. Even though most wines are made to hardly last a year, there's something momentous about buying a great wine early in your child's life (the wines made from grapes harvested during the birth year usually are available commercially by about the child's second birthday), storing it for a couple of decades as if it's a time capsule as your child grows, and pulling the cork on the day your offspring turns twenty-one. At least I hope it's momentous—again, my son was only born in 2003.

So what's a good approach for deciding which wine to buy and save for two decades? You can always just go with a favorite top producer, particularly from Bordeaux, the northern Rhône, a Barolo, or Champagne. But be wary of many producers in California—although the best wines made in the

1970s are drinking beautifully today, winemaking styles have changed and the jury is still out on whether this new style will be able to make it twenty-one years. And remember that what glitters with age can be gold: Riesling and Chenin Blanc are phenomenally age-worthy as is vintage Champagne.

Beyond simply selecting by producer, it's good to get a feel for the vintage itself. Weather and harvest reports give a preliminary indication, and detailed tasting notes from critics about individual wines will be available for you to peruse within six to nine months of the wine's release. I've tasted a lot of inky, tannic barrel samples, and it is a very difficult job to taste that and forecast how the wine will evolve. But Robert Parker is never one to back down from a challenge and he is confident in his forecasts. He made an early call that the 2003 vintage was superlative Bordeaux. But in scrutinizing his early notes on all but the top wines, which were priced stratospherically thanks to his praise, I found that he indicated he didn't think they would age. I took a pass. Since then, I've tasted wines from Bordeaux and other European regions affected by the 2003 heat wave, and I'm glad I didn't take the plunge. So, as always, be sure not to just buy based on scores, but read commentary from diverse sources about the wines and see if it is built for the long haul and if it sounds like *your* style since, after all, you'll be drinking the wine.

If you decide to buy a wine that is very in demand, you'll have to play the futures game (see May). If you do, consider taking advantage of futures by buying special format bottles, such as a magnum, since they are more celebratory and slower aging. But there are many age-worthy wines that don't have to be preordered, so don't fret if the whole futures campaign passes you by as you are changing diapers.

Since heat waves may become more common in our future, you might want to consider buying a birth year wine along the lines of the one I ended up getting for our son from the freakishly hot vintage: I opted for a few bottles of vintage port. It's extremely age-worthy, and the heat actually made for a good vintage of this fortified wine. And a little bit sweet, it's a good wine for newbies. Which I'm sure he will be at age twenty-one, right?

I eased the cork out of the 1971 Giacomo Conterno Barolo gingerly with a mix of hope and fear: I had just uncorked the most expensive bottle of wine I'd ever bought, and I wanted it to be good. I decanted it slowly to keep any sediment in the bottle. I looked at Michelle across the candle-lit table. We clinked glasses and inhaled the delicate perfume of the wine that was as old as us.

It was a random day in 2007—not even one of our birthdays. Oddly, the thought of drinking a wine from my birth year on my birthday had never crossed my mind (Michelle and I usually opt for a more recent vintage, from a place we've been together or an otherwise just plain old great bottle). But a reader of my Web site asked me if I drank wine from my birth year on my birthday. Never having done so, I just had to go on a quest to find a bottle of mature wine. The reward in our case was very worthwhile, and I recommend such a quest to all wine enthusiasts. In excellent mature wines, the youthful vigor and bite of tannins has mellowed into a supple and silky wine, one that caresses rather than bludgeons the palate. The attack diminishes and, as with humans, the weight of the wine shifts, this time to the finish, which can be long and beautiful.

You no doubt know that your birth year was a good one for you, but you might not know whether the world of wine was hit by hail, fire, brimstone, or biblical plagues. In order to get a quick overview, behold the magnificent infographic that is the Robert Parker vintage guide. At a glance, you can get his opinion about the quality of a vintage in wine regions around the world and how the wines are drinking now. It's a great place to get some preliminary information before moving on to the specifics of which producers excelled that year. Unfortunately, it only goes back to 1970; for birth years before that, consult a knowledgeable friend, specialty retailer, auctioneer, or Michael Broadbent's book, *Vintage Wine*, which tracks older vintages and gives estimates for the lifespan of specific wines.

Provenance matters tremendously when acquiring mature wine, and heat and fraud lurk in the back of every buyer's mind. Consider the story of William Koch, an inveterate collector and captain of industry who plunked down half a million dollars for four bottles of 1787 Lafitte (as it was spelled then) said to have belonged to Thomas Jefferson and engraved with a "Th. J." (The wines were supposedly found when a wall was removed from a Parisian apartment revealing a hidden cache.) He had assurances of the vitality of the wines from none other than Michael Broadbent, acting in his official capacity as the head of the wine division at Christie's in London. After stories started to circulate doubting the authenticity of these "Jefferson bottles," Koch assembled an FBI-caliber team to do forensic research and eventually draw up a lawsuit, which he filed in circuit court in New York against the seller of the bottles, the German collector known as Hardy Rodenstock. As of the writing of this book, the judge had thrown out the case on procedural grounds, and Koch was appealing the decision. For more background detail, see the excellent book *The Billionaire's Vinegar* by Benjamin Wallace.

Although the hunt for mature wine is not likely to be so colorful for nonbillionaires, the dramatic story does underscore an important point in buying older wine: The more coveted the bottle, the more likely it is to be a fraud. Serena Sutcliffe of Sotheby's has said that far more 1945 Lafite has been consumed in the world than was ever produced. Similar trophy bottlings include the 1947 Cheval Blanc, 1961 Lafite, and 1982 Pétrus and Mouton, to name a few. These wines had high critical praise and high prices, which is more likely to encourage fraudsters.

So, getting back to my thirty-five-year-old bottle. When I bought it the clerk told me that it had come from a private collector's cellar in Piedmont where the storage was excellent, which means "damp," so the label looked like hell. After thirty-five years, did I look like hell? Sure, I hadn't spent my life in a damp basement, but maybe it's a good idea to only serve fine, mature wines by candlelight to make the diners not seem too, um, mature.

*C*onsider this tip when deciding to drop five digits on a bottle of 1947 Domaine Romanée Conti, Romanée Conti: Reject it out of hand as a fake since the vineyard was replanted in 1945 and no wine was produced until 1952. Many a billionaire and his money have parted since the art of fraud has evolved, putting old wine in old bottles, as it were. To make all those bottles of 1945 Lafite that have been consumed, the duplicitous sellers of mature wine are often master blenders, putting wine from lesser vintages in a bottle in a suitably weathered and carbon-dated bottle. Although some leading Bordeaux houses have added security measures to their labels, wine does not come with a certification of authority. That's why some collectors have flocked to mature Champagne: It's much harder to fake the fizz.

Nonbillionaires buying wines worth mere hundreds of dollars need not fret about fraud as the main ruiner of mature wine, and can instead worry about storage conditions (wine can be spoiled by prolonged exposure to elevated temperatures or insufficient humidity). Buying from the winery virtually eliminates risk, and buying from a shop or auctioneer who deals with reputable private collectors can boost the chances of buying a good bottle. Wine auctions in America were virtually nonexistent in the mid-1980s (and in New York, the mid-1990s because of state laws), but the market has been on fire lately. The leading auctioneers are Christie's, Sotheby's, Wine Bid.com, Acker Merrall & Condit, Hart Davis Hart, and Zachys. These last three also have retail operations, which is how I found my bottle of Conterno Barolo. Even though you may want to channel your inner Carla Bruni and try to shop around (see page 11 for tips on how to do that successfully), when you're buying older wines it's worth being loyal to a single reputable retailer. Play the shops off each other when the wines are young.

Travel to: Piedmont—Where to Go When Truffles and Barolo Beckon

An October visit to Piedmont provides cool autumnal weather for sipping the local Nebbiolo and Barbera, as well as the thrill of the hunt—for good truffles.

I suppose that there are a good number of wine lovers who would think that heaven looks a lot like Burgundy. But there must be those who think it looks a lot like Piedmont, particularly around the hill towns of Barolo, Barbaresco, and Alba in northwestern Italy.

In the fall, the hills are often shrouded in fog. The late-ripening grape, Nebbiolo, predominates in the area so there's still activity in the vineyard and the winery on the foggy fall days. The turning leaves transform the hillsides to a blaze of yellows and reds. There are sounds of autumn in Piedmont too. In the lush hillsides you might hear an owner and his dog sniffing out the elusive white truffle for sale at high prices at the packed weekend market of Alba. But the unmistakable sound as the clouds roll in is of cannon fire. No, the area isn't under siege from a warring princedom. Rather, clouds can move in quickly and drop hailstones onto the ripe grapes. One bad squall and a vineyard's annual crop can be wiped out in minutes. Ever since the nineteenth century, locals have clung to the notion that blasting cannons at the clouds can break up the storms. Fortunately, now cannonballs are no longer careening around the hillsides threatening tourists and their rental cars. The blasters consider the sonic boom enough to repel the hailstones. Whether it's a giant placebo effect is anyone's guess.

A visitor who didn't know that the cannon blasts were to break up the hail might well have mistaken it for another battle, that currently being waged between the traditionalists and the modernists. As with so many regions, the fight over barrels and other accoutrements of "modern" winemaking has come to the pitched slopes of Piedmont. In the olden days, the vines were planted far apart and the wines fermented in large chestnut casks. Today, some reformers have chosen particular clones of Nebbiolo, replanted the vineyards closer together to cause the vines to stress and eke out only the most succulent fruit, and started aging the wines in small, sixty-gallon new oak barrels. Some of these modernists feel that the sweeter tannins of the new oak balances the harsher tannins of Nebbiolo. It's a major topic among the region's eight hundred producers and, no doubt, at the corner *enoteca*.

One thing nobody is disputing is the quality of the wines. One fall day back in New York I poured a twelve-year-old single-vineyard Nebbiolo for my thirty-three-year-old brother-in-law, the first Nebbiolo he'd ever had. He loved the lively acidity and the supple tannins and told me that the rest of the fall he kept ordering Nebbiolo, not only because he wanted to taste more but also because he wanted to impress clients on corporate dinners by not ordering Cab or Pinot. Nebbiolo, the most planted red grape in the region, comes in various forms up the desirability ladder. At the top is Barolo, the tremendously long-lived wines that have inspired cult follow-ings akin to some Burgundies. Barbaresco is another category from the towns just to the north of Barolo. And then there's some Nebbiolo from Langhe, a name for the region as a whole.

Beyond Nebbiolo, the region's Barbera is incredibly alluring. Although I would ideally save it for the spring or summer because of its low tannin and high acidity, it's hard to turn down the charms of the grape while in the place. Dolcetto, which produces user-friendly, robust wines better suited to autumnal and wintry dishes, can offer a rich and ready alternative while waiting for the Nebbiolos to come out of their tannic shell. And producers in the region make white wines too—by the boat load, actually—with the wines of sprightly, springlike wines of Gavi and the summery, poolside wines of Moscato d'Asti (again, smaller producers are usually better in these two categories). In fact, Piedmont is one of those regions where if I were locked in a wine bar and forced to drink only the wines of the region all year, I'd be happy to do so.

The wines and the local foods all have an earthy quality to them so pair-ing one with the other is easy. Risotto? Truffles? Mushrooms? Veal? These are all slam dunks with the reds of the region. Though I'm not quite sure where I come down on finanziera, a local dish of organ meat, butter, Marsala wine, and porcini mushrooms. But wine may have met its bitter end when the rich chocolates of the region, often blended with local hazelnuts (see

February for my thoughts on pairing wine and chocolate) appear at the end of the meal.

Even though the neighboring region of Emilia-Romagna has long been at the top of the foodie lists, Piedmont has gained greater renown: *New York Times* restaurant critic Frank Bruni grazed through the two regions in a week and declared Piedmont to have an edge.

So throw off the shroud of mystery and head southeast of Turin into the fog of Piedmont in the fall.

❋ *Wineries*

G. MASCARELLO: A traditional producer that makes wine of great subtlety and distinction; one of my favorites. The whole range is great even if the Barolos get most of the attention.

GIACOMO CONTERNO: Another traditional producer who makes top-notch Barolo and possibly the best Barbera in the Barbera d'Alba from the Cascina Francia vineyard.

VIETTI: With a foot firmly in the traditional and the modern these wines are often hugely rewarding. The beautiful art on the labels as well as the contents of the bottle always make them excellent gifts.

LUCIANO SANDRONE: This producer heard the gospel of globalization and shifted production styles. Although there are other producers who are relentlessly more "modern," the wines are a good test to see if you like the modern style.

The Slow Food movement is headquartered in the Piedmontese town of Bra (and a leading practitioner, the restaurant Guido, is just outside Bra).

While the *enoteca* may be what many American wine bars strive to be, the real deal is on every corner in every town in the region. They're not all fancy, but they almost always have some perfect pairing of local food and wine.

Accommodations: Still reasonably priced, charming B & Bs are available in the region from $90 to $140.

When to go: The fall is the ideal time for the truffles and the harvest.

Getting there: Milan is a hub from the U.S., and a rental car can easily complete the journey. Some European flights go directly to Turin, the regional capital.

Virginia Philip,

Master Sommelier, The Breakers, Palm Beach, Florida

How does context matter for enjoying wine?

Who you're with and where you were at the time really make a difference. Many people travel abroad and bring wine back home with them, and when they get home they open it and then say that it doesn't taste as good.

If someone ordered Cristal Champagne here at The Breakers while sunning themselves in front of the ocean, it would be a much different experience than at our restaurant, L'Escalier. It could be better or worse, but it sure would be different.

What is one of your favorite food-wine pairings?

Manzanilla sherry, olives, manchego, and toasted almonds as an apéritif.

How important is pairing wine with the seasons?

In south Florida or Palm Beach, pairing wine with the seasons is not as important, as the weather cycle remains pretty much the same year round. Obviously the summer months are much warmer and the shift to lighter reds is more predominant, but whites and south Florida go hand-and-hand. Up north, pairing wine with the seasons is crucial and critical, and this also applies to cocktails and liqueurs.

If you had to have one wine per season, what would it be?

Winter: Red Bordeaux
Spring: Sauvignon Blanc from anywhere
Summer: Champagne
Fall: Pinot Noir from anywhere

If you had to pick one season for drinking wine, what would it be? (and why?)

The fall is my favorite season of all. With the leaves turning color and the weather going from an Indian summer to mid-level temperatures to frosty, this season encompasses all the different possible wine categories.

What's one of your most memorable food-wine occasions where the location or company really mattered?

Definitely while traveling on a wine trip through Argentina. I traveled with a group of fellow sommeliers, many of whom were very good friends of mine. It was in the spring of 2003, and we had just gone to war with Iraq. Many people said the trip would be dangerous, but as a group, we just knew it would be fine and we would be well taken care of. And we were. The camaraderie between the winemakers and the sommeliers demonstrated once again, as always, that wine is able to smooth over international differences, even as big as politics and war.

NOVEMBER

The days are growing shorter, the holidays are approaching, and people seem to be bracing themselves for the worst of winter—it must be November. This month seems to be filled with anticipation. Thanksgiving weekend kicks off the holiday shopping season, but before you hit the mall you need to successfully maneuver your way through the feast, which presents familial and food-and-wine pairing challenges galore. And just in time to correspond with the stress of pulling off Thanksgiving, Beaujolais Nouveau descends upon store shelves, but I encourage you to "drink different." Solutions for some of these conundrums are found within this chapter— wines to prepare you for the upcoming winter, Thanksgiving picks, a gift suggestion for your favorite wine lover (better start saving up for it now), and a getaway on the other side of the world if the anxiety of the holidays proves to be too much.

Mourvèdre: The Next Big Red?

If game or fowl is on your plate this fall try matching it to a Mourvèdre in the glass. With so many big reds available today why not try the stinky Mourvèdre, hosting a tasting for your friends on a fall evening to try this fun macho wine.

As the world heats up, we are likely going to see more Mourvèdre varietal wines. Mourvèdre has started popping up around the world. Originally named after the Spanish town of Murviedro, the grape then came to cover much of southern France. In the late nineteenth century when phylloxera devastated vineyards in southern France, Mourvèdre lost out since it was difficult to graft onto phylloxera-resistant rootstock, which turned out to be the successful remedy against the root-eating louse. Only in the last fifty years was Mourvèdre able to be grafted, and as a result it has swung back into favor, though it still lags behind the other big reds in popularity. It's known in Spain as "Monastrell" and in California and Australia as "Mataro." But the best name for it is the colloquial one, from the south of France: Estrangle-Chien or "dog strangler," for its big tannins.

The Mourvèdre grape has a long hang time on the vine; it can produce powerful red wines that are high in alcohol. Further, its late bud break (the budding of the vine) and late ripening mean that it does well in warmer climates, such as its ancestral homeland, Spain. The grape has grown so well in Provence in the south of France that the Bandol appellation mandates all reds must have at least 50 percent Mourvèdre.

Mourvèdre is often blended with the grapes Grenache and Syrah in the southern Rhône: Mourvèdre provides the tannins and ageability; Syrah more tannins as well as aromatics; Grenache the fresh fruit notes and acidity. Mourvèdre is known for giving brambly, forest floor, rustic, leathery, or gamey aromas; it can take a wine to the wild side, so much so that *animale* is the most common descriptor. Australia also makes blends known as "GSM" after the three grape varieties (Grant Burge makes one called "The Holy Trinity").

The best wines from mostly Mourvèdre improve mightily with age. Château de Beaucastel from Châteauneuf can be drunk relatively early on but also can age considerably; Domaine Tempier from Bandol basically should not be touched for five or ten years after the vintage. But it's not just the high-end Mourvèdres that are age-worthy. I stumbled on the Castaño Hécula in my cellar six years after I bought it for seven dollars, and it was possibly the most profound under-$10 wine I've ever had.

Mourvèdre also produces some excellent big red values that will make you a star if you bring one to a cocktail party. Some of the big, lush wines are in vogue with the modern plush styling so they are showboaters that seem to turn heads. Although I am not a huge fan of these wines I do think they have their time and place: I keep a few on hand to serve as "ballast" when the evening is winding down and palates are dull, but there's still a thirst for more wine. Pour a leaner wine at this point, and it can get lost. Pour an expensive wine, and it may not get fully consumed. But pour an inexpensive Mourvèdre, and people will be happy and you won't mind if they don't finish the bottle.

Although Mourvèdre may have a macho reputation as a grape, it's not *too* manly since in my experience, both men and women enjoy the wines equally. And if we do see more of it in this era of global warming, that's fine by me—it is able to produce exciting wines, particularly when blended with the fruitiness of Grenache and the spiciness of Syrah. On its own, however, a great vineyard site and top winemaking skills appear needed to make a good one.

❋ Welcome to Flavor Country: Seven Mourvèdres

RIDGE (CALIFORNIA): This venerable American producer did some Mourvèdre (using the name "Mataro") bottlings but with only a few barrels made, this was a small production that is now unavailable in stores. Bottles sometimes appear at auction for not too much, gracefully aged. $$$

DOMAINE TEMPIER (BANDOL, FRANCE): This classic producer from Bandol makes long-living, succulent Mourvèdre blends, including several single-vineyard bottlings. The rosé is superlative (see July). $$$

TABLAS CREEK, ESPRIT DE BEAUCASTEL (PASO ROBLES, CALIFORNIA): Tablas Creek is a joint venture between the two families, the Perrins of Château de Beaucastel and their American importer, Robert Haas. Wonderfully balanced with notes of earthy rusticity, this wine is fifty percent Mourvèdre. The luscious black fruits, supple tannins, and mouth-filling charm with layers of complexity including faint clove, briars, and sage make this my favorite of the young wines. $$$

RAFAEL CAMBRA (VALENCIA, SPAIN): Modern in style, this wine exhibits the intensity of the grape in its youth: a slight minerality and acidity followed by solid but fun tannins from the oak as well as the grape. This one could benefit from three to five years in the cellar. $$$

CASTAÑO HECÚLA (YECLA, SPAIN): These wines are generally good values and are surprisingly age-worthy. $

JUAN GIL (JUMILLA, SPAIN): This Juan Gil is approachable (watch out for the alcohol level, though!) with big concentration and supple tannins and notes of dark fruit, bacon fat, and vanilla. Drink now, generally on its own since it is too burly for most foods. It's a great wine to bring and serve at cocktail parties. $$

LUZON (JUMILLA, SPAIN): The perfect ballast wine: big, lush, and under $10. There's an organic version too, called *verde*. Drink now. $

Crush This: How to Make Your Own Custom Barrel

For any gift situation to a fellow wine enthusiast, a fine bottle of wine is appropriate, but if you're not satisfied giving a bottle, consider splurging on a whole custom barrel. Sure the price tag might be daunting, but going in as a group can reduce the investment and increase the fun.

At some time over the course of a wine-enhanced life—or even a particularly good evening—every wine lover dreams about owning a winery and making their own wine. But then reality kicks in and all thoughts about killer red wine get drowned out in a sea of red ink, managing staff and inventory, and the risk of uncontrollable weather. As the saying goes, the best way to make a small fortune in the wine business is to start with a big one.

But thanks to an innovative company based in downtown San Francisco, the best part of the dream—making your own wine—can now become a reality. That's right, you can become an armchair winemaker crafting your own bottles of wine, thanks to Crushpad.

Here's how it works: Choose the style of wine you want to make, whether it's a lean Pinot or a fat Cab, and the winemakers on staff will steer you to a certain California vineyard from somewhere nearby, such as the Russian River Valley, Howell Mountain in Napa, or the Anderson Valley. Then the winemakers will help you work down the decision tree and will discuss with you whether the grapes should be crushed or destemmed, whether the fermentation should use natural yeasts or commercial, and whether to use new oak barrels or old. Be as active or as sedentary as you like: Visiting the winery at harvest time to oversee your grapes is encouraged, but you can also just kick back and wait for the three hundred bottles to be delivered to your door.

The Crushpad graphic designers will also work with you to develop a look for your label, and you can use any name you want—provided it isn't already trademarked. And the company suggests that the wine you make with them for $24 to $40 a bottle compares to a $50 to $100 bottle, if it is available at all.

So how do they do it? One reason is sheer volume. In order to make this worth their while you need to commit to making one barrel, the equivalent of about three hundred bottles. So while the per bottle cost is low, it remains a big ticket item with barrels ranging from $6,000 to $14,000 each, and some going even higher. That's a lot of bottles of the same wine so you'd better be sure you're a good armchair winemaker. To that end, Crushpad encourages sharing. You could go in with friends or clubs and design your own label. They even have a Web site that facilitates sharing a barrel among people who've never met offline, but share an interest: Bulldog lovers from Georgia to Jackson Hole could make their own canine critter label, for example.

The second reason for their lower per-bottle price is that they have a radical new business model in an industry that remains frustratingly ossified in its structure. Like Dell, who dropped prices by dropping the middleman, Crushpad also bypasses the distributor tier (more or less, they do have someone legally "clear" the wine) since they are selling directly to the (involved) consumer. That way, they claim, they can also afford to pay grape growers more money than many wineries, who have to pass their wines through the distributor tier. More money for growers, more profit for an innovative company, and a lower price for consumers? Sounds like an idea that's time is ripe.

Anybody want to go in on a barrel of Syrah?

Bojo Novo: Ditch the Nouveau, Go with the Local

The third Thursday of November may not be at the top of the list of most recognizable days around the world. But for wine lovers the day means one thing: The travesty that is Beaujolais Nouveau is airdropped on the world.

The grapes for this proto-wine, the first released every year from the French vintage, are harvested about three months prior to the airdrop. Often times they have not reached full ripeness, an issue that may become extinct thanks to global warming, so winemakers have to add sugar to boost the alcohol level. Unfortunately, the addition of enzymes to give the wine a common *gout de banane* (banana flavor) has nothing to do with global warming and the practice is unlikely to die out soon.

Regulations prohibit the bottling of Beaujolais Nouveau more than one week before the arbitrary date, when signs all around the world used to proclaim *le Beaujolais Noveau est arrivé* ("the Beaujolais Nouveau has arrived!"). Now, the dreadful slogan is "It's Beaujolais Nouveau time!", which sounds perilously close to a rip-off of a Miller ad.

This short time between bottling and marketing release means that the producers, notably the Beaujolais behemoth Georges Dubeouf, must send the bottles around the world by airfreight to Tokyo, San Francisco, and many points in between. As discussed in the April entry on the carbon footprint of wine, this is not the most earth-friendly method of shipment. If

Dubeouf sent the Nouveau to New York by sea, a bottle would have 1,500 grams of carbon dioxide emissions. By air, it emits 6,000 grams. So this year, just say no to Nouveau! Do it for the polar bears.

That said, it would be a pity to lose the sense of a global wine celebration caused by the arrival of Bojo Nouveau. So this third Thursday of November, why not grab a bottle of local wine, which has a relatively small carbon footprint? It's a great counterbalance to the air miles racked up by the Nouveau and can help support a (family) business in your home region. And if it's bad, this is the only time I'm asking you to do it. Just remember the baseline for comparing quality is, after all, that proto-wine less than three months in the making. Hopefully, somewhere near you, a local winery is aiming higher than that.

Thanksgiving: Bland Bird, Sweet Sides, and Relatives

Falling leaves to rake. Family to contend with. And dead bird to tackle. What could be better?

From a wine perspective, the turkey is the easiest part of Thanksgiving for pairings. The difficulty lies with those crazy side dishes (and the visiting relatives). But first, the bird.

The white meat of turkey is neutral, and there can be lots of ways to pair it. For white meat I'd go with a richer, fuller white just because the meat itself is kind of boring. Turkey leg, however, is more meaty and savory. This part of the bird likes red wine. A sparkling red would even be a good match!

But turkey never comes to the plate alone. Cranberry sauce? Fruity and tangy. Candied yams, redolent with maple syrup, butter, and topped with marshmallows? Yikes. Whoever invented this dish was not thinking about wine. So go sweet or light. I say a Riesling is a good way to go, particularly a fuller Riesling from the Rheinhessen or Nahe regions in Germany. I've found lighter reds to be popular too. Loire reds, Barbera from Italy, some Burgundy, or Oregon Pinot noir would go nicely with these dishes.

So now we've got the food-wine pairings covered, but we haven't talked about those guests. Because Thanksgiving involves so many people—friends and relatives, and sometimes friends of friends and relatives whom you might not know—you can't be sure where everyone is on their journey of wine. And being too ambitious with your selections can lead to trouble. For instance, if you go for a hipster bottle or wine geek pick, your aunt Ruth might not like it because she's used to drinking Chardonnay, and you'll be disappointed with the reaction you get.

My advice in a nutshell: Pour Prosecco or domestic sparkling wine instead of Champagne unless you know that everyone is into wine and values Champagne from Champagne. After spending money on the big bird and all that cranberry sauce, there may not be room left in the budget for expensive wine anyway. And if you spend a lot of money as the host, you might be disappointed if everyone is too busy catching up to notice your prized wines.

❈ *Some Excellent Choices to Pair with This Bird— and the Sides*

Sparkling Wines

BISOL "CREDE" PROSECCO: A nice dry bubbly to pour as an aperitif. $$

Whites

OFF-DRY RIESLING: See September. Always a great way to go, especially with the sweeter sides. Low-alcohol also helps pair with the foods.

GRECO DI TUFO: Great for Aunt Ruth since it is full-bodied yet unoaked. I poured the Benito Ferrara at my last Thanksgiving and the aunties loved it. "Greco di Fufo?" they said giggling. "I want some more!" $$

DRY CHENIN BLANC: the great aromatic lift of chenin will intrigue guests and dry wine will have refreshing acidity. Try the Francois Pinon, Cuvée Tradition from Vouvray. $$

CHÂTEAU DU HUREAU, SAUMUR-CHAMPIGNY: This red from the Loire has good acidity to pair with the food yet enough stuffing, aptly enough, to delight fans of red wine. $$

TEXIER CÔTES DU RHÔNE: good value and food friendly acidity level. $

CRU BEAUJOLAIS: Rather than go with the Beaujolais Nouveau and its big carbon footprint, try the food-friendly gamay grape from a cru Beaujolais such as the beautiful Marcel Lapierre. $$

OREGON PINOT NOIR: The delicate cranberry note of Oregon Pinot is a great pairing for the Thanksgiving meal. Try one from Domaine Drouhin, such as the excellent Laurène ($$$$) or Hamacher for a splurge. See Pinots under $25 (page 179) for a value.

Travel to: New Zealand—Escape to NZ Pinot Country

Can't deal with the depressingly short days, the cold weather, or the stress of the upcoming holidays? Skip town and go away this November—far away. It may be gray and slushy in your hometown, but it's summertime in New Zealand!

New Zealand may be best known for its Sauvignon Blanc, but it's the Pinot Noir country that is particularly worth visiting. So get ye to the South Island (aka Middle Earth for *Lord of the Rings* fans) and start sipping.

Marlborough, the hub of New Zealand winemaking, lies on the north end of the South Island. To get there from Wellington, on the south end of the North Island, hop on one of the ferries that traverses the Cook Strait and leads to the impressive Marlborough Sounds. (The ride takes about three hours.) The delicate fingers of land reach into the sea, bearing a striking resemblance to the fjords of Norway, to greet the ferry and practically pull it into the port at Picton. From there, it's a short drive down to Blenheim, the capital of Marlborough wine country, a region known for Sauvignon Blanc. Many of the big names of New Zealand wine, such as Cloudy Bay, are in the area, just a stone's throw from the ocean.

The real action is in Central Otago, recognized as the southernmost vineyard in the world at forty-five degrees south of the equator. In this remote area is a spectacular land of lakes and mountains better known locally as a top ski and extreme sports destination, which has given it a good infrastructure for tourism (indeed, some might go so far as to call it "touristy"), than as a land of great vines. But it's the Pinot Noir we're primarily interested in.

The region really puts the "new" in New World. Although settlers originally came to the region in 1860 in search of gold and happened to plant some grape vines, the Pinot gold rush only came in the 1990s. In 1996 there were eleven wineries in the region and 227 acres planted to grapes. By 2007 there were eighty-nine wineries with almost 3,500 acres planted to grapes, 78 percent of which were Pinot Noir. This rapid growth makes it an exciting place with lots of energy and momentum.

✳ *Wineries Worth Checking Out*

The New Zealand wineries are similar to the American wineries and welcome visitors to what they call the "cellar door." Here are a few that should not be missed if you find yourself in Middle Earth.

SERESIN ESTATE: Michal Seresin, a native Kiwi, left New Zealand for Italy in the 1960s to embark on a career in cinematography that included *Fame, Angela's Ashes,* and *Harry Potter and the Prisoner of Azkaban.* He returned to open his own winery in 1992 with the goal of making a "different" Sauvignon Blanc. The estate now farms organically and, in some areas, biodynamically.

CLOUDY BAY: Established in 1985, the winery that put Marlborough Sauvignon Blanc on the wine map is now owned by LVMH. Try the Sauvignon Blanc, of course, but try the Pinot Noir too. The cellar door is open seven days a week.

MT DIFFICULTY: The Bannockburn winery dates from 2001—but the wines a little longer since the winery structure came after the vineyards. Lunch, with great views, is available seven days a week (reservations recommended). Very solid wines.

FELTON ROAD: Near Mt Difficulty, the first vineyard here dates back to 1991. Open Monday through Friday afternoons; be sure to try the Block 5 if you can! Great stuff. And be sure to chat with owner Nigel Greening about the extensive recycling at the winery and his efforts to use lightweight bottles to reduce the carbon footprint of transit.

If your itinerary only includes a stop in Auckland but you want to get some wine on the agenda, there's always the option of Waiheke Island, a thirty-five-minute ferry ride from downtown and home of about a dozen wineries. Te Whau Vineyard has a restaurant and magnificent views over the Hauraki Gulf—the site of yachting clashes in the America's Cup—back toward Auckland.

Other activities: Take the train to Queenstown to hike the legendary Milford Track or bungee jump, even at night, where no experience is required. Queenstown is considered the "adventure sport capital of the world." There you'll have plenty of opportunities to ride rocket boats and glide-wires, or even try "Zorbing," an activity wherein a person is strapped in an enormous plastic ball and rolled down a hill. Best to save the Pinot Noir for afterward.

When to go: The New Zealand summer months are the best to take advantage of the better weather.

Getting there: Cars (and freight!) are allowed on the ferry, but there are several tour companies that operate out of Picton if you don't have a car. Alternately, fly to Blenheim, right in the middle of the vineyards, and pick up a car there. To get to Queenstown in Otago, there are direct flights (ninety minutes) from Auckland.

Richard Betts,

Master Sommelier, The Little Nell, Aspen, Colorado

How does context matter for enjoying wine?

Context is everything. I can tell you, no matter how good the bottle is, it cannot cheer up the Greyhound bus station. When you can align the stars (e.g., food, friends, music, setting, etc.) everything is just better. So often I hear from folks how good this Chianti or that Burgundy was in Italy or France and how bad it is here and I just want to say Duh! You were in Italy!

What is one of your favorite food-wine pairings?

Whatever I am craving with whatever I am craving. I do believe that certain things synergize and that we can dial it up if need be, but I also think that over-intellectualizing it can sap a lot of the fun. At the Little Nell I tell people to drink what they want and eat what they want. Recently we had a guy come in and drink a '69 Le Montrachet with a cheeseburger and I said, "Hell yeah!"

How important is pairing wine with the seasons?

We don't see folks knocking back a lot of ice-cold Muscadet in mid-January. Similarly, Amarone isn't a big hit in July. We have natural wants, desires, and tendencies, and if we pay attention to them, they will guide us to just what we feel like.

If you had to have one wine per season, what would it be?

Winter: Rustic, rich Rhône varietals like Grenache are very satisfying. You can taste the sun and feel the warmth.

Spring: I like many of the bright and aromatic whites of Italy—they are cheery with almost a sense of optimism. They also pair really well with all of the spring vegetables. Favorites include Tocai Friulano and Fiano di Avellini.

Summer: I love to drink a ton of rosé—it smells red, tastes white, and pairs with anything at all—especially the barbecue.

Fall: Well, if I have my druthers, I will drink a ton of old Nebbiolo and red Burgundy (I know that is two but I cannot pick just one) with all of the truffles I can lay my hands upon!

If you had to pick one season for drinking wine, what would it be? And why?

I cannot do it, it cannot be done. Wine, to me, is a grocery and not a luxury. No table is set until the wine—however modest—is set upon the table. At lunch, at dinner—this is very important to me.

What's one of your most memorable food-wine occasions where the location or company really mattered?

Gosh, there are so many! My friends and I have gotten really good at aligning the stars as mentioned above. Certainly my wedding in the Tuscan countryside stands out, but so does last Sunday afternoon's lunch. . . .

DECEMBER

Americans consume more wine in December than any other month as we buy, give, exchange, and ultimately uncork diverse wines for the holidays. In that spirit, I have tips for giving gift wines that have an impact as well as deciding what order to pour wines at a party. But the month opens on a note more bittersweet than holiday chocolate, with a look back at the legacy of Prohibition and a celebration of the repeal in 1933. For travel, if you are looking for a bright, twinkly holiday getaway, why not slip away to the city of lights for celebratory wining and dining?

December 5: A Toast to the End of a Dark Era

On the campus of Northwestern University in Evanston, Illinois, there's a rock with a brass plaque affixed to it that reads: "On this site in 1874, nothing happened."

You might think the same about the seemingly random date of December 5. But on this day in 1933, something *did* happen: The twenty-first amendment of the U.S. Constitution was ratified. Prohibition was repealed. There was a lot of celebration that evening, even if most of it was with beer and spirits. (But perhaps not in Evanston, which was the home of the Women's Christian Temperance Union.)

Can you imagine that for almost fourteen years, the production, distribution, sale, and consumption of wine, beer, and spirits was illegal? Me neither. Herbert Hoover called the period a "noble experiment." But it's not one that the wine industry or wine consumers would like to repeat.

After taking a decade and a half off from drinking legally, when Repeal finally came, U.S. winemaking equipment was outdated, research had ground to a halt, and barrel makers were hard to find. But, oddly enough, the grape acreage in California actually increased by 25 percent during Prohibition.

Unfortunately, while the quantity of grapes had gone up, quality had gone down. Thanks to a loophole in the law that enacted Prohibition, there was an exemption, originally intended for cider makers, which allowed people to ferment "nonalcoholic" juice from fruit, which led to a bustling trade in home winemaking as grapes grown in California were taken by rail to the big cities in the East. But the grapes that looked the best after such a long journey were the worst kind to make wine from (and making wine in the bathtub didn't help quality either). Sadly, over the course of Prohibition, wine became a way to get a cheap buzz in a legal gray area.

On December 5, 1933, the American wine industry started to shake off the effects of Prohibition, but it was a hangover that would last decades. Not until the late 1960s did the chances of getting a decent American wine rise much above zero. So henceforth, on December 5, as the weather outside is chilly, why not raise a glass of the full-bodied red that California makes so effortlessly today as a way to ward off those distant, dark memories of a bygone era.

At least on the winemaking side, the challenges of Prohibition are now behind us, but we are still feeling the effects of a seventy-five-year hangover with the structure of distribution. As part of the compromise in Congress to pass the legislation of Repeal, the lawmakers agreed to the Repeal at the federal level while letting states decide their own laws regarding the production and distribution of alcoholic beverages within their boundaries. The result is a patchwork of fifty different sets of laws that often mandate that wine must pass through the warehouse of a distributor in order to appear on the shelves of local retailers. According to Booz Allen Hamilton, a consulting firm, the wine industry has the most expensive distribution system of consumer packaged goods, with twice the margins of food distribution. Higher prices and limited selection are too often the main legacies of Prohibition, ones that many consumers still suffer with today. Although there is incremental change toward setting up freer trade in wine, many wine lovers are still waiting to shake off the vicious hangover that fourteen years of abstinence wrought.

❋ Suggestions for Celebrating the End of Prohibition

PETERSON ZINFANDEL TRADIZIONALE DRY CREEK VALLEY, $25: The vines in the West Vineyard, where this wine comes from, date back to Prohibition (the late 1920s). The cooler Dry Creek Valley tends to have more restraint and less jamminess than Lodi or Santa Barbara, and that's evident in this wine. But watch out: Those old vines still crank out a wine that has 15.6 percent alcohol even if the wine carries it well.

JUSTINO HENRIQUES, MALMSEY, MADEIRA 1933: Hey, it's from Portugal, but if you want to try something from the actual vintage of Repeal, Madeira is a great way to go since this oxidized wine is built to last—literally; barrels of the stuff were aged on sea journeys around the world. Oh, and you will need about $250 to try it. But it would be a great way to celebrate in style!

Or, simply, drink anything on this date. Those wine lovers who lived under Prohibition would be happy for you to simply have a choice between Burgundy and bathtub gin.

A Question of Timing: When to Pour the Good Stuff?

As we are in the home stretch of holiday entertaining, the question at the forefront of every host's mind regarding wine is no doubt: When should I serve the good stuff? There are several approaches to this problem:

1. Serve the good stuff first. This sort-by-price approach has the benefit of creating a strong first impression. And some guests might only want one glass anyway so this ensures they will get something good. However, wine style matters. For example, don't lead with a humongo Napa cult Cab—that's the kind of wine you have to work into.

2. Serve the good stuff second. This is my preferred strategy. I like to open with a strong wine that is intriguing yet not overwhelming. Good picks for whites are: a wine from Greco di Tufo or Falanghina, both indigenous white grapes of southern Italy; a Pinot Blanc (such as Léon Beyer); a bubbly; or a wine from the Savennières region of France. Then you and your guests will be ready for a great red, either light bodied such as a Pinot Noir, or a big red, such as a Cabernet Sauvignon or a Syrah. I'd recommend having two bottles on hand for four people at a dinner party, then having a decent third wine in reserve, what I call "ballast." Solid stuff, but easy on the wallet as well as the palate (check out my lists of wines under $10 on page 91).

3. Start with great stuff and keep it flowing. Who can argue with this approach? Just serve the wine by style—lightest bodied to fullest—and everybody will be happy.

4. Serve no good stuff. A sad strategy and one to avoid. However, some family get-togethers may require quantity over quality.

First Growth: Bordeaux and the Pabst Problem

As the holidays arrive, you might contemplate giving someone a top wine from Bordeaux, one of the "classified growths." But before you make your purchase and proudly tie a big red bow around the bottle, stop to ask yourself: Do you need to slavishly follow this 150-year-old classification system?

"Pabst still coasting on 1893 win," blared a headline in the satirical newspaper, *The Onion*. The blue ribbon that adorns the cans of the Milwaukee beer may indeed seem outdated. Similarly, a system created in 1855 for classifying the best producers of Bordeaux continues to be discussed and put on labels today. What's wrong with the 1855 classification? We can sum it up succinctly: the Pabst Problem. It's resting on its laurels. While the origins of the Pabst blue ribbon are murky at best, the story of the 1855 classification is crystal clear. Emperor Napoleon III requested members of the trade to draw up a list of the top wine producers in the Médoc, the flat vineyard land north of the city of Bordeaux and between the Bay of Biscay and the Gironde estuary. This ranking idea had been something of a sport for the previous seven decades and even Thomas Jefferson had tried his hand at it. So the *courtiers*, or brokers, obliged the emperor and drew up a classification that included sixty-one red wine properties (and a couple of dozen others in a sweet wine classification), divided into five categories or "growths" (crus).

In many ways it's surprising that the classification has limped into the twenty-first century. For starters, it was a snapshot in time and not a moving picture. The *courtiers* used price as their indicator of quality, which as any frugal wine lover can tell you, is not a great measure. Some of the producers had great vineyards but had fallen on rough times (e.g., Palmer, which was then in receivership) so they were ranked lower. Also, unlike Burgundy where the actual vineyards were classified, the Bordeaux system ranked the producers, where the better properties could acquire lesser ones and fold them into the production higher on the classified growth scheme.

Moreover, the classification only ranked the producers of the Médoc and thereby excluded several hundreds of producers in important other subregions, notably the entire right bank (Château Haut-Brion from the Graves, south of the city of Bordeaux, being the one exception). While there may have been qualitative reasons for doing so at the time, the rise of properties on the right bank, where Merlot is dominant, as opposed to the Médoc's Cabernet, has underscored the limitations of applying the 1855 classification to the current day. Consider excluding such estates as Châteaus Pétrus, Cheval Blanc, Le Pin, Ausone, Angelus, Figeac, and Lafleur, and the classification seems quite incomplete indeed, as several of these exceed the wines of the Médoc in price today. (The producers of Saint-Émilion on the right bank organized their own classification system in 1955 and have updated it approximately every decade since, to inject more dynamism. But the 2007 update was legally challenged by some downgraded properties showing the political difficulties inherent in such producer classifications.)

The 1855 classification now only lingers for the most part in auction catalogs and sales pitches from the producers. Instead, the quality indicator that almost everyone cares about is the score bestowed on a wine from wine critics, with the first and foremost being Robert Parker. For better or for worse, since his power has grown so great as to dictate his stylistic preference on the whole region's winemaking, the Parker rating is what matters most today for parsing which producer's fortunes are rising and which are falling. But for investment, the five top wines, called "first growths," which include Châteaus Lafite Rothschild, Latour, Margaux, Haut-Brion, and Mouton Rothschild (Mouton was added in 1973 after significant lobbying from Baron Philippe de Rothschild), are considered the "blue chips." But they are blue chips based on their reputations today, not the laurels earned in the past. Save the fake blue ribbons for the Pabst.

A Short List of Great Gift Wines

Wine makes a great gift for coworkers, friends, and relatives. While there are some one-size fits all solutions (Champagne), the best gifts are often those with some sort of meaning. It's rewarding to give a gift wine that ties in to something that you know about the person. If they lived in Spain or are married to an Argentine, for example, you might want to go with a wine from one of those countries. Or for a loved one, a wine from the birth year is always impressive. And if it's possible to find out something about the recipient's wine preferences, that can help fine-tune the selection. Below is a list of good gift wine recommendations to keep in your pocket all December long.

CHAMPAGNE: For gifts, why not give the real deal? Bollinger La Grande Année is a good way to go for a top-of-the-line prestige cuvée, and since it can be found for under $100, it won't break the bank for bling. Krug, for just over $100, is always good too. For a classy nonvintage, the Louis Roederer is an excellent way to go for about $40. For the more adventuresome recipients, try grower Champagnes from Larmandier-Bernier, the Terre de Vertus is north of $50, or from Pierre Peters for around $30. See February for more picks.

BORDEAUX: 2001, 2002, and 2004 offer many good values since the vintages were somewhat overlooked; 2005 is a way to impress those in the know since the wines are delicious (particularly in the Médoc) and expensive. In general, the past ten years have been very good to excellent—but for some reason, there is a curse of the "sevens" with bad harvests for years ending in seven.

Château Léoville Barton: Anthony Barton has been on a tear, and his wines just keep getting better. This Bordeaux used to be a great value, but it is generally $75 and up now.

Château d'Issan has a beautiful black and gold label that makes it perfect for when you're going for an elegant presentation. The 2005 wine—on the inside of the bottle—is gorgeous too.

Château Figeac: A great property from Saint-Émilion that will show all Merlot haters just how good Merlot can be in a blend.

MAISON TRIMBACH CUVÉE FRÉDÉRIC-EMILE: While some people might blanch at the sight of the tall fluted bottle characteristic of the Alsace, this is truly one of the great white wines of the world. This superb dry Riesling has sufficient acidity for aging so check for older vintages too. The current ones can be yours for only $35.

RIDGE MONTE BELLO: This iconic American wine is worth every penny. Despite winning accolades at home and abroad, and showing great aging potential (the 1971 won a significant tasting in 2006 against top wines of that era), it sells at a discount compared to the latest cult Napa winery, which generally fetches twice the price. The only trouble in giving Monte Bello as a gift is that it's so hard to let go of the bottle once you have it. Try to stick around for the present's opening.

CHÂTEAUNEUF-DU-PAPE: A great wine to give in winter since the big red goes so well with the wintry weather. Domaine du Vieux Télégraphe is one of my favorites in the region.

A RED WINE FROM WALLA WALLA: A big red from one of the top producers from this up-and-coming growing area in Washington State would make a good gift. Or make it a three-pack with a Pepper Bridge, Woodward Canyon and Cayuse, who makes impressive Merlot, Cabernet, and Syrah respectively.

BAROLO: Say happy holidays with a stylish Barolo, the best expression of the extremely slow-aging Nebbiolo grape. Giuseppe Mascarello, a traditional producer, makes the stunning blend of power and elegance that is the Monprivato bottling. Recipients should decant a young Barolo for at least an hour before consuming, while an older vintage is ready to drink upon opening but may need decanting to remove the sediment.

A MAGNUM: Supersize your present by giving someone a 1.5 liter bottle. It really makes an impressive gift. Several of the cru Beaujolais can be found for $50, while magnums of collectible wines fetch much more.

PORT: A good port in the winter is hard to beat. (See January for more details on whether you want to go for vintage or one of the cask-aged, ready-to-drink "wood" ports.)

QUINTA DO NOVAL NACIONAL: Heralded as one of the best vintage ports, while Taylor Fladgate makes a great twenty-year-old tawny as well as vintage port.

TAYLOR FLADGATE VINTAGE PORT: Patience is required—about twenty years worth—to enjoy the vintage port from this top house (they also make a great twenty-year-old tawny). Buy new and wait, or scout the auction markets for older vintages. This makes a great birth year wine gift.

New Year's Eve: A Celebration

Congratulations on successfully navigating a year of wine! You should raise a toast tonight to celebrate the accomplishment as well as to ring in the New Year. You've sampled so many wines in this year where you had a chance to "drink different." From off-the-beaten-path indigenous grapes to German Riesling to wines from independent American wine makers you've had a chance to try new wines. And you've had a chance to pair them with context, whether it's a glass of bubbly and chips at the Super Bowl, Lambrusco and grilled meat in the summer, or a stinky Mourvèdre with game in the fall. And you've also had the chance to travel near and far to some fun places and meet the people behind the wines.

So although tradition dictates that you should raise a glass of bubbly, which is always a good thing to do, why not make it your favorite wine from the past year? You've earned it.

Travel to: Paris—December in the City of Lights

Whether you're looking to take some time off from carols and wrapping paper, or skip town and ring in the New Year in style, Paris is the perfect December wine destination. Even if the outdoor seating has been put away, at least the City of Lights has even more abundant holiday lights to help you find your way from wine bar to wine bar.

On a nontouristy pedestrian street off Les Halles, you'll find Aux Tonneaux des Halles, one of a new wave of wine bars in Paris serving "natural" wines. Even if Paris only has a few vines remaining within the city limits (notably, in the twentieth arrondissement behind Sacré-Coeur), these natural wine bars and some related restaurants make Paris a great destination for wine lovers at any time of year.

The natural wines, as discussed in the Earth Day section (see April), hearken back to a bygone era of winemaking, one before commercial yeast strains had been invented and winemakers started favoring the richness of new oak. Almost all of the winemakers featured at Aux Tonneaux farm organically, but few actually state this anywhere on the bottle. Some don't even add sulfites. The wines can be cloudy and the aromas depart from the usual spectrum of fruits and vanilla aromas since they aren't enhanced using enzymes, micro-oxygenation, and oak barrels. But they are alive and alluring, so put Aux Tonneaux des Halles on your Paris wine itinerary.

Over at Le Verre Volé ("the stolen glass") in the trendy area near Canal Saint-Martin, Cyril Bordarier is a leader of the Paris natural wine scene. In a sensible arrangement that should be replicated around the world, the space doubles as a shop and a wine bar–restaurant. With less than twenty wooden chairs, be sure to call ahead for a reservation to sample the food. The wine list is the wall of wine itself, as each bottle has the retail price written on its neck. Take it away for that price as many pedestrians and scooter-riding locals do, or add a seven-euro corkage fee to have it with the often meaty main dishes served at the establishment.

Opened more recently is Racines ("roots"), in the bright arcade that dates back to Napoleon, known as the "Passage des Panoramas." The scruffy owner, Pierre Jancou, used to own a natural wine shop but found this (slightly) larger space and opened this wine bar–restaurant that features artisanal and natural wines and small-plate foods. The compelling destination is off the beaten tourist path but worth seeking out for lunch, dinner, or a glass of wine on weekdays (closed weekends). It has quickly become the "Must visit" on the natural wine itinerary of Paris.

Back in a center of tourism, the sixth arrondissement, Le Comptoir du Relais, is another must—providing you can get in. We met a friend for lunch there once; he arrived first and ferociously had to defend our seats. Chef Yves Camdeborde presides over this neo-bistro on the ground floor of the Hôtel Relais Saint-Germain with a focus on natural foods and wines. The food is not only terrific but reasonably priced (particularly at lunch); ditto the wine list where we enjoyed a one-liter carafe of natural wine for only 15 euros. But word is out so come early or late for lunch when reservations are not allowed (dinner is pretty much impossible). *Bonne chance*, as they say.

Natural wines have reached the heights of gastronomy in France and nowhere more so than the Michelin three-star wine list at Pierre Gagnaire. The wine list is compact and seasonal, like the food, and Gagnaire remains a leading chef of haute cuisine. Lunch is always a great way to cut the bill at top restaurants in Paris. To wit: At Pierre Gagnaire it is 90 euros, while dinner can easily be 225 to 400 euros—without cracking open the wine list.

Another way to stretch your feeble dollar and increase your square footage during your stay in Paris is to rent an apartment. We have done this several times, and for wine lovers it has the bonus of allowing you to take advantage of some of the great wine shops and drink the wine there without having to bother with the *schlepfaktor* of bringing it home (even though that too is possible). Feel like a local and buy food at the markets and cook it yourself while sipping great wine.

At the top of the list of wine shops to visit is the iconoclastic Cave Augé on the Boulevard Haussmann. Allegedly the oldest wine shop in Paris, the store is packed with bottles on top of bottles of fine wine and armagnac. Even though the manager is *un peu* grumpy, it does help to ask the staff if you are looking for something specific since there is a storage space below the store where they keep many of the gems out of sight. And if you happen to visit during one of the two weekends a year (which occur in the spring and fall) when they have a wine tasting that spills out onto the broad sidewalk, you can swirl and spit with some of the finest natural producers in France.

Great Wine Destinations in Paris

❋ *Top Wine Bars*

RACINES: Pierre Jancou's all natural wine bar and micro-restaurant in a beautiful old *passage*. 8, Passage des Panoramas, 75002.

LE VERRE VOLÉ: 67, Rue de Lancry, 75010.

AUX TONNEAUX DES HALLES: Patrick Fabre's retro-shabby wine bar caters mostly to a crowd of locals and offers wines from many of the leading natural producers in France. 28 Rue Montorgueil, 75001.

WILLI'S WINE BAR: A staple among Anglophone tourists and locals for two decades, owner Mark Williamson is often on hand to greet guests. 13 Rue des Petits Champs, 75001.

CAVES LEGRAND: One of the oldest wine shops in Paris also has a wine bar looking out onto a charming pedestrian passageway. About one hundred yards from Willi's. 1 Rue de la Banque, 75002.

❋ *Notable Wine Restaurants*

LE BARATIN: A natural wine institution for a quarter of a century, visiting natural winemakers often come here, drawn in part by the three-course, 15 euro lunch. 3 Rue Jouye-Rouve, 75020.

LE COMPTOIR DU RELAIS: 9 Carrefour de l'Odéon, 75006.

FISH: Excellent seafood and a strong, if concise, wine list: 69 Rue de Seine, 75006.

TAILLEVENT: This gourmet address is renowned for spectacular service as well as excellent food and a long wine list. Reserve for dinner at least a month in advance. 15 Rue Lamennais, 75008.

IL VINO D'ENRICO BERNARDO: This restaurant, run by the thirtysomething former sommelier of the Four Seasons Hotel George, has a twist on traditional ordering: Diners select only the wine; they pair it with the food.

❋ *Top Shops*

CAVE AUGÉ: Strong focus on fine and natural wines. 116 Boulevard Haussmann, 75008.

LA DERNIÈRE GOUTTE ("THE LAST DROP"): Owned by American Juan Sanchez, this micro-shop has many natural wines with a focus on wines from the South of France. 6 Rue de Bourbon le Château, 75006.

LES CAVES TAILLEVENT: The sommelier from the restaurant also chooses the wines at this shop. 199 Rue du Faubourg Saint-Honoré 75008.

LA CAVE DE L'INSOLITE: One of the city's top selections of natural wine. 30 Rue de la Folie Méricourt, 75011.

LA CAVE DES PAPILLES: An excellent selection of natural wines. 35 Rue Daguerre, 75014.

LAVINIA: A large, modern shop in the financial district. Grab a bottle in the store and there's no corkage fee in the sleek restaurant on the top floor. 3 Boulevard de la Madeleine, 75001.

✻ *Top Natural Wine Producers*

DARD & RIBO (RHÔNE)

GEORGES DESCOMBES (BEAUJOLAIS)

MARIELLE LAPIERRE (BEAUJOLAIS)

PHILIPPE PACALET (BURGUNDY)

CATHERINE & PIERRE BRETON (LOIRE)

DOMAINE BERNARD BAUDRY (LOIRE)

ANSELME SELOSSE (CHAMPAGNE)

When to go: Avoid going in August since many places are closed. If you do go in December and have extra time, consider taking the TGV (France's high-speed rail service) to Alsace. The wine-producing region lays on the Christmas spirit with great verve, giving it a fairy-tale atmosphere.

Getting there: Direct flights from main U.S. hubs make this an easy getaway.

Belinda Chang,

Wine Director, The Modern, New York, New York

How does context matter for enjoying wine?

When it comes to enjoying wine, context is everything! If I am throwing a DJ party for one hundred of my closest friends, budget restrictions aside, we are not going to be drinking and contemplating the greatness of Salon Le Mesnil Blanc de Blancs 1973, so much as we are going to be happily taking slugs from magnums of Nino Franco Rustico Prosecco as we bust a move on the dance floor. There is an appropriate time, place, friend, occasion, and mood for every wine.

What is one of your favorite food-wine pairings?

The answer to this question changes about every millisecond for me, as I am a little tired about obsessing about the what-the-sommelier-believes-that-you-are-*supposed*-to-drink-with-that-dish dilemma. I have opened dozens of bottles from Charlie Trotter's cellar in order to determine exactly which wine, from which vineyard, from which vintage, from which importer was the exact, precise, indisputable, perfect match for a dish from the *Meat and Game Cookbook*, for which I wrote the wine notes. Nevertheless, some of my favorite food and wine combinations past and present include:

❊ Australian sparkling Shiraz with Chinese roast duck: Under normal circumstances, I never touch that crazy, bubbly red stuff, but this is a great match!

❊ Chef Laurent Gras's lobster cappucino with Yves Cuilleron Condrieu Essence d'Automne: decadence on decadence—unctuous, rich, foamy bisque with unctuous, rich, botrytis-affected Viognier—over the top!

❊ Chef Rick Tramonto's papardelle with meat ragu with Bruno Verdi Sangue di Giuda from Lombardy: It freaked my guests out when we poured it to pair, but this slightly sweet, slightly fizzy red is an unbelievable match with that classic savory dish. I converted every taster!

❊ Lambrusco with salumi and formaggio! The moment I enter Emilia-Romagna, the first wine that I order (always to the surprise of my travel companions) with my first plate of meat and cheese is sparkling Lambrusco! Oily cured meats and nutty cheese with the refreshing, fruity red is soooo good. The simplest adage holds true: what grows together, goes together!

✳ Chef Gabriel Kreuther's chorizo-encrusted cod with Finca Allende Rioja 2003: fish with red wine, hell yeah! Smoky with smoky, Spanish with Spanish.

How important is pairing wine with the seasons?

I look at this question from a sommelier-in-a-restaurant's perspective, in that the great chefs that I have worked for always respected the seasonality of food. Although, there are truffles (and just about every other ingredient) to be found year round these days, there is nothing more delicious than the white Alba truffle shaved at the height of the cold season or the heirloom tomatoes of the summer, or the peas and asparagus harvested in the spring.

So, in my restaurants, we are pouring wines to accompany the bounty and the harvest of the season. Luxurious Barolo and Chardonnay swathed in oak are some of the wines poured with the Alba white truffle risotto and rich braised meats of the cold season. Elegant, bright Chinon from the Loire, high-toned Pinot Noirs, and racy Sauvignon Blancs are poured for the dishes and the menus for warmer weather.

Just as our palates crave different foods with different weather, the wines that are best suited change as well.

If you had to have one wine per season, what would it be?

Winter: Amarone della Valpolicella from Quintarelli or Dal Forno for all of the braises, stews, and hearty meals that keep me warm!

Spring: Vielles Vignes Roussanne from Château de Beaucastel is my go-to wine for tricky dishes with lots of green, and a lot of them seem to turn up in the spring.

Summer: Bardolino Chiaretto or other delicious rosé for all of the great salads, vinaigrettes, and simple dishes highlighting the flavors of summer.

Fall: Echézeaux from Henri Jayer, the perfect Pinot Noir for rabbit, poussin, squab, duck, root vegetables, and the myriad dishes of the fall. Maybe the perfect Pinot Noir, period.

If you had to pick one season for drinking wine, what would it be? And why?

I would choose winter, because it is the season of luxury and decadence. The foods of winter take longer to prepare, and we tend to enjoy the wines with more of a sense of relaxation. Meals take longer, and it is the time to order a throw-down for a bottle of Bordeaux, a serious Syrah, a grand cru white Burgundy or whatever wine to you seems like an indulgence.

continued on next page

What's one of your most memorable food-wine occasions where the location or company really mattered?

It always matters!

If the first date does not include a fabulous bottle of wine, the relationship is doomed!

If you order a lame bottle in front of a prospective new employer, forget about it!

If you don't celebrate the occasion with a wonderful wine, it is not a celebration!

Okay, my final answer would be: A few years ago, I was recovering from a potentially career-devastating sinus surgery, and my long-distance boyfriend came to stay with me and tend to me. Over a delicious home-cooked meal in my Chicago condo, the menu for which I do not specifically remember, he dropped to one knee and proposed—the bottle of wine was an $18 Chariot Sangiovese from the Central Coast, California. Of all of the bottles that I have tasted in my career, 1900 Latour, 1847 Château d'Yquem, 1929 Richebourg, this one was the most delicious!

ACKNOWLEDGMENTS

Like humans, books take months to gestate. But this one had a parallel gestation with our second son since he arrived only shortly after I delivered the manuscript. The harvest for 2008 came early to our house.

For the very existence of this book, I thank Rick Richter of Simon & Schuster as well as John Chapin and Lucy Crotty for making a key connection.

The whole team at Simon Spotlight Entertainment has been terrific to work with. I'd like to thank Jennifer Bergstrom, Emily Westlake, Michael Nagin, Ursula Cary, Trish Boczkowski, and Kristin Dwyer. They all came to our original summer meeting that turned into a tasting and were won over by the joys of a Soave, a Provencal rosé, and an unoaked Malbec. But I'd particularly like to thank Emily, who has moved his book along with good humor and at an impressive speed.

My gratitude goes to Mark Ashley, Steve De Long, Martin Gillam, John Gilman, and Mike Steinberger, who all provided thoughts, suggestions, facts, or feedback along the way. The sommeliers who participated in the survey took time from their busy schedules to talk with me or reply to the questionnaire, and I thank them for bringing their voices to this project.

But most of all I'd like to thank my wife, Michelle, for supporting this project in many ways, from acting as an unofficial agent, to proofing, to brainstorming—often on the deck over a glass of Pinot Noir.

APPENDIX A

Dr. Vino's Cheat Sheet to the World's
Main Wine Regions and Their Grape Varieties

In the Old World (Europe), the regional name often becomes better known and synonymous with a grape variety—think Pinot Noir and Burgundy, for example—because producer groups mandate which grapes are allowed to be grown in many regions. In the New World, the situation is more fluid as growers experiment with different grape varieties. Here's a list of some important regions and the main types of grapes grown in them.

Region	Main grape(s)
Burgundy, France	Pinot Noir Chardonnay
Champagne, France	Pinot Noir Pinot Meunier Chardonnay
Bordeaux, France	Cabernet Sauvignon Merlot Cabernet Franc Sauvignon Blanc Sémillon
Loire, France	Cabernet Franc Chenin Blanc Sauvignon Blanc
Beaujolais, France	Gamay
Alsace, France	Riesling Gewürztraminer Pinot Gris
Northern Rhône, France	Syrah Viognier Roussanne Marsanne
Southern Rhône, France	Grenache Mourvèdre
Piedmont, Italy	Nebbiolo Barbera Dolcetto Moscato Arneis
Tuscany, Italy	Sangiovese
Friuli-Venezia Giulia, Italy	Tocai Friulano Pinot Grigio
Emilia-Romagna, Italy	Lambrusco Trebbiano Romagnolo
Sicily, Italy	Nero d'Avola
Rioja and Ribera del Duero, Spain	Tempranillo
Priorat, Spain	Grenache

Region	Main grape(s)
Rias Baixas, Spain	Albariño
Jerez (aka sherry), Spain	Pedro Ximénez Palomino Fino
Douro Valley, Portugal	Touriga Nacional
Germany	Riesling Blauburgunder (Pinot Noir)
Austria	Grüner Veltliner Riesling Blauburgunder (Pinot Noir)
Napa Valley, California	Cabernet Sauvignon Chardonnay
Sonoma Valley, California	Zinfandel Pinot Noir Chardonnay
California Central Coast	Rhône varieties
Willamette Valley, Oregon	Pinot Noir Pinot Gris
Walla Walla, Washington	Merlot Cabernet Sauvignon Syrah
Barossa Valley, Clare Valley, Australia	Shiraz (Syrah) Riesling
Margaret River, Australia	Cabernet Sauvignon Riesling
Marlborough, New Zealand	Sauvignon Blanc
Central Otago, New Zealand	Pinot Noir
Mendoza, Argentina	Malbec Barbera Syrah
Maipo, Rapel, Casablanca, Chile	Cabernet Sauvignon Merlot Carménère Chardonnay Sauvignon Blanc
Stellenbosch, South Africa	Pinotage Chenin Blanc (Steen)

APPENDIX B

Judge This Wine by Its Label: A List of Good Importers

If you're stumped by what's on the front label, check the back label for the importer's name as an indicator of whether what's in the bottle is good. Here's a list of some great ones.

KERMIT LYNCH: France

TERRY THEISE: Germany, Austria, Champagne

ROBERT KACHER: France

ROBERT CHADDERDON: France, Italy

LOUIS/DRESSNER: France

KESELA PÈRE ET FILS: France

WEYGANDT-METZLER: France

THE AUSTRALIAN PREMIUM WINE COLLECTION: Australia

BROADBENT SELECTIONS: Port, Madeira

VINTUS: various European countries

VINE CONNECTIONS: Argentina

ERIC SOLOMON/EUROPEAN CELLARS SELECTIONS: France, Spain

JON DAVID HEADRICK: France

JENNY & FRANCOIS SELECTIONS: France

DAN KRAVITZ/HAND PICKED SELECTIONS: France

WILSON DANIELS: France, Italy

MARTINE'S WINES: France

APPENDIX C:
SOMMELIER SURVEY

Paul Grieco,

Partner and Wine Director at Hearth and Insieme Restaurants and Terroir wine bar,
New York, New York

How does context matter for enjoying wine?

Context is everything. As much as wine can be the sole focus and sole determining factor of the so-called success of an event or gathering, the context in which the wine plays the starring role allows the grape juice to shine even better. Moscato d'Asti never tasted so good as it does gazing out over the setting sun in Piedmont or sitting on the beach in Montauk watching the waves roll in.

What is one of your favorite food-wine pairings?

Milk and Oreo cookies (While not an alcohol/food pairing, I'll let this one slide because it's a classic)
Beer and salt-and-vinegar chips
Riesling and everything
Grüner Veltliner *Smaragd* with Brebis Pyrenées
Barolo with roasted leg of lamb
Bourgueil with hen of the woods mushrooms

How important is pairing wine with the seasons?

Well, this is a Paul Grieco specialty and while quite a subjective practice, it should be de riguer in all places. Don't drink massive red wine in the summer; lighten up, have a little Chinon in place of that Napa Cabernet. In this context, there is context.

If you had to have one wine per season, what would it be?

Winter: Barolo
Spring: Mosel Riesling
Summer: Loire Valley Chenin Blanc
Fall: old school Rioja

If you had to pick one season for drinking wine, what would it be? (and why?)

Winter: the flavors of the earth dominate, which allows for terroir to shine through in wine. And with the sun setting at five p.m., I feel better about starting to drink earlier in the day.

What's one of your most memorable food-wine occasions where the location or company really mattered?

I was with my buddy Chris Cannon at his family's home on the coast of Greece. He was cooking an entire baby lamb on a spit . . . the bougainvillea was in full bloom . . . the Aegean was radiating (with fisherman dropping dynamite into the water to fish—yeah, baby!) . . . and the Naoussa red by Kir Yianni was like nectar from Zeus.

GLOSSARY

ACIDITY—Grapes have a natural acidity, though the level varies both across grapes and growing areas. I find that a higher level of acidity makes the wine go better with food. Warmer climates tend to produce grapes with lower acidity.

APPELLATION—A geographical designation of the wine's origin. To get the AOC France (or DOC or DO in Italy and Spain) the wine must be made in accordance to various production techniques that can control the type of grapes grown and whether irrigation is allowed in the vineyard.

ATTACK—The initial sensation of wine on the palate.

BALANCE—The best wines have a perfect interplay with the various components such as fruit and oak, acidity and sweetness, and alcohol and tannins.

CLOSED—When a wine appears shut down, lacking in aroma. Some wines go through such a period in their evolution, called a "dumb period."

CORKED—The wine has become tainted by chemical compounds in the cork, resulting in a nasty, moldy odor. The problem, only recognized scientifically in the 1980s, has driven the wine industry to alternative closures, such as screw caps.

DISJOINTED—Unbalanced in some way, as in too much tannin, alcohol, or acidity.

FINISH—The lingering impression the wine leaves after swallowing it.

LEES—Dead yeast cells that fall to the bottom of the fermentation vessel. A white wine aged "on the lees" has a richer mouthfeel.

MALOLACTIC FERMENTATION—A second fermentation that turns sometimes harsh malic acid into softer lactic acid. It makes red wines taste softer and whites taste buttery (think California Chardonnay).

MIDPALATE—The sensations on the palate that occur temporally between the attack and the finish.

MOUTHFEEL—The general impression of how the wine tastes in the mouth.

NEW WORLD—Refers to the wine world outside of Europe. Stylistically, the wines are fruitier, fuller, and often higher in alcohol.

NOSE—The aroma of the wine.

OAK—Oak barrels are often a preferred choice for aging wine because wood is porous and allows the wine to have delicate interplay with oxygen. Oak has become controversial when it is pronounced, particularly in white wines, which occurs when 225-liter barrels of new oak are used.

OLD WORLD—Refers to the wine-producing countries of Europe. Stylistically, the wines tend to be less fruity and more subtle.

OXIDIZED—This can be a fault in young wines that have spoiled with exposure to oxygen but sherry and Madeira strive for this character.

REDUCED—The opposite of oxidation. Much modern winemaking minimizes contact with oxygen to preserve the fresh fruit character, which can add volatile sulfur compounds and make the wine have a whiff of rotten eggs or burnt match. Decanting can remove reduction.

SPOOFULATED—A term used among some wine geeks to deride a wine that has been extensively manipulated in the winery, presumably to make up for a lack of distinctiveness of the vineyard.

TANNINS—Phenolic compounds derived from skins and seeds that are found in many red wines that contribute to the overall flavor profile and the age-ability. High levels of tannins in young wines can make them taste chewy. With age, the tannins soften and the wine assumes a more supple character.

TERROIR [TEHR-WAHR]—The French term for growing environment, which includes the soil and the microclimate (heat, rain, sunshine, and wind) and the effect it has on the wine. Certain grapes are likely to do better in certain *terroirs*.

VARIETAL WINE—A wine labeled according to its main grape variety. Such a wine should have varietal character or the aromas and palate impressions of wines from that grape variety.

VINTAGE—The year that the grapes were harvested.

YEASTS—Single-celled organisms that convert sugars into alcohol in winemaking.

INDEX

NOTES

Page 28

SWIRL WINE TO "VOLATISE the ESTERS" sm aromatic compounds that lie on the surface of the wine Swirling shoots them out + ↑ towards your nose

P 34   LBV = Late bottle vintage – PORT